W9-COS-386

Bangladesh — Equitable Growth?

Pergamon Titles of Related Interest

Brown—*Disaster Preparedness and the United Nations: Advance Planning for Disaster Relief*

Demir—*Arab Development Funds in the Middle East*

Golany—*Arid Zone Settlement Planning: The Israeli Experience*

Goodman & Love—*Management of Development Projects: An International Case Study Approach*

Laszlo, Baker, Jr., Eisenberg & Raman—*The Objectives of the New International Economic Order*

Meagher—*An International Redistribution of Wealth and Power: A Study of the Charter of Economic Rights and Duties of State*

Renninger—*Multinational Cooperation for Development in West Africa*

Bangladesh — Equitable Growth?

Joseph F. Stepanek

Pergamon Press

NEW YORK • OXFORD • TORONTO • SYDNEY • FRANKFURT • PARIS

Pergamon Press Offices:

U.S.A.	Pergamon Press Inc., Maxwell House, Fairview Park, Elmsford, New York 10523, U.S.A.
U.K.	Pergamon Press Ltd., Headington Hill Hall, Oxford OX3 0BW, England
CANADA	Pergamon of Canada, Ltd., 150 Consumers Road, Willowdale, Ontario M2J, 1P9, Canada
AUSTRALIA	Pergamon Press (Aust) Pty. Ltd., P O Box 544, Potts Point, NSW 2011, Australia
FRANCE	Pergamon Press SARL, 24 rue des Ecoles, 75240 Paris, Cedex 05, France
FEDERAL REPUBLIC OF GERMANY	Pergamon Press GmbH, 6242 Kronberg/Taunus, Pferdstrasse 1, Federal Republic of Germany

Library of Congress Cataloging in Publication Data

Stepanek, Joseph F 1943-
Bangladesh, equitable growth?

(Pergamon policy studies)
Bibliography: p.
Includes index.
1. Bangladesh—Economic conditions. 2. Bangladesh—Economic policy. 3. Bangladesh—Rural conditions.
I. Title.
HC440.8.S75 1978 330.9'549'2 78-16797
ISBN 0-08-023335-X

The views expressed here are those of the author and not necessarily those of the United States Agency for International Development.

Printed in the United States of America

For Caroline

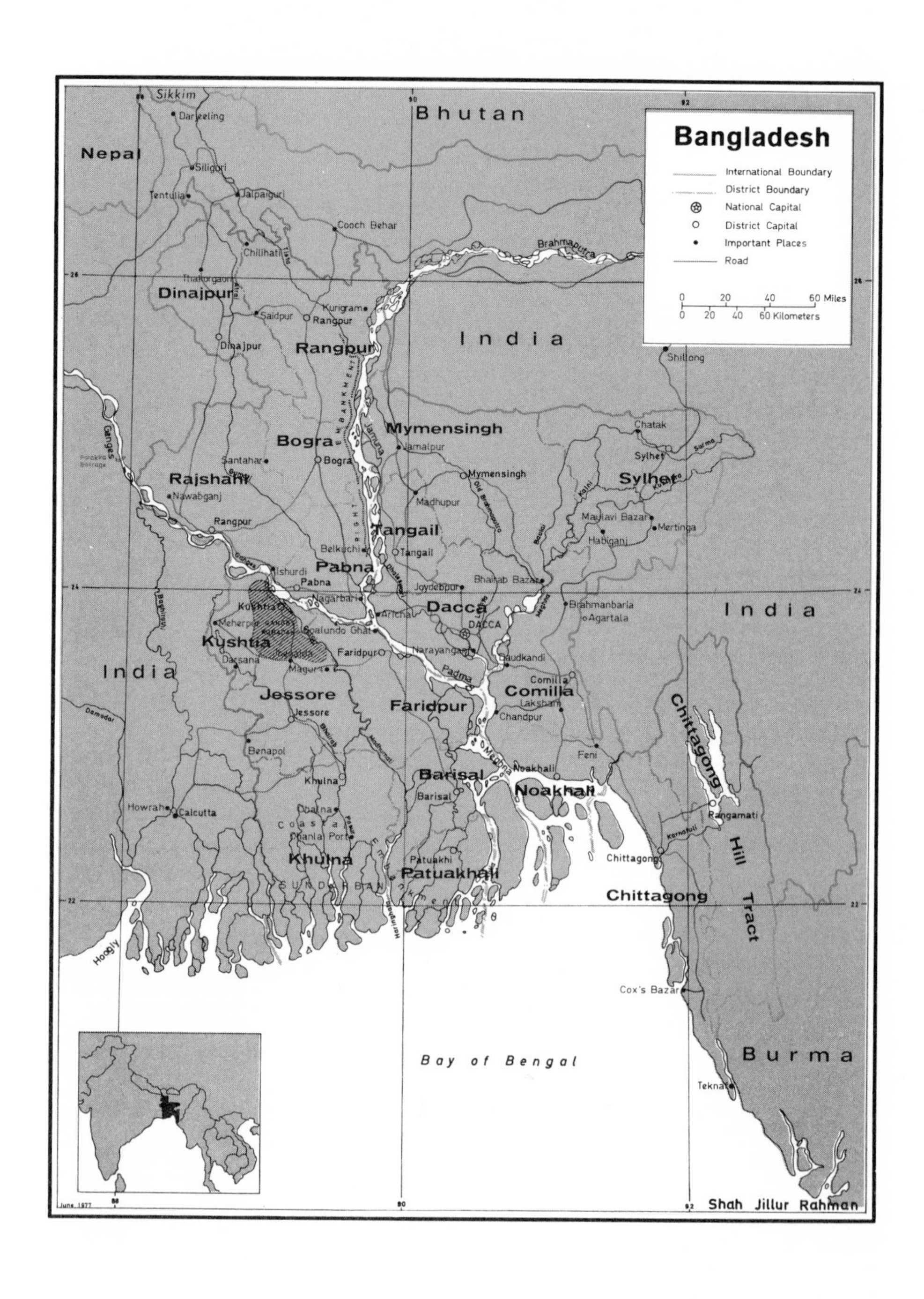
Bangladesh
International Boundary
District Boundary
National Capital
District Capital
Important Places
Road
0 20 40 60 Miles
0 20 40 60 Kilometers
Sikkim
Bhutan
Nepal
India
Burma
Bay of Bengal
Darjeeling
Siliguri
Tentulia
Jalpaiguri
Cooch Behar
Chilihati
Brahmaputra
Thakurgaon
Dinajpur
Saidpur
Kurigram
Rangpur
Shillong
Mymensingh
Jamalpur
Bogra
Santahar
Rajshahi
Nawabganj
Ganges
Jamuna
Madhupur
Chatak
Sylhet
Maulavi Bazar
Mertinga
Habiganj
Tangail
Belkuchi
Pabna
Ishurdi
Nagarbari
Aricha
Joydebpur
Bhairab Bazar
Dacca
DACCA
Brahmanbaria
Agartala
Kushtia
Meherpur
Goalundo Ghat
Faridpur
Narayanganj
Darsana
Magura
Daudkandi
Padma
Jessore
Comilla
Laksham
Chandpur
Chittagong
Benapol
Meghna
Feni
Khulna
Barisal
Noakhali
Howrah
Calcutta
Rangamati
Hill
Tract
Patuakhali
Chittagong
Cox's Bazar
Teknaf
Hoogly
Shah Jillur Rahman

Contents

Preface

A visitor to Bangladesh from the world's richest country cannot be unaffected by the massive poverty of its people. Every day of a long stay in Bangladesh I experienced an evolution of reactions into ideas, and ideas into prescriptions, that have resulted in this book. During a five-year tour as economist for the United States Agency for International Development, I viewed with discomfort the juxtaposition of the country's poverty and its development potential. This book represents my efforts to understand the reasons for this poverty, and to suggest how it can be alleviated; a development strategy is offered that can guide millions toward individual well-being. The country's present course does not ensure this outcome.

The United States Congress passed legislation in 1973 requiring AID to focus on the "poor majority" in developing countries. The Bangladesh AID mission's Development Assistance Program (DAP) became a guide for meeting this mandate. This book, like the DAP, is not content to be a legislatively-directed project list, with accompanying introductory language. Instead, it focuses on the theoretical rationale for defining the development process to include the poor in this agrarian nation. In doing so, we find much that explains the massive poverty of this historically rich region, and thereby we can identify several national economic policies that need reordering.

The trickle of benefits for the poor from an urban-oriented growth model has turned to drops. Is the Bangladesh government prepared to ensure the participation of its people in productive activity? Why should it enlarge the economic franchise? How can this be done? I undertake to answer these questions with a good deal of trepidation. I present my argument, for this book is essentially an argument, without the support of a parallel country experience. Moreover, I recognize that I enter upon a highly subjective field; there are as many views on development as there are contending interests. The government of Bangladesh has opened its doors to the world's development experience, but has yet to formulate and implement an effective development strategy of its own. I draw on these lessons, as well as on my own field experience in Bangladesh during its first years, to make the case for more appropriate solutions to domestic development problems.

The government and several aid donors have amply described the Bangladesh economy, its development plans, and its project portfolio. Although the country has passed through trying times in its first six years, I have kept redescription and evaluation of these reports to a minimum; rather, the focus is on the future consequences of present realities.

This book holds out hope for development in difficult circumstances, and provides an argument for an alternate strategy. It is written in the belief that it will be of value to the reader as a source of ideas on development, even if we may not agree on the overall strategy. Bangladesh is a test development case for the poorest of the poor countries, a test case operating under most perplexing circumstances. However, while Bangladesh is unique, its problems and their solutions are not. For this reason, I hope this book will contribute to the understanding of students and aid practitioners who are interested in Bangladesh and in the labor-rich, poor world in general.

Many look upon the future of Bangladesh with pessimism, even alarm. An effective development strategy remains elusive. While I do not believe Bangladesh is a hopeless case, this book does pile evidence upon evidence that circumstances there are more difficult than previously imagined. Unfortunately, the country's critics will certainly use these analyses to their own short-sighted advantage, yet the same analyses dramatize the country's potential. The problems and aspirations of this poor nation bear sympathetic understanding.

Washington, D.C.
December 1978

Joseph F. Stepanek

Acknowledgements

A few statements of attribution and gratitude are required from a second generation development wallah. I am indebted to many for contributing to this book. I am grateful to my parents, Joseph Edward and Antoinette Farnham Stepanek, for a procession of Asian experiences that led to China in 1947, then to Indonesia, Burma, and India. I am grateful to them and to others for their faith and support during my formal education. It is to Professor George Zinke of the University of Colorado Department of Economics that I owe an appreciation of political economy.

The first United States AID mission to newly-independent Bangladesh was responsible for channeling nearly $500 million into relief activities. Our small staff then turned to the challenge of transferring relief grants into development programs. I am indebted to the AID coordinator in Dacca, Anthony Schwarzwalder, and to my co-authors Michael Jordan, David Garms, and James Dalton for their assistance in writing the guiding Development Assistance Program. That guidance paper remains a draft for lively discussion. My AID compatriots and I are all indebted to the late C. Herbert Rees of AID/Washington for constantly challenging our perceptions.

Bangladeshi and foreign scholars and development practitioners continue to enhance the accumulated analyses that describe the country's problems and prognosticate its future. I have drawn upon my conversations with them, and their many writings. I wish to express my thanks to M. M. Abdullah, Raisuddin Ahmed, Stephen Allison, Stephen Biggs, Donald Born, Hugh Brammer, David Catling, Edward Clay, Guy De Brichambuat, Arthut Defehr, Thomas Gibson, Edward Glaeser, Eric Griffel, Azharul Haq, Tomasson Jannuzi, Charles Johnson, Fred King, Andrew Koval, Borje Ljunggren, Colin McCord, William Oliver, Trevor Page, and John Thomas.

Several people have reviewed the book in various stages of repair. I thank James Peach, Vernon Ruttan, and James Weaver for critical advice. For individual chapters, I benefited from comments by Mohiuddin Alamgir and Craig Baxter on Chapter 2, Edward Clay on Chapter 6, Tom Jannuzi and Jim Peach on Chapter 7, Robert Morton and Keith Pitman on Chapter 8, and Obaidullah Khan and Lutfur Rahman Khan on Chapter 9.

The wide range of reports by my assistant, Nizam Uddin Ahmed, has added immeasurably to my understanding of Bangladesh and its problems. Without his assistance this book would not have been possible. Mr. Nizam Uddin took an active part in the War of Liberation. I am also indebted to others of the USAID staff, including Robert Gonsalves, Ziaul Haq, Latifur Rahman, Harun-al Rashid, David Sarker, and M. A. Wahhab. For typing the manuscript and its many drafts, I thank Marian Boch, Carol Kling, Nicole Risafi, and Siddika Talukdar. I am indebted to Constance Texeira for her work on the transcriptions, and I am grateful Jean Joyce and Virginia Locke for their editorial assistance.

A great debt is due AID itself, and its many people who have encouraged my work even as we discussed often-divergent strategy, policy, and project possibilities; I am especially grateful to Joseph Toner, USAID Director in Bangladesh, in this regard. I alone remain responsible for the book's judgments and prescriptions.

I also feel a keen sense of appreciation to Robert Beckman, the Bangladesh Desk Officer for AID in Washington, and to David Wilson and Cynthia Bryant of the USAID mission. Lastly, I thank my daughters, Julia, Ahlia, and Vanessa, for their continued high spirits despite my evening absences. ("Daddy, is Mr. Toner <u>making</u> you write this book?")

List of Tables

List of Figures

1 Introduction

For 25 years Bangladesh was a portion of Pakistan and, before that, of India. In 1971, it stood alone as a new country. Images of golden harvests faded in the face of a devastating cyclone, an independence struggle, and millions of hungry people. A former provincial government was left with staggering national problems. Massive poverty now had to be squarely faced. Maintenance and stability soon became the standards of success. The colonial days of Sonar Bangla, or "Golden Bengal," had come to an end. (1)

THE CHALLENGE

Population growth has caught up with and possibly surpassed the region's ability to support its people. Material well-being is eroding towards a subsistence level of living. Even if drastic population control measures are taken now to reduce the birthrate, twice the present popuation will strive to exist on a similar resource base in 23 years; each person now gives a little of his present livelihood to support additional people, and will do so again year after year. Each year two and a half million more people are absorbed in Bangladesh; that is, 3% compounded annually. Nearly a million added people are looking for work each year. "In a starvation condition" may come to describe a large proportion of the population, as it did during the flood of 1974. No other nation faces this Malthusian reality so immediately, yet with so little sense of urgency or direction.

The economic institutions of Bangladesh evolved over centuries to serve an urban elite of colonial merchants and administrators. This institutional legacy is now tragically inappropriate to the task of development. As a consequence the basic resource dilemma, too few resources spread among too many people, is severely compounded by institutions that continue to serve the few. "There is already a large degree of tension over land, income, and opportunity in Bangladesh today which will be increased substantially if the population doubles, and tries to work the land under the same general set of institutions and conditions..." (2)

It is the alteration of these entrenched economic institutions of inequitable control of land and opportunity that is the challenge to Bangladesh today. Present development plans build on these institutions because their shortcomings are not well understood. Development planners are in need of another point of view, of an agriculturally-led development model that postulates economic growth and individual well-being and explains how these may be accomplished short of revolution.

DEVELOPMENT PROSPECTS

The country's assets remain the ones that gave this region the name Sonar Bangla; golden harvests of paddy and jute are assured by ample labor, water, and a twelve-month growing season. Much of the year the countryside is a carpet of green. There is an abundance of natural gas, a basic ingredient for nitrogen fertilizer, which can speed crop production, and may one day contribute more than jute does to foreign exchange earnings. Although the country has suffered a double depletion of economic leadership, at Partition and again at Independence, the formerly provincial economy now has a national identity. The country is socially cohesive and is unified by an elaborate rural administrative structure, both vital assets if development is to be brought about among a population soon to double. In addition, Bangladesh is small; government officials can travel from the capital to isolated villages in a matter of hours.

However, the country's one unknown resource is organization. Rhetoric must be translated into leadership and skill to alter institutions designed for an earlier age. Ample resources, whether of domestic or foreign origin, are not easily translated into improved well-being. This book's development model holds hope for increasing production and improving individual well-being, provided the political will is brought to bear on the task. Lessons from selected developing countries are instructive.

> One should never underestimate the importance of adopting the right policies for the progress of developing countries. It bears remembering that many countries have had even more outside assistance than Taiwan or Korea without achieving the same improvements in livelihood for the poorer half of their people. The cumulative total of $150 per capita in economic aid that Taiwan received between 1950 and 1965 is equal to Venezuela's per capita earnings from petroleum exports over a period of only seven months, and equal to Chile's per capita earnings from mineral exports in just eighteen months. Yet Taiwan - like Korea in the early 1960s, Puerto Rico in the 1950s, and parts of India and Pakistan (the two Punjabs) in the mid-1960s - did not begin its spectacular performance until it had made a series of highly important policy changes: changes in its rural areas in the early 1950s, and in its industrial export sector in about 1960. (3)

What are the right policies for Bangladesh? On what basis can judgments be made?

A SKETCH OF THE BOOK

Pessimism can easily overwhelm reasons for being optimistic about the future of Bangladesh. The country faces severe difficulties, but these do not foreclose the opportunity for equitable growth. This book is about these development opportunities and the institutional preconditions needed for their achievement. Macroeconomic comparisons with other countries tell us little of a country's potential, or how it can be mobilized for development. (4) An institutional analysis of Bangladesh does identify the sources of economic growth for the population as a whole. (5)

Chapter 2 describes Bangladesh's nation-building experience since independence. In the course of six short years the country has faced immense economic difficulties. The translation of aspirations into reality has failed. An analysis of this experience dramatizes the institutional hindrances to equitable growth, and even to growth itself.

In Chapter 3 the nation's brief economic history is described in western theoretical terms which buttress urban-industrial aspirations. Chapters 2 and 3 together explain why the country's present development plans are failing.

A development model for Bangladesh is examined in Chapter 4. The new high-yielding rice seed can ensure growth with equity in an agrarian economy, thereby providing a nexus between the country's productive and distributive aspirations. Growth linkages emanate in several directions from the new seed to generate foodgrain, farm employment, improved rural incomes, and the growth of market towns. In important ways the new seed also furnishes a foundation for industrial and export expansion. However, this theoretical model is too simplistic in the face of reality. For this reason the body of the book is devoted to an examination of the new country's institutional legacy; I offer a prescription for turning this green delta, in fact as well as theory, into fertile ground for the new seed revolution.

In Chapter 5 an economic tradition is examined which increasingly smothers the incentive for agricultural growth. The urban middle class relies heavily upon subsidized imported food, leaving the nation's cultivators to sell their harvests in stunted commercial markets. Until the urban and the rural food systems are combined to serve a unified developmental purpose, this country's agrarian potential and the well-being of its people will remain in question. "Food for development" is a new slogan that may mask a growing dependence upon concessional food aid.

The new high-yielding seed are said to be a highly divisible, labor-intensive technology; that is, they are easily utilized on small farms. In Chapter 6 it is shown that the new seed provide windfalls to the credit and land-owning elite, but not to agricultural laborers. Unless technological processes and products are further adapted to the labor-rich, resource-poor land of Bangladesh, these seed, as well as other types of technical change, will not become vehicles for broad-based, widely-shared development.

In Chapter 7 it is documented that Bangladesh is a land of tenant cultivators and laborers rather than of small farm owner-operators, as has been widely proclaimed. As in the control of credit, adverse tenancy conditions may prevent rapid acceptance of the new seed technology and, therefore, arrest the country's capacity to employ and feed its millions.

The importance of water to this delta is examined in Chapter 8. Here I show that a recent strategy has slowed the rate at which irrigation coverage is extended to the nation's cultivators. A narrow focus on the control of the major rivers has delayed achievement of irrigation targets. India's Farakka Barrage, and the Bangladeshi cultivators themselves, are only now forcing the government to consider alternative land and water development strategies.

In Chapter 9 Comilla's cooperative institutions and their associated rural programs are examined. In the name of modernizing the country's poor farmers, Comilla's procedures and resource policies have become unwitting vehicles for the exploitation of small farm owners by the rural elite. Comilla's programs could achieve little else in the face of the country's resource and administrative policies. However, Comilla's basic institutional concepts, when seen in the context of a dynamic agriculture, remain appropriate for effecting development for a population soon to double.

During the course of this rural analysis, I find that it is by design and not accident that the county's poor are being pushed out of economic processes. The economic institutions and policies inherited by Bangladesh, which are the subjects of Chapters 5 through 9, will test any equitable development plan. An economic strategy designed for the poor is reassessed in Chapter 10. Whether it will succeed depends upon a sense of national economic purpose which is yet to be defined.

NOTES

(1) The term Sonar Bangla, or "Golden Bengal," originated with the region's rich harvests and with its muslin cloth that was renowned in 18th century Europe. British textile exports to Bengal in the late 18th and early 19th centuries destroyed this native industry and drove a third of the total labor force out of work. The region's first economic crisis brought on its first depletion of entrepreneurial leadership.

(2) A.Z. Obaidullah Kahn, page 6. (Complete references for partial citations are found in the bibliography.)

(3) Robert Hunter, et al., "A New Development Strategy? Greater Equity, Faster Growth, and Smaller Families," Washington, D.C.: Overseas Development Council, 1972, page 16.

(4) In 1975, Bangladesh, with 81 million people, ranked among the five most populous countries: Japan had 111 million; Brazil, 110 million; Nigeria, 70 million; and Pakistan, 71 million. These same countries, ranked by population density, appear quite differently: Japan has 775 people per square mile; Brazil, 35; Nigeria, 195; and Pakistan, 230. Bangladesh has 1,450 people per square mile. It is surpassed in population density only by the states of Singapore, with 9,800 people per square mile, Hong Kong, with 11,000, and

Malta, with 2,649. Another small country, the Netherlands, has only 60% of Bangladesh's population density. Wisconsin, which is only about the size of Bangladesh, has only 6% of Bangladesh's population density.

North Korea, Malaysia, Morocco, Ireland, Cuba, and Bangladesh all have similar gross national products of between $4 and $5 billion, yet the population densities of the first four cluster in the area of between 100 and 200 people per square mile. North Korea has the highest population density of this group, with 345 people per square mile. Export earnings of about $350 million place Bangladesh with the Cameroons, El Salvador, and the Sudan.

"Years to double" (population) has become a new index; for Bangladesh, with a population growth rate of 3%, this will take 23 years. Her "years to double" neighbors are Libya, Tanzania, and Syria; these countries have present population densities of 3, 42, and 102 people per square mile, respectively. Bangladesh's years to double have been shrinking: Between 1650 and 1860, a span of 210 years, her population doubled to 20 million; between then and 1940, 80 years, it had doubled again to 40 million; 36 years later, in 1976, it stood at 80 million; and by the turn of the century, in 24 years, it may double again.

India, Burma, and Nepal, Bangladesh's immediate neighbors, have densities of 485, 120, and 232, people per square mile, respectively. Per capita aid flows show Bangladesh to be on top, with $5.80; India receives $1.30; Burma, $2.30; and Nepal, $2.50.

However comparisons are made in macroeconomic terms, Bangladesh's population denominator is always the largest.

Sources: USAID, "Population Growth in Bangladesh," Dacca: June 1975; National Geographic, Atlas of the World, 4th Edition, 1975; World Bank, Atlas - Population, Per Capita Product, and Growth Rates, 1975; and ODC, The U.S. and World Development - Agenda for Action, 1975, pp. 198-200.

(5) An explanation may be necessary of my use of the terms "institution," "tradition," and "legacy." The term "institution" is used to refer to many national organizations and practices, such as government administration, the political system, and educational and health structures. Economic institutions include the public sector food ration system, the industrial sector, the land tenure structure, the "institution" or "tradition" of providing public subsidies on a wide range of goods and services, and the rural "institutional" structure through which public development plans are implemented. In Chapters 6 and 8, the term "institution" is applied loosely to the new seed technology and to the water development strategy. All of these institutions are in a sense a "legacy," inherited first from the British by Pakistan and then, with minor changes, from Pakistan by Bangladesh. These institutions, therefore, predate Bangladesh, and some have deep historic roots. In the text I identify five of the economic institutions for analysis.

2 Nation-Building – The First Years

A devastating cyclone struck the Bengali coast in November of 1970 and a military crackdown the following March galvanized an East Pakistani autonomy movement into an independence struggle. The central Pakistani Government in the west responded belatedly to the cyclonic devastation that fall, and yet had ample military resources to suppress the simmering resentment the following spring. After independence was won in December, 1971, further crises followed in rapid succession, severely straining the new government and casting doubt on the ability of the country's political and economic institutions to resolve its problems. The country's institutional heritage requires analysis for, as will be shown, equitable growth depends fundamentally upon an alteration of this legacy.

The country's first leader recognized that political independence would be only a first step. However, no sooner were new political and economic mandates issued than sharp cleavages developed between government rhetoric and the realities of daily life. Why was this so? Were resources inadequate, or population density so great? Did the country suffer more seriously from the war and from a depletion of its commercial leaders than had been previously expected? Or were the problems even more deeply rooted? (1)

I will review briefly the East Pakistani era, and leave to later chapters more detailed discussions of the institutional legacies that first the British, then the Indians, and still later the Pakistanis, left to Bangladesh. I will examine the country's first nation-building aspirations in order to explain why these first efforts failed. In Chapter 3, we will probe the economic difficulties, which also explain why rhetoric and reality separated so easily in the country's first years. These two introductory chapters (Chapter 2 on the economic and political crises, and Chapter 3 on the theoretical underpinnings of present and future development plans) explain why a new developmental point of view is required.

THE FORMER EAST WING OF PAKISTAN

Between the first partition from India in 1947 and the one from Pakistan in 1971, life in East Pakistan was relatively tranquil. Crop production kept pace with consumer demand, and high death rates checked population growth and its consequent burden on the land. The fourfold price increase during 1973 and 1974 contrasts sharply with the price stability and relative abundance during the 1950s and 1960s. The East Wing's economy appeared stable and its harvests rich, but these masked the political and economic price being paid during this period. Stability was purchased at the price of growing food imports and a protected import market for West Wing goods. The East Wing's case for greater autonomy was fueled by the claim that her jute earnings were financing much of the West Wing's growth. The data certainly do suggest inequity and stagnation. The per capita gross domestic product in East Pakistan grew 6.2% between fiscal year 1950 and fiscal year 1968; this represents an annual compounded rate of only .3%. As a consequence of this meager growth and of an inequitable inter-wing allocation of development resources, per capita gross domestic product in the East eroded seriously; between fiscal year 1953 and fiscal year 1968 it fell from 91% of that in the West Wing to 59%.(2) Belated central government attention to this deteriorating inter-wing relationship came too late to head off redoubled efforts for greater autonomy. In the spring of 1970 the Pakistan Government proposed that 55% of the fourth Five-Year Plan be allocated to the East Wing, but time had run out.

TRANSLATING RHETORIC INTO REALITY - AN ADMINISTRATIVE FAILURE

Independence - 1971-72

Sheikh Mujibur Rahman returned to his new country from imprisonment in Pakistan in January, 1972. The Prime Minister, known as *Bangabandhu*, "Friend of Bengal," recognized that his popularly-acclaimed legitimacy and authority had to be translated into nation-building programs. He had successfully led his largely rural *Awami*, (People's) League Party to independence, but this experience was of little value when it came to running a country. Greater autonomy for the East Wing, not independence, had been his life's ambition. The fledgling government did clear ports, repair bridges, and administer $1.5 billion of relief and rehabilitation assistance in its first 18 months. When the rehabilitation period stretched on for many more months, with hundreds of millions of dollars at the government's disposal, the country's administrative fabric started to tear apart. (3)

The Socialistic Transformation - 1973-74

In reaction to what had been perceived as the worst abuses of Pakistani control, the new government implemented a wide-ranging "Socialistic

Transformation" which had been promised during the independence struggle. The Sheikh personalized this political and economic revolution into the "Four Pillars of Mujibism" named for the people for whom the Sheikh always spoke. These Four Pillars proclaimed that nation-building was to be founded upon the principles of secularism, democracy, nationalism, and socialism. Like the independence struggle itself, these Four Pillars represented as much a reaction to Pakistani methods as a proclamation of national aspirations. A policy of secularism was adopted because the former Pakistani Government had used Islam to promote political ends. Parliamentary and rural elections were promised soon after independence, for here, too, the Pakistanis had controlled the "democratic" electoral process through which the Awami League had hoped to win greater autonomy. Nationalism represented freedom from cultural domination; the new country gloried in its ancient language, its heroes and its literature.

The fourth Pillar of Mujibism, socialism, also had deep roots in the country's previous exploitation. Ten public-sector corporations were established in March of 1972 to bring the largely private Pakistani industrial sector under government control. This type of socialism included the country's jute and cotton textile industries, its tea estates and sugar refineries, the former Pakistani banks, insurance companies, inland water and air transport, and a major portion of the foreign trade. In spite of the appearances of a sweeping reform, only 6 to 7% of the gross domestic product was nationalized. (4) As most of the nationalized firms had been abandoned at independence, the government take-over did not significantly disrupt private Bangladeshi investments. The socialistic reforms did exempt farm lands of less than 8.3 acres from agricultural taxation, and the earlier land-holding ceiling of 33.3 acres was reinstated. Aside from these modest changes, agricultural lands were not redistributed, urban real estate was not nationalized or taxed, and the system of subsidized consumer goods for the middle class remained intact.

The implementation of these Four Pillars fell to the former East Pakistan civil service and to the Pakistani-trained army. Awami League mistrust of these administrators grew steadily after independence because the two groups had served the central government more readily than provincial interests prior to their achieving independence. Senior civil servants were soon being intimidated by the Sheikh's personal friends and political allies, and the army's role was gradually made secondary to that of a new paramilitary force. During 1972 and 1973, Awami League members on whom the Sheikh relied found themselves in most of the key positions of government, from ministers and secretaries down to the relief chairmen at the village level. The administration of government became highly politicized.

The long promised parliamentary elections were held in March of 1973, and the union, or sub-county level, elections were held later in December of the same year. The parliamentary elections were easily dominated by the Awami League for two reasons: the older conservative Muslim League was still discredited, and the paramilitary Rakkhi Bahini, or Protection Army, was used to control and threaten where the Awami League was challenged. Later in 1973, elections in the far more numerous union councils proved very difficult to control, and the population came to see the Rakkhi Bahini and the Awami League as vandals. The Sheikh's party lost its first election, and thana, or county, elections were put off indefinitely.

The increasing degree of personal cronyism and Awami League control of the public sector led to further centralization of the governmental decision-making process and to economic strangulation. One British legacy, the well-disciplined Bengali Civil Service, fell into disarray. Information channels were thoroughly clogged and administrative decisions and orders were seldom made or carried out without the personal intervention of the Sheikh. Unlike the Sheikh, his friends and associates had little sense of ideological commitment to the Four Pillars; they were neither administrators nor were they disciplined. They saw instead the immediate personal gain made possible by their new positions and that was, they felt, justified by the political oppression and economic exploitation of the past. The country's relief assistance must have appeared to them as a bonanza. Massive amounts of soft money consumed an already soft state.

The Second Revolution - 1974-75

The Four Pillars of Mujibism raised popular expectations that daily life would improve. However, instead of reforms the population saw political tyranny and economic chaos. Belatedly, the Sheikh became aware of the popular resentment boiling up around his party and himself. In an effort to break free of his Awami League, he declared emergency powers on December 28, 1974 and suspended the constitution and the civil liberties it had promised. A single party presidential form of government was announced on January 26, 1975. The Awami League party was dissolved, reemerging as the Bangladesh Krishak Sramik Awami League, popularly known by its acronym BAKSAL. This new party was to include farmers, laborers, and other representatives of the people, including dissenting political groups.

In another attempt to translate his remaining popularity into action, the Sheikh announced a "Second Revolution" to end corruption, to achieve industrial and agricultural self-sufficiency, to control population, and to bolster the eroding sense of national unity. Economic centralization was to be deemphasized and the private sector was to be given greater scope. At least on economic policy matters, the Second Revolution was to reverse the direction of the first - Four Pillars - revolution.

On March 26th, 1975 the Sheikh announced further reforms. For the landless, compulsory agricultural cooperatives were to be introduced in every district. This was the first time that a post-independence program addressed the growing numbers of landless and tenant farmers. Because the Sheikh was unwilling to trust the civil service and unable to conduct rural elections, he planned to appoint new district governors to sit with rural civil servants to effect these reforms. In short, to escape his own party, he further personalized and centralized his control of the government.

The Sheikh's efforts to translate programs into action disintegrated because of the innumerable decisions and resources that generated handsome rewards. Influence, not public administration, became an important allocator of public resources. During the first three years of independence, consumer goods were scarce and smuggling to India was presumed to be at a high level. The black market rate for foreign currencies was three and four times its official rate, and public resources were often diverted from public purpose to private ends. The phrase "black money" gained popularity as a description of the illegal windfall profits that accrued to those with political and bureaucratic positions. In the name of improving social welfare, the government continued an old policy of subsidizing imported goods for the urban middle class. Any diversion of these commodities to the inflated open market, upon which the poor relied, brought generous windfalls, provided financing for additional bribes and commodity "purchases," and further stimulated the price spiral.

These domestic abuses, justified in part by low public salaries and high inflation, went hand in glove with smuggling. The unofficial taka rate with the Indian rupee reached three to one and made smuggling all the more profitable. (5) Jute, rice, imported wheat, fertilizer, pesticides, and pharmaceuticals flowed across the border in exchange for a wide range of manufactured consumer goods. The consequence of these economic conditions for the people was an inflation rate that climbed from a near-stable level in the 1960s to 75% in 1974. The rice price jumped to nearly ten times its pre-independence level for a few months in late 1974, and the general price index tripled by late 1975. Economic chaos and smuggling meant death from starvation for tens of thousands of people in late 1974.

The Coups in 1975

Future histories of these years may set the bloody coups of 1975 slightly apart from the economic turmoil of this period. Political rivalries and personality clashes precipitated the first coup. The Sheikh, most of his family, and several of his associates were slain on August 15, 1975; others were jailed and a few were later murdered in their cells. With the second countercoup in November, the army stepped in directly. None of the three coups threatened the country's economic and social structure.

The grim days of 1973, 1974, and 1975 did give way to better ones in 1976 and 1977. Economic policy changes initiated by the Awami League government were carried on by the military. A sequence of good harvests helped to moderate prices. A tighter control of the border and reduced profits curtailed smuggling by 1976. Industrial capacity utilization and export earnings improved. (6) Public revenues recovered. Inflation was brought to a near standstill by strict controls on public and private spending.

To the Sheikh's credit, the economy started to improve well before the coups. Rice prices began to decline, prices in general stabilized, and difficult economic decisions were made in early 1975 (see Fig. 5.1 on page 57). In April of 1975 the demonetization of the 100-taka note put a clamp on the inflation and speculative gains; in May, the taka was devalued and private and foreign investment regulations were further liberalized. A few of the nationalized firms, including tea estates and tanneries, were sold or returned to their previous owners. Prior to the coups, subsidies on a wide range of rationed goods were reduced.

Most of these economic changes were substantive but a few were illusory. Agricultural production grew by 17% in 1975-76 which acted to raise the gross national product and per capita income. However, when the monsoon turns malevolent, the vulnerability of the country's macroeconomic indicators to poor crops will once again be obvious. (7) The government is still very reluctant to let decentralized decisions and market prices improve efficiency or determine investment priorities. Although the government has a responsibility for the public welfare, socialistic controls in Bangladesh have proven to be handsomely self-rewarding for a few.

Political liberalizations joined the economic ones in 1976. Union elections in early 1977 were accomplished without violence; and in future elections the desires of the people may be welded into national political parties at the top. However, despite the turmoil of independence, early years of economic chaos, and the coups, the integration of the country's economic and political system remains far from complete. The following quote says it well: "Politics is still a subject of parlor discussion in our society, contributing little or nothing to the production of society's wealth and goods in agricultural, industrial or any other sphere of economy; but the purveyors of such policies live on, and, what is more, usurp and expropriate the production of others . . ." (8)

DEVELOPMENT PLANNING - A SIDE SHOW

At the time, the new government's annual development plans and, certainly, its First Five-Year Plan seemed important documents. With the advantage of hindsight, it is now clear that the planning process became a side show in the political turmoil of the time, and with reason. The Planning Commission's assumptions and targets, and its manner of interministerial negotiation and implementation, reflected little understanding of the civil service or of the political and economic events of the post-independence years.

The country's first Annual Development Plan was drafted to guide its relief and reconstruction task. (9) A second annual plan in 1973 continued to guide this recovery effort, and set self-sufficiency in rice production as the country's central developmental goal. By the time of the third annual plan, in 1974, it was recognized that the relief effort could not be left behind easily. Increasingly, the annual plans passively reflected the allocation of resources instead of guiding them. Rehabilitation projects, and later developmental ones, were slowed by economic difficulties, political interference, and by the sheer inability to design and implement projects that could absorb high levels of foreign assistance. Annual plans fell short of available resources, as is evident from a comparison of columns 1, 2, and 3 in Table 2.1.

The country's First Five-Year Plan for 1973-78 was announced in late 1973. This first long-range plan stressed the broad goals of increased production, improved income distribution, and national self-reliance, the Sheikh's "Socialistic Transformation." Real per capita income was to grow at a rate of 2.5% by a public sector outlay of $5.1 billion. Forty-five percent of the plan was to be financed by foreign aid. The primary focus was on

Table 2.1
Annual Development Plans for Five Fiscal Years, 1973-77, in millions of current takas

Fiscal Year	ADP Budget Target	ADP Actual Disburse-ment	% Short fall	Total Aid in millions of dollars	Disbursed in millions of takas	Actual ADP as % of Aid Taka Equiva-lent
	(1)	(2)	(3)	(4)	(5)	(6)
1973	5,010	2,131	57	420	3,318	64
1974	5,253	3,050	42	640	5,056	60
1975	5,250	3,932	25	924	7,276	54
1976	9,500	8,500	11	814	12,210	70
1977	12,220	9,000	26	502	7,530	120

Source: Annual Development Plans and Budgets, Bangladesh Government.

Notes: For FY 73-75, \$1 = Tk. 7.9; for FY 76-77, \$1 = Tk. 15.00.

The balance of payments aid receipts are accounted for on a c.i.f. basis, but the contribution of this aid to domestic budgets is valued in terms of the actual taka revenue it generates. A large discrepancy results between the two (the difference between columns 2 and 5), and is a consequence of the following: (1) subsidies, which represent the different between the cost of the importer commodity to the donors, and the (lower) revenue receipts from their domestic sale; (2) technical assistance that is non-revenue producing; and (3) other minor valuation problems. Agricultural inputs such as fertilizer, pesticides, and irrigation equipment, and foodgrain and edible oil, are imported and subsidized. As a consequence largely of subsidies, the c.i.f. value of foreign assistance is larger than each annual plan. The actual ADP as a percent of aid taka equivalent (column 6) varies widely because of varying c.i.f. prices, and levels of aid and ADP disbursement.

foodgrain self-sufficiency; emphasis was also placed on price stability, creation of employment for the nearly one million new entrants to the labor force each year, and an industrial policy of import substitution and export promotion. The plan was based upon an input-output model formulated by Planning Commission economists. (10) It was assumed at the outset of the planning process that foreign assistance would finance the resource gap implicit in the use of existing prices and capital coefficients. Domestic taxation and subsidy reductions were also treated lightly for the same reason: the assumed availability and absorptive capacity of foreign assistance (11)

Actual capital costs, resource flows, and administrative abilities were sharply out of line with the plan's assumptions. These led not to adjustments, as flexibility was assumed away, but to shortfalls in physical targets and the erosion of individual well-being. As will be shown in later chapters, no account was taken of the country's institutional legacy. The plan, as a theoretical exercise, was irrelevant from its very inception.

In the months following the release of the Five -Year Plan several factors conspired to render its physical targets as unrealistic as earlier annual targets had become. Each year witnessed an inability to mobilize administrative managerial ability and to physically import and implement the resource levels made financially possible by donor commitments (see Table 2.2). Sluggish imports and idle production capacity caused duties, excise taxes, and public sector revenues to fall below the projections for 1973 and 1974. At the same time expenditures continually exceeded projected figures because of increased subsidy and military costs, and the occurrence of natural disasters. The burden of government subsidies on a wide range of consumer goods and agricultural inputs explains why each annual plan mobilized less than the full value of foreign aid available to finance it (see columns 4, 5, and 6 of Table 2.1). The flight of scarce managerial and technical talent to overseas opportunities still continues, and makes administrative problems all the more acute. And with the departure of qualified people, the country loses many of its enthusiastic leaders.

International commodity prices soared in 1973 and 1974. The cost of foodgrain and edible oil imports went up sharply at a time when domestic crops were poor; as a consequence, the government spent itself into a foreign exchange crisis in early 1974. Relief appeals for cash during early 1974, and for flood damage assistance during the summer, diverted the government's attention from development.

Following this troubled period, annual plan priorities were altered to deal with the difficulties facing the country. Emphasis was shifted to the completion of ongoing, quick-yielding projects and to the supply of agricultural inputs. This was done at the expense of the earlier emphasis upon distributive justice and the planning of development priorities. (The sector expenditures of each annual plan are provided in Table 2.3.)

Although there was talk of a Second Five-Year Plan in 1976, the planning process had become little more than the circulation of old project lists to aid donors. One development document is entitled simply Aid Worthy Projects, and it bears no date. In 1978 an interim Two-Year Plan was released to cover the period until the Second Plan is ready in 1980.

Table 2.2 Foreign Assistance for Bangladesh - in $ millions

	Fiscal Year					
	1972	1973	1974	1975	1976	1977
Aid Disbursements						
Food	103	121	300	379	307	106
Commodities	217	217	186	386	378	188
Cash	-[a]	-[a]	-[a]	14	-[a]	61
Projects	7	82	154	145	129	147
Total	327	420	640	924	814	502
Aid Commitments	591	973	587	1,299	930	657
Aid Pipeline	431	984	931	1,306	1,422	1,577

Source: Ministry of Planning, Bangladesh Government

Notes: (a) For these years, the cash disbursements are included in commodities. Aid commitments take place during each fiscal year. "Pipeline" refers to total assistance available at the end of each fiscal year, and is calculated as a residual. Therefore, the closing FY 73 pipeline ($984 million) minus the FY 74 disbursements ($640 million) plus the FY 74 aid commitments ($587 million) equals the FY 74 closing pipeline ($931 million).

Table 2.3 Annual Development Plan Expenditures by Sector in millions of takas

	Revised Budget 1973/74	%	Revised Budget 1974/75	%	Revised Budget 1975/76	%	Revised Budget 1976/77	%	Budget 1977/78	%
Agriculture, Rural Development & Water	1,579	34.0	1,784	34.0	2,990	31.5	3,148	31.3	3,348	29.1
Agriculture	(576)	(12.4)	(639)	(12.2)	(1,150)	(12.1)	(1,529)	(15.2)	(1,514)	(13.1)
Rural Development	(306)	(6.6)	(285)	(5.4)	(480)	(5.1)	(420)	(4.2)	(482)	(4.2)
Water and Flood Control	(697)	(15.0)	(860)	(16.4)	(1,360)	(14.3)	(1,199)	(11.9)	(1,352)	(11.8)
Industry	525	11.3	650	12.3	1,360	14.3	1,430	14.2	1,480	12.9
Power, Scientific Research and Natural Resources	537	11.6	712	13.6	1,510	15.9	1,313	13.0	1,764	15.3
Transport	965	20.9	812	15.7	1,250	13.2	1,962	19.5	1,815	15.7
Communication	131	2.8	186	3.5	345	3.6	307	3.1	524	4.6
Physical Planning and Housing	233	5.0	340	6.5	660	7.0	630	6.3	933	8.1
Education and Training	307	6.6	288	5.5	450	4.7	473	4.7	562	4.9
Health	207	4.5	218	4.0	330	3.5	320	3.2	383	3.3
Population Planning	50	1.1	77	1.5	250	2.6	216	2.1	288	2.5
Social Welfare	21	0.5	20	0.4	40	0.4	29	0.3	33	0.3
Manpower and Employment	3	-	13	0.2	30	0.3	20	0.2	42	0.4
Cyclone Reconstruction	80	1.7	150	2.8	285	3.0	80	0.8	113	1.0
Other	-	-	-	-	-	-	129	1.3	222	1.9
Total Development Expenditure	4,638	100.0	5,250	100.0	9,500	100.0	10,057	100.0	11,506	100.0

Source: Ministry of Finance, Bangladesh Government

Note: For FY 1973/74 and 1974/75, $1 = taka 7.9; for FY 1975/76 - 1977/78, $1 = taka 15.

NUMERICAL RUINATION

In discussing the political and economic events of the first years of independence, I have only touched on the conditions of the poor in Bangladesh. In this section, I describe the effects of population growth on the economy; and in the following section, I recount how the poor endured these early chaotic years.

Population growth adds 2.4 million people each year to the country's 83 million inhabitants, according to 1977 figures. The needs of the newborn increase the backlog of unmet needs for the population as a whole. Fifty percent of the population is under 15 years of age and largely dependent. Moreover, because of the youthfulness of the population, as many as 900,000 to 1.1 million more adults seek work every year. A portion of each year's national output has to be spent to maintain this existing economy, which subtracts from the economy's ability to supply the new arrivals with the goods and services required by the existing population. (12) As a consequence, providing for the additional population becomes more costly, and the unmet needs of the existing population remain unmet. Real per capita income fell 20% in the two years following independence; it has yet to recover fully.

Family burdens are more difficult to evaluate than public ones. Each economic crisis pushes people into a state of destitution, many to stay. Additional children cannot receive schooling, and still more of the family's resources have to go for food, clothing, and housing.

Of the present school-age population of 22 million children, only 9.3 million are currently enrolled in primary and secondary schools. In order to provide primary education for just the additional school-age children, 11,000 more schools and 60,000 more teachers are needed each year; yet only 9,000 new teachers are graduated each year. At least 165,000 additional teachers would be needed if all eligible children were in school. (13) Stagnant plans and population growth are depriving the country of its future human capital.

PLIGHT OF THE POOR

For the poor people of Bangladesh life clearly became more difficult in the first years of independence. In the face of inflation and scarcities, those in the urban economy - the labor union members, rickshaw wallahs, day laborers, and those in the innumerable services - were able to demand higher wages. Commercial people were partially protected by the increased value of their goods. Salaried people were partially protected by access to subsidized consumer goods. However, the urban poor and most of the rural population had neither ration card nor full-time employment, and they had to fend for themselves in the inflated market. The price of rice went up twofold between 1971 and 1973,and another threefold in 1974. Dry chili prices went up eightfold in the three years following independence; cigarettes, sixfold; razor blades, tenfold; and soap, fivefold. Bengali newspaper articles were vociferous in their attacks on higher prices, smuggling, starvation deaths, and misuse of relief and ration supplies.

Bangladesh is rural. Ninety-three percent of the population lives in villages of less than 5,000 people. The nation's 7 million farm families live in 19 districts, 423 thanas, 4351 unions, and some 65,000 villages. On foot, by boat, and by cart, villagers have access to weekly village markets, or hats, and to union and thana officials; these institutions are their contact with the larger world. Three-quarters of a rural family's income is spent on food, yet caloric, protein, and vitamin deficiencies remain seasonal, if not endemic, problems. Very few families can rely entirely on their own crop production for their livelihood. The gap is made up by laboring in others' fields, by providing various services, and by simply reducing expectations. Extreme poverty was plainly visible in towns and cities in late 1974; the economic and political tyranny in the countryside drove hundreds of thousands from their villages. The following descriptions of Dacca during 1974 are drawn from reports by Nizam Uddin Ahmed. (14)

> People from different walks of life struck by starvation, famine, and disease started pouring into Dacca in late September 1974 (after the summer flood) with the desperate hope of getting some food, shelter, cloth and if possible, work. The present population of Dacca city is estimated to be no less than 2,000,000 and is comprised of permanent city dwellers, service holders, traders, etc. and floating citizens from all over the country. Out of the total population, 500,000 are estimated to be slum dwellers, 50% of whom had come to Dacca earlier, after the liberation of Bangladesh, in search of food and work, having become jobless and landless in their respective rural homes. It is estimated that over the last three months another 300,000 people from all over the country have joined the already miserable jobless people in Dacca. They are the floating population who occupy street corners, verandas of unoccupied old houses, railway station platforms, market places, and open fields.
>
> There are many more slums around Dacca and the slums now have no accommodations yet people are pouring in everyday in Dacca from villages far and wide in search of work. They have old and worn-out rags to sleep on and hardly a worn-out lungi, or vest, to put on against the winter cold. The women have hardly a tattered sari. They collect dry rubbish, bushes, straws and rejected tires to cook their food. They hardly ever eat meat, big fish, milk, eggs, butter, oil, fruits and now not even dal, a lentil.
>
> Shamsul Huq, aged about 38, came to Dacca one month back from his village home in Chandpur Thana of Comilla District with his family consisting of his wife aged about 30 years, a widowed daughter aged about 16, and four more children of the ages 14, 12, 8, and 8 months. He is a landless laborer having nothing more than a homestead and no farm. Before he left his village home he sold his little hut for taka 40 ($5) having no other alternative as he could no longer get loans or work or food. In Dacca he started begging with his family from door to door until he was picked up by police and brought to Nazrul Islam College Relief Camp. According to him, since his birth he saw his parents

tilling others' land and working as agricultural laborers. The only land that he possessed from his father was sold to the moneylender who helped him from time to time until his marriage when he had to hand it over completely. He has no plans to go back to his village home where he apprehends there will be no work or food. He hopes to find work in Dacca or otherwise he will start begging upon closing down of the gruel kitchens.

Had Anjuman Mufidul Islam, a charitable burial institute, not existed in Dacca city, street corners would have now been filled with decaying dead bodies of unclaimed corpses. Starvation deaths of unidentified and unclaimed persons in Bangladesh are not new but the number has increased alarmingly.

Bullock carts and bullock-pulled drums are provided to these sweepers for cleaning filth and night soil. The condition of the bullocks is as bad as their masters except that bullocks get food every day which their masters do not. Out of 72 bullocks two were dead for the last 6-7 days, giving out a horrible decaying odor. The dead bullocks cannot be removed unless the Government Inspector comes and inspects the incident and reports the matter to higher authorities for necessary action. Several representations by sweepers so far have failed to bring the Inspector to their colony as he was said to be otherwise busy. The sweepers reported that unless the Inspector was given taka 100 ($13) as a bribe, the dead bullocks will never be removed from their colony. It is reported that they are collecting taka 0.25 (3 cents) from each sweeper as donation towards the taka 100 for the Inspector Saheb.

On the basis of real wage and foodgrain consumption analyses, A.R. Khan has established that "the living standards of the vast majority of the rural population in Bangladesh declined in absolute terms during recent decades. The real wages of agricultural laborers fell. These phenomena have been particularly pronounced in recent years. Comparing the decline in recent years with the already dreadful poverty in the benchmark year of 1949, it is clear that the vast majority of the rural population today must be suffering from severe undernutrition and starvation of various degrees." (15) This 1974 calamity, more man-made than natural, is another page in the region's history.

THE DEVELOPMENT CHALLENGE HAS YET TO BE DEFINED

Contrary to political rhetoric and plan goals, the actual economic processes at work during these first years caused broader participation in poverty. Even in the face of the continued economic crises and a literal flood of poor people into Dacca, public policies were altered only slowly. Good harvests and more food imports saved the day.

Economic liberalizations have taken place to improve efficiency and management, but no new conceptual planning framework has been put forward. Population control has yet to receive the attention it so desperately needs. Budget priorities clearly favor the urban minority. In short, the economic legacy from Pakistani days prevails.

The relief and rehabilitation era has been closed; the country has survived a period of economic chaos. Conventional economic indicators have signaled that these improvements mean economic restoration. The real challenge ahead may now become apparent. As will be explained in later chapters, improvements in the distribution of rural income in the 1960s were reversed in the 1970s, and throughout this period real wages continued their decline. (16) These are only symptoms of underlying pressures at work in an overpopulated agrarian economy. Before turning to an equitable growth model in Chapter 4, and to practical strategies for ensuring broad participation in agricultural development in the following chapters, Chapter 3 examines the theoretical reasons why the urban-industrial perspective retains its orthodoxy.

NOTES

(1) Since independence, the economy has been studied closely. The International Monetary Fund, the World Bank, the Asian Development Bank, and others have conducted many economic analyses of the short-term perspective. Longer term perspectives have been provided by Austin Robinson, John Lewis, John Mellor, Gus Ranis, Rene Dumont, and Brian Reddaway, among others who visited Bangladesh in its early years. These visits, and subsequent reports, provide temporal and international perspective to seemingly insoluble problems.

The country's planners have also benefited from the work of Basil Kavalsky and his eleven member mission from the World Bank. Their Bangladesh - Development in a Rural Economy, 1974 (in three volumes), was the first study to transcend the crises of 1972-74 and offer an appropriate development model for Bangladesh.

(2) USAID, East Pakistan Economy, Dacca: November, 1968, "Section IX - Disparity." The fiscal year for the Governments of Pakistan and Bangladesh runs from July 1st to June 30th.

(3) These sections have been drawn from the works of Rounaq Jahan; Edward A. Glaeser, "The Political Economy of Bangladesh under Sheikh Mujibur Rahman," Cornell (draft), 1975, p. 36; and Peter J. Bertocci, "The Politics of Mass Poverty in Bangladesh," Oakland University (draft), 1976, p. 20.

(4) The country's total industrial sector - to keep its size in perspective - generates 10% of a $7 billion gross domestic product and employs less than 5% of the available labor.

(5) The rupee currency unit - used for centuries in the subcontinent - was changed to the taka with independence and devalued 53% to place it on a par with the Indian rupee. The official rate, like that of the Indian rupee, remained tied to the pound at taka 18.98 to 1 and floated with respect to the

dollar at approximately taka 7.9 to 1. In May of 1975, the taka was devalued 56% to taka 30 to the pound sterling, which placed it at approximately taka 15 to the dollar.

The terms lakh and crore, one hundred thousand and ten million, respectively, are, like the word rupee, Hindi words used throughout the subcontinent. One lakh and one crore taka are worth $12,700 and $1.27 million, respectively, at the pre-devaluation official exchange rate of taka 7.9 to $1.00. After the May 1975 devaluation to taka 15 to $1.00, taka one lakh and one crore were worth $6,700 and $670,000, respectively. Before this devaluation, the approximate black market rate for the dollar was taka 18 to 25 during 1973 and 1974, and taka 16 to 22 during 1976 and 1977. Unless otherwise stated the official exchange rate is used in the text.

(6) The country's foreign exchange earnings are heavily dependent upon the export of raw jute and jute manufactures such as sacking and carpet backing. Expressed in current dollars, the jute export "benchmark" was $341 million in FY 1970. Following independence the earnings have been: in FY 1973, $305 million; in FY 1974, $318 million; in FY 1975 $299 million; FY 1976, $291 million; and in FY 1977, $295 million. These values in current dollars disguise a decrease in the quantity of jute exported.

The decline in jute earnings reflects several problems, such as a decline in the country's terms of trade, a declining market for natural fibers as a result of the development of polypropylene, weak domestic manufacturing and export management, and the competition between jute and rice. Although these two crops compete on only 15% of the total rice acreage, any shift away from jute, as happened during 1973-75 because of relatively higher rice prices, causes adverse foreign exchange consequences. Although the factors that influence this competition have important implications for labor use and rural income distribution, I have not had occasion to study them.

(7) During 1970-71, the gross domestic product fell by 5.5%, and by an additional 14% in 1972. A turn-around of 8.2% in 1972-73, and of a further 11.5% the following year, were caused primarily by good harvests and better utilization of industrial capacity. No change occurred in 1974-75; the growth in 1975-76 was 11%, and in 1976-77, 4 to 5%, again because of good harvests. The overall change has, therefore, been about 2% per year, which the 3% population growth rate diminishes to less than nothing. Real per capita income, unchanged in the 1960s, suffered a decline after independence.

(8) S.H. Khan, "Politics, Politicians and the People," Holiday, September 25, 1976.

(9) In the late spring, the Bangladesh Government publishes its budget, which covers its fiscal and monetary policies, annual development plan, and targets for the coming fiscal year. These documents also include a review of, and budgetary revisions for, the previous fiscal year.

(10) Bangladesh Government, Planning Commission, "Some Alternatives for the First Five-Year Plan," Dacca, April 12, 1973.

(11) In the case of subsidies for agricultural inputs, for example, the plan projected a total cost of $2.5 billion, of which only 49% was to have been

recovered from farmers. The efficiency and equity ramifications of these subsidies are examined in later chapters.

(12) These "demographic investments" are amply described by Austin Robinson in "The Economic Development of Malthusia," The Bangladesh Development Studies, Vol. II No. 3, July 1974, pp. 647-660.

(13) From USAID, Bangladesh Development Assistance Program, Dacca: 1974, pp. 140-191.

(14) Throughout the book I will quote occasionally from papers and field reports prepared by Nizam Uddin Ahmed, my economic research assistant in Dacca, and by me. Some of this material is of joint authorship, and some was written by one or the other of us, but I use the term "USAID Staff" to refer to all of it. The particular quotations here are drawn from reports based on interviews conducted by Mr. Ahmed between April and December of 1974.

(15) A. R. Khan, 1976, p. 24.

(16) Recent work by Mohiuddin Alamgir documents that the distribution of rural income improved during the 1960s and then deteriorated during the 1970s. See "Some Analysis of Distribution of Income, Consumption, Saving and Poverty in Bangladesh," The Bangladesh Development Studies, (BDS) Vol. II No. 4, October 1974, pp. 737-818; and "Poverty, Inequality and Social Welfare: Measurement, Evidence and Policy," BDS, Vol. III No. 2, April 1975, pp. 153-180.

3 Theoretical Legacies and Future Development Options

In the years following independence Bangladesh suffered severe economic jolts caused by extreme price and supply fluctuations, and by governmental aspirations to revitalize the country's small export-oriented urban sector. Despite plan priorities, which focus on agriculture and employment creation, political priorities and budgetary decisions continue to reinforce what remains in effect an export-oriented Pakistani industrial growth model. It is understandable that Bangladesh has fixed its sights on industry and other symbols of western wealth. To replicate these western successes, many poor countries have embarked on development planning processes drawn from the European planning experience. They have done so with little recognition of either their own resources and institutional endowment, or the conditions in developed countries that have made an industrial model exemplary. The availability of foreign advice and assistance has made this basic model all the more attractive.

I will show in this chapter that the Bangladesh people are heir to an economic model that is entirely inappropriate for the development of an agrarian economy. The country's lack of resources and massive population provide few options and little time for experimentation. Yet development must take place. In the face of continuing poverty in Bangladesh and in several other countries (and growth in others), western development theory is breaking with its past prescriptions.

LEGACIES OF WESTERN THEORY

Although Bangladesh is unique in its difficulties, it is but one of several poor countries which have embarked on a development course more encumbered with inappropriate theoretical baggage than is generally recognized. A brief review of economic growth models is necessary to understand the difficulties facing Bangladesh. (1) Examples of several economic precepts are noted here; they explain the failures of earlier models and dramatize Bangladesh's need for an altered theoretical approach.

The Preeminent Role of Savings

The importance of savings has been long established in classical economic thinking as the source of growth. Deferred consumption, said to be crucial to the supply of funds for capital-consuming investments, has been pursued by theoreticians and planners with single-minded attention. (2) Since the 18th century this emphasis has served to strengthen the economic status quo, whether represented by western commercial interests or the interests of the urban elite in developing countries. By relying upon this one-factor-of-growth model in developing countries, the recognition of how domestic savings have historically been used, the consumption requirements of a healthy and skilled labor force, and, most importantly, the size and composition of aggregate demand as an additional engine of growth have been overlooked. For Bangladesh and other poor agrarian countries, the emphasis upon savings seems sadly misplaced.

"The old problem of how to squeeze the peasantry is very much with us today." (3) Individual well-being will never flow from the developmental implications of such a statement. The peasantry is being "squeezed" severely, with adverse consequences for both growth and equity. The motives and sources of economic growth must be defined more generously.

Capital-Biased Growth

Western technical choices are largely reflections of processes induced by scarce labor and abundant natural resources. As a result, western growth models are largely ex post facto explanations of a relative factor endowment and resource price structure that encourages heavy capitalization. Western economics is, therefore, a product of labor-poor, resource-rich countries. Massive urban unemployment in Europe during the Industrial Revolution would have led to social unrest, and possibly altered political structures, if 40 million people had not migrated to the resource-rich frontiers of the New World and Australia. (4) In labor-rich developing countries similar migrations cannot now take place, and capital-growth models do not stress the underlying social and ethical changes that enabled and later reinforced the industrialization of Europe. The actual resource endowment of Bangladesh is, in a sense, entirely "foreign" to the development theory and aspirations of her outward-looking elite. Western experience offers neither a labor-rich, resource-poor development model nor the nicely packaged ethical and institutional underpinnings upon which countries such as Bangladesh can build.

Inherent in the commitment to imported models and aspirations is a faith in technological choices drawn from the western technical shelf. Because manufacturing processes are thought to be rigid, many policy makers and planners conclude that domestic market prices cannot influence technological choices and processes. Labor, the abundant resource, remains underemployed, and imported technologies and aspirations, often packaged in concessional foreign assistance, further reinforce an artificial price structure. As a consequence, economists - and their plans - do not threaten the existing economic system. Much of the following analysis identifies the economic distortions caused by the perception that domestic "prices don't matter."

Economic Production or Improved Welfare

A third fundamental consequence of western growth theory is the perceived conflict between increased production and improved well-being. It is a sad commentary on economics as a social science that it has taken decades to come to the theoretical and practical realization that these social goals are jointly determined. The economists' proclivity for marginal analyses has obscured the basic issue; production and organizational technologies contain their own distributive formulas. How plentiful are land, labor, capital, and managerial ability? Who benefits from their use? Who purchases the final product? Income distribution is both a consequence and a cause of growth.

All too often in developing countries the proportion of the factors employed and the composition of the national output reflect the preferences of an urban elite. As a consequence, production is capital-intensive, labor is underemployed, and the growth of existing urban-industrial centers becomes increasingly costly to achieve. With this kind of economic structure, production and human well-being do become inconsistent objectives. Poor people are the victims. An agriculturally-led growth model is offered in the next chapter as one route out of this costly impasse.

The Quality and Quantity of Human Capital

In retrospect, western models have underestimated the importance of other factors that contribute to growth in developed countries. During the development of industrialized countries, for example, human skills closely matched the tasks at hand. (5) In Bangladesh, however, educational aspirations and budgets are seriously out of step with manpower needs, as was pointed out in Chapter 2. Little adjustment is being made to find either less costly educational techniques or to fulfill manpower requirements. (6)

Just as the quality of human skills was not an explicit variable in western economic theory, inattention to human numbers has proven to be an oversight of historic consequence. Until very recently most development economists gave very little attention to the limitation of population. A century ago western developing countries had the advantage of far lower population densities and, in many cases, rich natural resources. Bangladesh - already the most densely populated country in the world - enjoys neither of these advantages that made rapid labor-force growth something to be encouraged rather than checked.

Combining the Strengths of Capitalism and Socialism

With the western economic legacy came models for implementation. The efficiency of capitalism was readily acknowledged by the newly-independent countries of the subcontinent, but this efficiency was seen to result in inequitable distributions of income and in inadequate supplies of social services. Therefore, the efficiency of capitalism was to be guided by the welfare aspirations of European social planners. In Pakistan, and now in Bangladesh, the vehicle for ensuring both efficiency and welfare has become the ministerial administration of plans, priorities, and prices. A wide range of urban consumer goods and services, and agricultural inputs are sold at subsidized prices to ensure that they are within reach of poor people. However, despite an effort to combine the best of two systems, this administrative experience is often described as having combined the practical difficulties of each. Public controls have led to inefficient administration and high costs; and subsidized public resources have ensured their limited supply, their allocation to those with influence, and the stifling of private sector incentives. In short, governmental efforts to control the private sector have caused inefficiencies and inequities.

This brief discussion has touched on the more visible of the theoretical legacies from the west. Subtle ones, of individual and social aspirations, of land and capital distribution, and of political institutions, are equally as important in understanding the bases of western growth theory. That these are not easily transplanted to poor countries has been often said and little understood. Before turning to a discussion of what development models may be relevant to Bangladesh, I review the implications of these western growth strategies as they relate to agriculture.

THE RESIDUAL ROLE OF AGRICULTURE

The previously-described theoretical precepts were the basic building blocks of growth theories for many developing countries in the 1950s and 1960s. Whether the emphases was on industrial growth, import substitution, export diversification, or some other leading edge of urban growth, agriculture and the rural population played a secondary role during these two decades. Whatever theories of agricultural development enjoyed prominence during this era, they were defined in terms of their contribution to the prevailing urban-industrial strategy rather than to the well-being of the rural population. Agriculture has remained for too long the supplier of food, labor, and capital which fuel urban-industrial growth. (7) In the 1950s, and continuing into the 1960s, little attention was paid to the requirements for ensuring the flow of these agricultural surpluses to the cities, or to the consequences of an unchecked population growth rate on the ability of agriculture to sustain these flows. It was assumed that agricultural production would grow to feed the cities and that industrial growth would generate employment to absorb displaced agricultural laborers, as had been the case in developed countries.

It is important to note that the early agricultural development theories place great emphasis upon broad participation of rural people in agricultural processes. The communal farming and community development models are notable for this emphasis. Land reform is an even more direct way of achieving the same social objective. (8) Since the mid-1960s, the introduction of high-yielding seed varieties has become the production basis of most "integrated rural development programs" world-wide. It is now axiomatic to say that agricultural modernization means new seed varieties of major crops and markedly increased supplies of modern agricultural inputs. This technological shift in the agricultural production function is of singular importance, yet it overshadows the remaining institutional and distributive problems which were front and center of older rural development strategies.

For Bangladesh, urban-industrial priorities continue to command attention and resources. The green revolution,based on the new high-yielding seed, has become another development "priority" without becoming an effective development strategy.

OLD GROWTH THEORIES IN A NEW AGE

One repercussion of these imported theoretical conceptions for Bangladesh, is the artificial division between efficient increases in production and improvements in the distribution of income - between economic growth and well-being. Foreign assistance does not bridge the two development objectives; it is not an adequate substitute for expanding frontiers, vast natural wealth, or domestic institutions appropriate to the challenge of equitable growth. Bangladesh must find solutions to its development problems within its boundaries, and this necessarily requires recognition of its own resources and institutions.

Development goals will have to mean life-style aspirations other than those exemplified by the heavily urbanized and industrial regions of developed countries. The capital intensity of a western growth model cannot be replicated across Bangladesh. Ex post facto explanations of developed countries are proving to be totally inadequate guides for late-developing countries in other cultures. Tens of millions of rural people "... will see Haley's comet before the growth effects spread beyond the urban fringe." (9) Instead urbanization must be actively discouraged; capital deepening must be balanced with capital sharing. Continuing efforts by the government to close a resource gap inherent in an urban-industrial strategy has led to stagnation. In short, poverty is man-made; it is the result of a largely-imported institutional heritage. With national independence the alleviation of this poverty has become a domestic responsibility. From what models can Bangladesh draw?

NEW THEORIES OF ECONOMIC GROWTH

The high-yielding varieties of seed and the emphasis on population control in the 1960s became twin elements of a new theory of "equitable growth" for developing countries in the 1970s. The emphasis on industrialization was increasingly seen as the cause of rural stagnation; conventional models were not working. The new seed technology - in the right policy environment - facilitated the combination of production and distributive objectives into one development strategy. No prior technical change had made this so obviously possible and on such a grand scale. The new seed is highly divisible for small farm agricultural systems; large farms and heavy equipment were found not to be the keys to rural growth, and because the new seed dramatized the possibilities for labor-using techniques in agriculture, other non-agricultural growth processes were examined for their job-creating opportunities.

With the use of the new seed and associated policy changes, it became apparent to researchers and planners that the small-family norm could be accepted at per capita income levels beneath those previously thought necessary to effect a demographic transition. These twin events, more heralded after the fact than recognized at the outset, have provided the theoretical base for several new equity-oriented strategies for economic growth. A short review of this thinking is useful for it not only dramatizes the conceptual advances that have been made but points up their inadequacy as a strategy appropriate for Bangladesh.

The roots of this new economic theory belong in the institutional school of economic thought rather than in the capital-growth school. Thorstein Veblen, Clarence Ayres, and Gunnar Myrdal have identified the social and institutional preconditions for human progress: those "larger forces moving obscurely in the background." (10) Works by Gunnar Myrdal in the subcontinent, Bruce Johnston in Japan, John Mellor in India, and others have helped to unify the theory and institution of popular participation in economic growth processes.

In the middle 1960s attention was focused on the new seed and the growth linkages to other sectors that emanate from the widespread use of this seed. This agricultural production priority, identified with John Mellor's work in India, underlies the development strategy proposed for Bangladesh. The application of his new seed-based growth model is discussed at length in the next chapter.

Several authors have warned that the high-yielding seed cannot be treated as the new single growth factor. Albert Waterston and Barbara Ward have voiced discontent with development strategies that rely on agricultural production priorities alone. Unless additional strategies accompany a priority placed on agricultural production, the new seed harvests will fall largely to the rural elite. Waterston and Ward stress that poor farmers must have access to agricultural inputs, to markets, and to rural infrastructure. Labor-intensive construction programs and industry are also seen as methods for ensuring broader participation in productive processes. Education and health services must be decentralized to rural areas. Waterston emphasizes the need for rural self-reliance, and Ward stresses rural participation in decision-making processes. Ward suggests that larger resource flows from rich to poor countries can finance these developmental priorities. (11)

James P. Grant and Mahbub ul Haq charge that broad-based programs such as the above will be very slow to improve the well-being of the poor; they favor a more direct attack on poverty. These authors note that reliance on capitalism's efficiency, socialism's welfarism, and foreign aid have all led to inefficient elitism. The products of such growth strategies cannot be redistributed to the poor because fiscal systems are weak, the consumer goods and services of the urban elite are inappropriate to the needs of the poor, and the institutions of industry are not neutral to the distribution of their own products. "Trickle down" has failed. Grant and Haq stress the redistribution of land, credit, health, education, and family planning service. They do not, however, explain how these are to be implemented. This minimum, basic human-needs approach is necessarily expensive, and can be financed, according to Haq, by North-South resource transfers and other transfer mechanisms for poor developing countries. (12)

Examining the East Asian experience, Irma Adelman and Cynthia Taft Morris come to different conclusions from those of Grant and Haq about the origins of growth with equity. They point out that land reforms were implemented early in the development process, giving the poor direct access to productive resources. Also at an early point in the development process, great emphasis was given to primary, secondary, technical, and university education. This early redistribution of physical and human capital, particularly in Taiwan, provided the basis for a commercial middle class and for sophisticated exports. (13)

Unlike the authors of development advice, institutions providing foreign assistance must face political realities and translate theory into practice. Their approach is to improve whatever participatory processes exist by redirecting project investments to agricultural and rural service sectors. These priorities bring us full circle in many "soft states," for such an approach must rely on existing institutions, and so upon "trickle down." (14)

This brief review of new development strategies cannot be concluded without pointing out that the generality of this new thinking limits its prescriptive usefulness. Furthermore, the absence of authoritarian regimes, disciplined societies, and large middle classes in many of the poorest countries makes it all the more difficult to translate developmental strategies that are drawn from other cultures into useful programs. There is a reluctance in this new thinking to ask why the world's poor are poor, and to identify the institutions that cause poverty in these least developed countries. The strategies suggested by Grant and Haq come closest to identifying the institutional difficulties that prevent millions of people from being drawn into growth processes. It is within the framework of these institutional difficulties that I examine one equitable growth strategy for Bangladesh.

NEW INCOMES AND SMALLER FAMILIES

Development planners believed in the 1960s that many poor countries could not enjoy per capita income growth until high population growth rates were reduced. In developed countries the manifold processes of industrialization and urbanization were assoicated with demographic transitions marked by reduced death rates and lowered birth rates. As a result, it was assumed that low death and birth rates could be equated with relatively high per capita income levels. However, it became clear in many poor countries that population growth had to be sharply curtailed before there could be a substantial improvement in economic well-being. Otherwise, population growth would consume resources designed for development. Western-style public health systems have brought about lowered death-rates in developing countries with relative ease. Bringing birth rates down is proving to be a difficult task. Individual and social consensus are needed to accomplish this; the motivation to have smaller families must be developed.

A new understanding of population dynamics has been circulating among demographers since the late 1960s; demographic transitions are occurring in some poor countries prior to the achievement of the individual income standards of developed countries. This transition is being achieved at relatively low levels of per capita income, as conventionally measured, because the development strategies in these countries are predicated upon popular participation in productive activities. Economic security can be improved for the poor. In a few developing countries a strong relationship is found between equity-oriented strategies and acceptance of the small family norm; together, these result in more rapid per capita income growth. Analyses by William Rich and Robert Hunter illustrate that falling population growth rates are associated with, or soon follow, governmental efforts to improve individual access to productive activity and to social services. (15) Although their analyses do not prove that expanding the economic franchise causes the birth rate to fall, their evidence that the development strategies of Taiwan and South Korea are contributing to a reduced population growth rate, whereas the strategies of Mexico and Brazil are not, is persuasive. It is also evident from their work that no single social or economic variable is the key; governments must introduce reforms across a broad front of economic policies and institutions. (16)

PROSPECTS FOR DEVELOPMENT IN BANGLADESH

The people of Bangladesh are so poor that improvement in their well-being can only come from the development of all facets of economic life. A generalized strategy for development must create employment and provide a host of services. However, for reasons that will be elaborated upon in the following chapters, it is premature to recommend a multifaceted development strategy in Bangladesh. It may even be premature to focus on the more sophisticated later generation problems of the green revolution because the new seed, the primary vehicle for development, is forcing recognition of severe institutional constraints to growth. Waterston's and Ward's concern that agricultural production increases will be enjoyed by the rural elite is well-founded. No agricultural strategy that hopes to include all citizens can afford to ignore the existing institutional blocks to broad participation in economic processes, and even to increased agricultural production. Although the approach I recommend for Bangladesh is based on an equitable growth strategy and, of necessity, is centered on agricultural production, most of our attention must be devoted to the basic institutional underpinnings of the economy. No participatory strategy appears relevant until the institutional heritage is understood. The causes of poverty must be identified. The country's existing institutions of price, technology, tenure, land and water development, and rural programs do not support the translation of a broadly participatory agricultural production strategy into reality.

NOTES

(1) For disussions of the major theories of economic growth, see Benjamin Higgins, Economic Development (Norton) and Gerald Meier, Leading Issues in Development Economics (Oxford). For critiques of selected economic growth models, see Wassily Leontief, "Theoretical Assumptions and Nonobserved Facts," The American Economic Review, Vol. 61, March 1971, pp. 1-7; Michael Lipton, Why Poor People Stay Poor - Urban Bias in World Development, Cambridge: Harvard, 1977; and Wendel C. Gordon, Economics from an Institutional View Point.

(2) See Ragnar Nurkse, Problems of Capital Formation in Underdeveloped Countries, New York: Oxford University Press, 1953, and P. N. Rosenstein-Rodan, "Problems of Industrialization of Eastern and Southeastern Europe," Economic Journal, Vol. 53, June 1943.

(3) Abu Abdullah, "Land Reform and Agrarian Change in Bangladesh," The Bangladesh Development Studies, Vol. IV No. 1, January 1976, p. 94.

(4) Barbara Ward, "A 'People' Strategy of Development," Washington, D.C.: Overseas Development Council, 1973, p. 3.

(5) This is an over-generalized statement of the U.S. educational experience but it permits a broad comparison of western educational priorities with those common in the subcontinent.

(6) Edward Denison, in The Sources of Economic Growth in the United States (New York: Committee for Economic Development, 1962), has calculated that 70 to 80% of the growth in the United States is explained by qualitative improvements in labor's productivity.

(7) See John C. H. Fei and Gustav Ranis, "A Theory of Economic Development," The American Economic Review, Vol. 51 No. 4, September 1961, pp. 533-565.

(8) The problems with these several agricultural development strategies are noteworthy. Cooperative farming successes are few because it is difficult to sustain a spirit of communal enterprise from generation to generation. The community development philosophy has suffered in practice because its tenets have been poorly understood and inadequately funded and implemented. Possibly the basic assumption is weak; given existing rural resources and power structure, and a little outside help, villagers can improve their lives through coordinated work. Traditional villagers may be like traditional

farmers; they, too, have wrung the last benefit out of their existing resource base and organizational structure. Where land reforms have been associated with the new seed technology, as in several East Asian countries, an expansion of the economic franchise is greatly in evidence. More commonly, however, as in Latin America and South Asia, land reforms have proven to be exercises in definitional obfuscation.

(9) James B. Stepanek, "A Comment on the Doctrines of the International Monetary Fund," (draft) 1975, p. 13.

(10) Clarence Ayres, p. 19.

(11) Albert Waterston, "A Viable Model for Rural Development," Finance and Development, Vol. 11 No. 4, December 1974, pp. 22-25; and Barbara Ward, op. cit.

(12) James P. Grant, "Development: The End of Trickle Down?" Foreign Policy, No. 12, Fall 1973, pp. 43-65; Mahbub ul Haq, "The Crisis in Development Strategies," in The Political Economy of Development and Underdevelopment, pp. 367-372, edited by Charles K. Wilber, New York: Random House, 1973; and his "The Third World and the International Economic Order," Washington, D.C.: Overseas Development Council, September 1976.

Although these authors clearly intend the International Labor Organization phrase "basic human needs" to encompass job and income creation, other authors use the phrase to refer only to the public provisions of services such as education, health, nutrition, and family planning. The risk for development programs in this distinction is that public services can absorb a great deal of foreign assistance without addressing basic institutional reforms to enlarge the economic franchise.

(13) Irma Adelman and Cynthia Taft Morris, "Who Benefits from Economic Development," Chapter 4 of the authors' Economic Growth and Social Equity in Developing Countries, Stanford University Press, 1973.

(14) In varying degrees this approach to "growth with equity" is practiced by the World Bank, ILO, the United Nations Development Program, the Food and Agriculture Organization of the United Nations, and several bilateral foreign assistance programs.

(15) See William Rich, "Smaller Families Through Social and Economic Progress," Overseas Development Council, Washington, D.C., January 1973, and Robert Hunter et al.,"A New Development Strategy? Greater Equity, Faster Growth, and Smaller Families," Overseas Development Council, Washington, D.C., October 1972.

(16) The tentative nature of this thesis is highlighted by contradictory evidence from countries other than those cited. Data for southern European countries illustrate that fertility rates may fall before socioeconomic development occurs and that no single indicator or group of indicators appears to be associated with the transition. (See Alan Sweezy, "Recent Light on the Relation between Socioeconomic Development and Fertility Decline," Caltech Population Program Occasional Papers, 1973.) On the other hand, a demographic transition has occurred at low levels of income in

Sri Lanka where it was caused not by development but by the public supply of risk-reducing social services. These services have been provided at the cost of slowed development. Sri Lanka spent her foreign exchange earnings on free education and health services, subsidized food, and an anti-malaria campaign. According to Frederick Roche, high fertility is a consequence of a high infant mortality rate; when this is reduced, the fertility rate will fall. A massive redistribution of public resources for political, not economic, reasons has served to control population growth in Sri Lanka. (See Frederick C. Roche, "The Demographic Transition in Sri Lanka: Is Development Really a Prerequisite?" Cornell Agricultural Economics Staff Paper, January 1976.)

4 A Modern Rice Culture – The Foundation for Equitable Growth

Rapid growth of a modern rice culture can be the foundation for Bangladesh's development. The new high-yielding rice varieties and related growth processes can provide increased employment and income for an economy that cannot ignore its poor. My theoretical model is drawn largely from the work of John Mellor. (1) According to his model, adapted to Bangladesh, the new high-yielding seed technology, the creation of rural infrastructure, and market-town growth are the basic building blocks for achievement of the Five-Year Plan's goals. A dynamic rural economy will contribute to the plan's three goals of increased production, improved income distribution, and national self-reliance. Although I keep this model before me to guide the analysis and my hopes for the country, the remaining chapters spell out the institutional conditions that can make theoretical prescriptions a reality.

It is not enough to increase supplies of agricultural inputs, improve agriculture research institutions, and speed the rate of agricultural growth. Increasing yields is a technical matter; expanding and then sustaining these harvests countrywide will severely strain the present institutional structure. Not only must there be a political and administrative commitment to a complex biological technology, but major alterations are required in the country's economic institutions. This institutional analysis in the following chapters focuses on the country's food system, the new seed technology, traditions of land tenure, the country's water development strategy, and rural institutions for equitable growth.

Before turning to the rich institutional mosaic of Bangladesh and to those changes of policy and program which are needed to implement an equitable growth strategy, the model's logic needs further elaboration. The growth linkages of the new seed technology can encompass the whole economy. To ensure that this does happen, in theory as well as practice, the model is strengthened to include crop diversification that will extend the green revolution to all crops, and to include rural earthworks and market-town growth that will expand rural employment and purchasing power. Emphasis has to be placed upon earthworks and upon market-town development because under-employment far surpasses the labor requirements of the most intensive use of the country's arable land. Although I do not address population control as a separate subject, the model may also speed acceptance of the small family norm. However, this achievement, like the achievement of a seed-based equitable growth strategy, cannot be taken for granted.

AGRICULTURAL DEVELOPMENT - THE MODEL BROADLY DEFINED

The Five-Year Plan's priority on foodgrain self-sufficiency does not represent the fullest exploitation of agriculture's contribution to development, nor does it necessarily call for the participation of all the country's laborers and cultivators. If the new seed technology provided bumper crops on some portion of the country's 22 million acres and the grain price trend fell for lack of adequate demand, the green revolution's expansion could end before the country's under-employed were included in the modernization process. The revolution would be over because consumer demand did not grow as fast as crop production. Consequently, the new seed, which requires costly doses of fertilizer and water, would be unprofitable. Growth of on-farm employment and income generated by the new seed could stagnate. Because only the high-yielding new seed can ensure income growth, its use cannot be allowed to falter. Foodgrain self-sufficiency is within the country's grasp now, yet its achievement will do little to translate the new seed technology into improved rural well-being. (The country's new and old seed are described in this chapter's Appendix A.)

Over the long term, crop production increases have to be purchased so that farmer expectations of continued profitability are ensured. Grain prices often decline dramatically with good harvests; if this decline occurs over a number of years, farmers will curtail their use of the new seed and expensive inputs. How can high harvest prices be assured year after year?

Foodgrain purchases dominate the meager budgets of the poor; well over half of their income is spent on foodgrain and other food items. As incomes grow with larger harvests and better crop prices, the poorest laborers and cultivators will spend as much as 60% of their new income on foodgrain. (2)

Herein lies a vital link between larger harvests and their purchase. If there is broad participation in the new seeds' harvests, it will generate additional purchasing power by laborers and sustain cultivators' price expectations.

Foodgrain self-sufficiency does not address this price maintenance requirement. In fact it suggests a different growth process. A goal of self-sufficiency alone, without regard to wide acceptance of the new seed, can be achieved by crop-yield increases on the farms of the fewer, relatively more progressive farmers. This will mean larger harvests but fewer new food consumers. The few large producers will consume only a small proportion of their increased harvests because their position of relative wealth, as absentee owners and farm managers, has long since allowed them to spend most of their income on non-food items. With added incomes, these "farmers" will spend proportionately more on goods and services imported into the rural economy.

An agricultural strategy that emphasizes broad acceptance of the new seed will generate a different consumption pattern and a different level of food demand than a strategy that simply stresses foodgrain increases. When food self-sufficiency is achieved by policies oriented only to production increases, a lower absolute level of food production will satisfy the demand for grain because the rural majority will not have the income to make their food needs felt. Malnutrition will remain veiled. As will be shown in later chapters, the population of rural Bangladesh can be divided into these two broad food consumption groups.

An agricultural strategy that assures broad access to agricultural inputs will enable more cultivators and agricultural laborers to exploit the new seed, thereby earning the incomes with which to purchase and retain larger amounts of each harvest. Their demand for food will help to sustain an agricultural growth process that might otherwise lapse or be sustained only by a costly price support program or export drive. Although price supports and grain exports can sustain the demand for grain, these approaches are typical of enclave economies that leave most cultivators outside modernization processes. The point is not the achievement of foodgrain production per se, but economic viability for millions of the rural poor. Participation in agricultural processes is their only option.

Fortuitously, the new seed's divisibility for small-farm use ensures technical compatibility between increased crop production and greater rural participation. In addition, the country's basic agricultural input systems are in place. Programs for new seed, credit, fertilizers, pesticides, and irrigation have been established since the 1960s.

New income in the hands of a wide range of rural people ensures more than higher grain prices during harvests. More income will also be spent on non-grain foods and consumer goods and services. (3) The expansion of rural purchasing power provides a vital link to consumer goods, to manufacturing, and to foreign trade. A sustained rate of rural income growth will encourage a diversification of expenditure patterns and further rounds of investments in the production of other crops and in the local manufacture of consumer goods. Because new goods can be produced by labor-intensive techniques in market towns, yet another round of investment and employment is created. Consumer goods production for domestic demand can lead to export markets for higher-value crops, western-style consumer goods, and high technology products. Therefore, growth linkages emanate from the new seed in several directions: to income and employment growth from the expansion of agricultural production; to agricultural marketing, processing, and storage; to the growth and diversification of consumer demand; and to export markets.

These processes represent new purchasing power in the hands of millions of rural families, an impressive engine for growth. This broad rural development strategy also may encourage acceptance of the small-family norm by providing economic security that heretofore has been absent. This growth is generated not by the evolution of urban-based growth linkages as they are classifically understood, but by the promotion of these same processes among millions of people in rural Bangladesh. (Will the mountain come to Mohammed?)

Three aspects of this model are required in order to strengthen its growth linkages. Although the new rice seed is the fundamental technological revolution that makes this equitable growth model possible, higher rice yields are only one factor in a comprehensive rural strategy. Crop diversification, rural works, and market-town growth are also essential for ensuring that laborers share in rural growth processes.

One other aspect of the model, the quality of human capital, is discussed in this chapter's Appendix B. As I have emphasized, the model in all of its aspects remains only a model. Whether the policies and programs that flow from its conceptualization will improve the well-being of millions of people depends upon the assumptions underlying this seed-based model. These assumptions, and the prescriptions that follow from their analysis in this instititutional milieu, hold the key to the new seed's relevance for Bangladesh.

SUSTAINING AGRICULTURAL GROWTH

Crop Diversification

The model's growth linkages emanate from increased agricultural incomes made possible by higher rice yields and remunerative harvest prices. Maintaining this seed-based growth process in the years to come will depend upon the supply of improved varieties of all the major crops. A rice culture alone - even though this one grain dominates the economy - cannot sustain the income linkages of a dynamic agriculture. At present, vistas of golden paddy, which seemingly stretch forever, disguise very low yields and low cropping intensities. Even with the added purchasing power prescribed by our model, rice prices will soften as multiple increases in yields occur. Because this price trend is likely to happen well before a majority of farms are modernized and unemployment is significantly reduced, other seed vehicles are needed to carry the new seed revolution forward. Therefore, a policy of crop diversification is required in order to expand the model's technological seed base. This expansion will encourage a more intensive utilization of land and labor and will create higher net returns per acre. The country's agricultural research and extension systems are beginning to offer improved varieties of a wide range of crops. Income growth and the diversification of family spending patterns in the future will create markets for a greater variety of foods.

Rural Earthworks

Just as a wider range of new seed varieties is needed to carry the seed revolution to more cultivators and agricultural laborers, so too must other methods be found to expand rural purchasing power. To do so, agricultural laborers should be able to find off-season employment in the construction of rural infrastructure. Rural works laborers could construct irrigation canals and roads to provide the physical linkages necessary to ensure the growth of economic ones. With these projects, rural purchasing power could be put in the hands of hundreds of thousands of laborers who would otherwise remain under-employed during a portion of the year.

Rural wage payments could result in modest increases in total rural demand. Ninety percent of the cost of canals and minor roads would be in the form of wages for rural laborers. These laborers in turn would spend more than half of their wage payments for foodgrain and other food commodities. This added income would be spent at a time of year when the main aman (summer) harvest comes in and grain prices are seasonally low. Whether earthworks are required to create purchasing power, build rural infrastructure, or provide humanitarian assistance, they can provide a multi-faceted strengthening of the model's growth linkages.

A works program for the purposes just described was started before Bangladesh became independent. Throughout most of the 1960s, the Rural Works Program provided hundreds of thousands of jobs on rural road and irrigation projects. Since independence the Rural Works Program has become dispirited for political and financial reasons, while a new Food For Work Program based on a wage payment in food instead of cash has expanded. These two parallel work programs have come to exemplify contrasting philosophies of rural development.

For the purpose of highlighting the price-based linkages of the growth model, I draw attention to the use of grain payments in lieu of cash wage payments. The introduction of food payments, which are largely imported, represents an increased grain supply during those times of year when purchasing power, not food supply, is typically the problem. In the spring of 1976, when the country's largest wheat crop was being harvested, wheat payments contributed to a further decline in the cultivators' harvest price. (4) Should this food-based program become significant, it will undercut the production and expenditure growth linkages upon which development depends.

Market Towns

Village markets, called hats, and larger ones, called bazaars, are the commercial centers of rural Bangladesh. Weekly, and often daily, 6,600 of these markets come alive in the late afternoon as tradesmen - kumars, kamars, and chasis (potters, blacksmiths, and farmers) - exchange their goods. (5) There are very few permanent buildings and a motorized vehicle is rarely seen, yet the manufactured goods of a massive rural population are purchased and traded for foods of all kinds. Grain and jute traders dominate the centers of these markets, while potters, carpenters, blacksmiths, and toolmakers conduct their business along their edges. These craftsmen are sought out for utensils, furniture, cloth, bicycle repairs, and pump maintenance; they are the kamars and mistries (mechanics) of the model's evolution into rural industry and market-town growth. (6)

As my emphasis upon rural earth works serves several purposes, so, too, is the promotion of market-town growth the coincidence of several developmental objectives. Farm income and wages will be increasingly spent for non-farm goods. The unemployed must be able to find work without having to resort to a futile search for work in the cities. On-farm and public earth work will not provide adequate employment alone.

Although most market towns are small, often no more than a weekly gathering, they function well. Thana and some 500 district centers have developed into full-time commercial centers. In keeping with the model's prescriptions, market-town growth must be guided by public policy. Governmental reluctance to encourage large private industry is understandable, for the concentrations of economic power in Pakistan contributed to inter-wing injustices. Now the country must give scope to its own entrepreneurs. A rural industrial strategy will generate employment, produce consumer goods, and stimulate decentralized urban growth centers at a cost to the public far lower than that which has been tolerated in the past. (7) When writing of Bangladesh, Gustav Ranis noted this potential: "Giving too short shrift to small-scale industrial entrepreneurial capacity in LDCs is analogous to our previous error in underestimating the wisdom and entrepreneurial capacity of LDC farmers." (8)

There is a more subtle reason for including market towns in the model; these towns must become centers for rural investment opportunities. The proceeds of the new seed technology and related commerce need productive outlets. Land purchases by the rural elite speed poor farmers into a state of landlessness. If poor cultivators and landless agricultural laborers are to be drawn into the processes of agricultural modernization, then the wealthier landowners and traders must have investment opportunities that are more closely aligned with productive activities. Private resources can put the disenfranchised to work.

Small-scale fabricating, processing, and marketing firms are an alternative way to meet consumer demand and even export growth. Experience in East Asian countries makes it clear that most consumer goods - and certainly their fabricating and assembling stages - can be completed in shops employing from five to 50 people. (9) It is not economically sound to fulfill consumer demand with imports and the products of large-scale industry.

Market-town growth may always depend upon the importation of capital-intensive basic materials, such as iron and steel, aluminum, plastics and most chemicals, petroleum products, and drugs; however, it makes little sense to import labor-intensive goods to labor-surplus areas, and particularly to a vast rural market. Increasingly, Bangladesh should import capital-intensive raw and intermediate goods, and export goods that are labor-intensive and complete. Sophisticated electronic equipment, quality clothing, and high-value food and animal products can be produced in rural Bangladesh for its own population and for export. (10)

The Urban-Industrial Complement to a Rural Model

The industrial "leading edge" of western growth models now becomes a co-partner with agriculture in development. The final growth stage for some growth models of high mass consumption becomes a first or second stage in this model. Productive opportunities and consumer demand, not single-minded attention to the savings rate, are the keys to development in this agrarian economy. (11) The growth of manufacturing, stimulated by increasing purchasing power, depends upon reducing the inequalities of rural life.

However, old models die hard:

> "It is well to recognize that economic growth is a brutal, sordid process. There are no short cuts to it. The essence of it lies in making the laborer produce more than he is allowed to consume for his immediate needs, and to invest and reinvest the surplus thus obtained.... The underdeveloped countries must consciously accept a philosophy of growth and shelve for the distant future all ideas of equitable distribution and welfare state. It should be recognized that these are luxuries which only developed countries can afford.... Historically, growth has never been 'balanced'. There have always been leading and lagging sectors as well as regions." (12)

While I agree that growth may be a brutal process and that there are certainly no shortcuts, the burden of this growth need not fall so directly on laborers. The fallacy in the above quote is the failure to recognize that broad-based access to productive activities, self-generated welfare, is a necessary substitute for older growth models that ensured ex post facto "welfare" for the urban few.

Fundamental to my model is the rationalization of prices, that is, the alteration of prices to reflect the relative domestic supplies of labor and capital. Subsidies on consumer and capital goods seriously inhibit the search for less costly solutions to the goals of increased production, employment growth, and national self-reliance. In a country of 80 million people, the price of capital should reflect its relative scarcity and not the ready supply of foreign aid.

All sectors of the economy should contribute to job creation. Heavy manufacturing can play a role by using multiple shifts, redesigning plant layouts, and decentralizing some of the operations that can be carried out effectively in market towns: raw material processing, product fabrication, and packaging. Even technologically rigid plants, such as those manufacturing steel and chemicals, have potential for efficient job expansion in the areas of final product handling and distribution. However, the redirection of industry will be difficult, in part because management may view labor as undisciplined and, therefore, expensive; a public wage goods policy would help to change this perception.

Agriculture must contribute to the considerable cost of its own modernization. Agricultural input subsidies should be reduced. It may be more efficient to mobilize private resources by encouraging private investment in market-town growth rather than struggling in vain to tax rural incomes. The cities and towns must also support development; reducing urban food subsidies taxes the cities and allows agricultural prices to rise.

The dangers of rapid urbanization are appreciated by the government. Its policies governing the free distribution of food and the location of industry discourage further growth of the largest urban centers. The government provides some incentives to civil servants in rural posts and encourages Dacca-based officials "to go on tour." However, in the face of a rapidly increasing population, the piecemeal attention to land use problems must give way to planning for market-town development.

CONDITIONS OF THE MODEL'S CONTRIBUTION TO EQUITY AND GROWTH

The model's linkages are only theoretical; their practical effect depends on a host of assumptions. Among these the most obvious are the supply and effective delivery of agricultural inputs, remunerative agricultural prices, and expenditure linkages. Past experience dictates considerable passimism with respect to the fulfillment of these first assumptions. As Albert Hirschman has pointed out, "Agriculture certainly stands convicted on the count of its lack of direct stimulus to the setting up of new activities through linkages effects - the superiority of manufacturing in this respect is crushing. (13)

Even if these linkages can be assured, the growth processes that are initiated may not be important or widely shared. To ensure that these new resource flows do not dwindle to another trickle, more subtle assumptions must be analyzed. Will urban Bangladesh depend on her cultivators for food? Will cultivators respond to higher prices? Can agricultural production programs be designed to ensure participation in growth processes? My reply to Hirschman anticipates the institutional emphasis in chapters to come. The "superiority" of manufacturing is a reflection of the institutional and policy biases, discussed in Chapters 2 and 3, rather than the exclusive qualities of industry itself. Although these qualities do not necessarily have to be exclusive, their absence severely constrains an agriculturally based model.

I have selected five institutions for detailed analysis in the remaining chapters. These institutions - the food system, the new seed, tenure, water, and rural development programs - have been treated individually and, I believe, inadequately by others. (14) These institutional analyses are to be seen within the framework of the seed-based growth model which has been described. Will the rural poor have access to rural growth processes? This is the basic question addressed in the remaining chapters.

Labor's Share in the New Seed Revolution

Agricultural growth will improve the well-being of those who participate; owners of land and capital will share amply in these growth processes. However, it cannot be said *a priori* that millions of rural laborers will benefit.

Because this model is designed to ensure broad participation, and because it depends on the consumption patterns created by this participation, we must focus on those institutions that determine laborers' share in the new seed technology.

We first examine the macroeconomics of agricultural production in Bangladesh and its institutional rigidities. At the farm level, the new seed are a mixed blessing. Acceptance of this technology is very much in question. There is also growing evidence that tenure traditions, as well as water and rural institutional programs, are keeping laborers and cultivators from public resources.

Our conclusion is inescapable. In order to assure equitable rural income growth for millions of people who are disenfranchised from all but their own two hands, a direct confrontation with existing institutions is required.

Growth of Per Capita Income

A high population growth rate nullifies the powers of this model since it destroys the per capita income growth required for the diversification of consumption patterns. If population growth consumes the added output made possible by the new seed, per capita well-being will not improve. Though total demand may grow with population, each person's material well-being will not improve. Individual diets will not expand and diversify, nor will the secondary income and employment growth linkages emanating from additional rural incomes be significant. (15)

Population growth also intensifies pressures on the land. Family labor is displacing hired labor; farm sizes are decreasing; landlessness is increasing; a smaller proportion of the rural population is finding full-time employment. Population growth must be stopped.

PROSPECTS FOR JOB CREATION

Achieving foodgrain self-sufficiency is not a major issue in my view; the food gap is small and basic production techniques and programs are in place. Full-time employment is a different matter. The gap between the number of laborers and the number of jobs is widening, and the techniques of job creation - on a large scale and in this institutional milieu - are not known. Laborers are coming of age two and three times faster than jobs are being created.

The prospects for employment expansion are sobering. Because of the youthfulness of the population, the percentage increase in the labor force is larger than that of the population as a whole - a staggering 4 to 4½% each year. This places the annual increment of those looking for work in the range of 850,000 to 1.1 million.

Estimating actual job growth is more difficult to assess because the coefficients of crop-acre/man-days in agriculture and in industrial and commercial employment are very hard to generalize to the economy as a

Table 4.1. Prospects for Employment Growth in Bangladesh, 1976

Supply or Demand for Labor in 1976, mid-year in millions	Sector Employment, in millions	Annual Increment in Labor or Employment	Assumed Percentage Growth Rate
Supply of Labor			
Total population	81	2,430,000	3%
Total labor force	28.4	1,140,000	4%
Agricultural labor force	21.6	860,000	4%
Demand for Rural Labor			
1. Agriculture			
Rice, new varieties	1.22		
Rice, local	5.00		
Jute	.88		
Sugarcane	.18		
Tea	.14		
Livestock, forestries, and fisheries	3.00		
Other	.50		
Agriculture Subtotal	10.92	220,000	2%
		(550,000)	(5%)
2. Non-Agriculture			
Rural Earthworks	.17	134,000	20%
Market Towns			
Industries	.30		
Trade and services	.80		
Non-agricultural Subtotal	1.27	55,000	5%
		(110,000)	(10%)
Rural Subtotal	12.19		
Urban Employment:			
Industries, based on imported materials	.44		
Industries, based on indigenous materials	.66		
Trades and services	1.50		
Urban Subtotal	2.60	130,000	5%
		260,000	(10%)
TOTAL	14.79	260,000	(10%)

Source: Calculated by author from coefficients and statistics in Government, International Labor Organization, and World Bank documents.

Note: Figures in parentheses are from the Five-Year Plan.

whole. Estimates are offered in Table 4.1. (16) Local varieties of rice generate half the total employment in agriculture. A 2% expansion rate in on-farm employment, created by a new seed-based production growth rate of 4%, will generate 220,000 jobs per year. The Five-Year Plan, in unrealistically high projection, places this estimate at 550,000 new jobs per year.

Man-day increases per crop acre year are a direct function of the supply and acceptance of agricultural inputs. Dramatic man-day increases come with costly irrigation systems which permit the double and triple cropping of fallow land. Although many man-days were expended on rural earthworks in the 1960s, these represent relatively few "whole" jobs each year.

Market-town employment, the hardest to estimate, has been calculated on the basis of 10% of the employment created in agricultural production. (17) The industrial employment numbers are firm, but it must be admitted that the figure of 1.5 million for trades and services is an approximation.

The percentage increases used in Table 4.1 reflect what has happened in the 1960s. All told, 439,000 additional jobs can be created each year, assuming that existing plan targets are implemented. The estimate of 920,000, which assumes heroic efforts, would narrow the gap considerably for the new entrants to the labor force. However, there is little evidence from the past to suggest that even the plan's projected job growth rate of 4.5% can be achieved. The long-term employment creation growth rate is likely to be under 2% because agriculture is already labor intensive, and a realistic growth rate for agricultural production is likely to be no more than 3.5 to 3.9%. Experience in other countries indicates that rural employment growth is approximately one-half the rate of growth in agricultural production itself. (18) In recent years the growth in agricultural production averaged less than 2% in Bangladesh.

A dispassionate review of Table 4.1 indicates that the prospect for employment growth is dismal. Only a radical change in the entire institutional structure can put these numbers of people to work. There is no comparable lesson to draw from other countries. Short, intensive periods of labor mobilization have occurred under authoritarian regimes, but they are not applicable here.

My model may be called too little and too late because the numbers of unemployed appear so formidable. In the present institutional context of Bangladesh, the model's prescriptions may be too radical. In the following chapters I develop the case for the reorientation of existing institutions which retard agricultural growth and erode rural well-being. Paper strategies and plans can easily project a job creation rate high enough to close an employment gap. Such exercises are irrelevant; planning targets must be predicated upon an institutional foundation appropriate to the challenge.

NOTES

(1) John Mellor, The New Economics of Growth, Cornell, 1976. The model is based on Mellor's work in India and on the numerous supporting studies Mellor and his students have conducted in recent years. Mellor's mathematical model (with Uma J. Lele) is contained in Cornell Agricultural Economics Occasional Paper No. 43 entitled "Technological Change and Distributive Bias in a Duel Economy" (revised, October 1972). (The World Bank's study Bangladesh - Development in a Rural Economy, prescribes a similar agricultural production model for Bangladesh.) The wealth of Indian data upon which Mellor's work is based is becoming available in Bangladesh; surveys of household income and expenditures, and land holdings are now being conducted.

(2) The Statistical Division of the Ministry of Planning has recently completed a household expenditure survey for 1973-74 and others are under way. This survey indicates that the lowest household income quartile spends approximately 85% of its income on major food items. See The Statistical Year Book of Bangladesh, 1975, pp. 269-284.

(3) Indian data drawn from Mellor (May 1972, pp. 13, 15) illustrate that with each higher decile of rural income, the proportion of income expended for non-grain agricultural products and for urban goods and services increases. Analyses of consumer data for East Pakistan from the 1960s by M. Raquibuz Zaman (unpublished tables) illustrate the same expenditure patterns among a poorer population.

(4) The first official mention of this problem is made in a Bangladesh Agricultural Research document entitled "Group Discussion on HYV Wheat - Recommendations," Dacca: September 1976, pp. 2, 6. There is another reason to question rural works' contribution to equitable growth. Because of the degree of landlessness and tenancy, an expansion of rural works may cause a deterioration in the distribution of income and land as farm owners enjoy larger harvests and are able to buy out smaller holdings. In other words, rural works, as well as other development programs, are not "neutral" with respect to their impact on the existing distribution of income and assets. For works programs to contribute to equitable growth, there must be a change in the distribution of land. This point is discussed in following chapters.

(5) The phrase "kumars, kamars, and chasis" (potters, blacksmiths, and farmers, is a popular Bengal expression for rural commerce.

(6) The term mistri is used throughout the subcontinent to mean a general mechanic.

(7) The importance of market-town growth can be appreciated by contemplating the alternative in the plan. The capital cost per unit of additional production - the incremental capital output ratio (ICOR) - was to have increased each year. For the First Five-Year Plan, from FY 1974 to 1978, the ICOR for agriculture was to grow from .8 to 1.6. For manufacturing, the ICOR was to grow from 3.6 to 5.0, and for other sectors, from 2.6 to 4.0. In

aggregate the ICOR was to have increased from 1.9 to 3.1 In other words, the cost of each additional unit of output was projected to go up by two-thirds during the Five-Year Plan period. (World Bank, Bangladesh - Development in a Rural Economy, pp. 298-99.) It is clear from Chapter 2 that this objective is not being met. A.R. Khan has calculated that, with respect to industrial employment, "....the sluggish growth in nonagricultural employment was due partly to the failure of the nonagricultural activities to expand fast and particularly to the use of inappropriate technology in these activities.... The share of the manufacturing sector (both modern and traditional) in total employment declined from 5.81% in the benchmark year (1949) to 5.39% in 1967-68 ... to 3.69% in August 1974." (A.R. Khan, March 1976, pp. 25-26). The resources may be available to finance this degree of capital deepening for a small industrial enclave, but at a cost of relatively fewer consumer goods and jobs for the country as a whole.

(8) Gustav Ranis, p. 844. Through the pioneering work of David C. McClelland it is now known that entrepreneurial spirit can be identified in a population and that training can strengthen this motivation to achieve. See David C. McClelland and David G. Winter, Motivating Economic Achievement, New York: The Free Press, 1971.

(9) For an excellent analysis of the Indonesian case, see Louis T. Wells, Jr. "Economic Man and Engineering Man: Choice of Technology in a Low Wage Country," Harvard: Economic Development Report No. 226, November 1972, (Also in Timmer, 1975). For other small-scale industry comparisons see Joseph E. Stepanek, "New Perspectives: Industrial Development in the Third World," Wien: Osterr. Bundesverl., 1972.

(10) The case for market-town growth is one thing; its promotion has proven to be quite another. Past efforts to decentralize industries have focused on the industrial estate model, subsidized credit, and ready access to imported capital goods. However, efforts to decentralize industry have not been successful. What is it that will induce the entrepreneur to select more socially optimal production techniques and locations?

Credit may be a problem for the small entrepreneur, but those already capitalized with land and equipment are the first to receive cheap credit from public resources. Because the rural entrepreneur can be characterized as having a need for relatively larger amounts of working capital, collateral requirements need to be based on production, not on assets. (The parallel with the small farmer is noteworthy.) Public credit, industrial estates, and particularly import licenses have traditionally favored the larger firms, thereby causing distortions in the very processes and products development plans seek to encourage. Promotion of market-town growth must avoid this trap.

Ranis suggested, during a visit to Dacca, that functioning transportation and communications systems may be more important to rural industries than has been recognized. Good communications in rural towns are a partial substitute for long trips, high inventories, and needless risks. A working telephone and telegraph system may be more important than the public provision of cheap land. This type of infrastructure will enable manufacturers and traders to maintain their vital low margins.

For a study of the promotion of small industry in India see Joseph E. Stepanek, "An Entrepreneurial Approach to Accelerated Small Industry Development in Selected Indian Districts - An Exploratory Study Undertaken at the Request of the Ministry of Industry and Civil Supplies, Government of India," ILO, April 1976.

(11) For a growth stages model see Walter W. Rostow, The Stages of Economic Growth: A Non-Communist Manifesto, Cambridge: Cambridge University Press, 1960.

(12) Mahbub ul Haq, The Strategy of Economic Planning, Karachi: Oxford University Press, 1963, p. 30.

(13) Albert O. Hirschman, The Strategy of Economic Development, New Haven: Yale University Press, 1958, pp. 109-110.

(14) The topics analyzed in Chapter 5 through 9 reflect those on which I focused much of my time while in Dacca. These five chapters, therefore, do not represent the distillation of all those factors, economic and non-economic, that may be central to the development of Bangladesh. Subjects that may warrant greater attention than those analyzed here include family planning, public administration, and educational aspirations.

(15) According to a recent (unpublished) study by the Statistical Division of the Ministry of Planning, the proportion of household expenditures spent for foodgrain increased from .57 to .83 between 1960 and 1973-74. Even though 1973-74 was an extremely inflationary year, particularly for foodgrain (see Fig. 5.1), I believe that when data for 1975-77 become available they will show that the trend expenditure elasticity has varied little since 1960. Not only is this an index of poverty, but it bodes ill for the per capita income increases and expenditure diversifications that are vital to a market-based development strategy.

(16) There are several employment projection studies in Bangladesh. We have drawn upon ones in the Five-Year Plan, and those offered by Mellor and Zaman, by Clay and Khan, and by Raisuddin Ahmed of the Planning Commission. The work by Clay and Khan is based upon their own field surveys and is the most comprehensive of the studies cited. The labor-force participation rate is approximately 35%, and the agricultural labor-force, as a percentage of the total labor force, is conventionally assumed to be 76%.

(17) This may be high. The employment created off-farm, in direct support of the new seed technology, is surprisingly low. For two Indian states, S.D. Thapar has estimated that for each 1,000 acres of new seed, a net of 6.4 new jobs are created. S.D. Thapar, "The Green Revolution and Its Impact on Employment in the Tertiary Sector: A Case Study in Punjab and Haryana," in Ridker and Lubell, editors, Employment and Unemployment Problems of the Near East and South Asia, Vol. II, Delhi: Vikas, 1971.

(18) World Bank, Bangladesh - Development in a Rural Economy, pp. 129-30.

APPENDIX A

NEW RICE FOR OLD - THE CHALLENGE

"Traditional" and "HYV" seed varieties are brief terms for elaborate crop cultures. (1) The phrase "new seed technology" applies to the package of modern agricultural inputs which includes the new seed. New crop varieties of jute, wheat, pulses, and oils are also being developed in Bangladesh. I introduce these complex crop cultures by focusing on the one crop that dominates village life - rice.

Rice is native to the Ganges-Brahmaputa Delta, to Burma, and to southern China. New rice varieties developed by the International Rice Research Institute (IRRI) at Los Baños in the Philippines are being spread throughout the world. China has made similar independent advances in seed breeding. (2) Bangladesh has the full range of traditional rice types - deep-water, saline, rain-fed, and irrigated - that challenge seed research institutions to supply each traditional rice zone with higher-yielding varieties. Only the mountainous rice, a type grown in other parts of Asia, is absent.

Bangladesh has three crop seasons - boro (winter), aus (spring), and aman (summer) - that are described by contrasting water, temperature, photoperiod, and pest conditons. (3) The boro crop supplies about 20% of the total rice harvest, and the aus provides 24%. Aman, which is the principal crop, supplies 54%, and thereby defines the rice economy for much of the year. As is illustrated in Table 5.1 the relative contributions of these seasonal rice crops are changing as the boro harvest rapidly increases. Wheat production has also grown dramatically, although the crop provides only 2% of the total grain production.

Because the new seed make shorter growing periods possible, five rice crops can be grown successively on the same acreage over the course of two years, and in isolated cases as many as three crops can be grown in one year. The yields of the new seed are also multiples of present traditional levels. In the face of these possibilties, the typical pattern of one and two low yielding crops each year is being displaced. Irrigation of fallow land is increasing the cropping intensity in the winter. Under winter's flood-free, relatively controlled conditions, the new high-yielding seed are being readily adopted to more acreage. Traditional summer aus and aman varieties, on the other hand, have evolved over the centuries by means of adaptive, albeit unconscious, selection by cultivators. These hardy monsoon-resistant but low-yielding varieties will not be easy to displace. Increasing rice yields on this flood-vulnerable acreage presents seed breeders with their greatest challenge.

In 1965, the International Rice Research Institute sent new rice strains for winter field trials to Comilla District, East Pakistan. A threefold yield increase to a ton and a half per acre soon established this import as a popular variety; only then did IRRI give it the now well known name of IR8. This seed's responsiveness to fertilizer and irrigation was remarkable, but its long stem could not hold its heavy harvest. IR8 was not accepted for the aus and aman seasons because of its pest susceptibility and inability to endure shallow flooding. Nonetheless, IR8 did represent the first new rice variety in Bangledesh; imported and domestic contributions soon followed. IR20, a second import from IRRI, was introduced in 1970 as an aman variety. Its strong stem length provided early flood protection, and its popularity was further ensured by its resistance to a virulent aman disease. Unlike IR8, IR20 proved to be the real breakthrough for the new seed's acceptance in Bangladesh.

During its first years, the Bangladesh Rice Research Institute (BRRI) field-tested seed varieties from IRRI. By the early 1970s this national institute was breeding its own seed to combine the advantages of imported IRRI varieties with the hardiness and quality of native strains. Early work at IRRI and BRRI focused on yield increases made possible by breeding-in fertilizer responsiveness. Recognition of farmers problems, however, soon forced compromises; yield potential had to be de-emphasized in favor of other beneficial traits. Fertilizer expenditures often made little sense if irrigation was unavailable, if risks of pest vulnerability and of lodging (falling over) were high, or if credit was absent. In addition, the fact that grain cannot be easily dried during the monsoon often prevented the adoption of new seed that would otherwise have been favorably received; "odd" growing periods upset traditional cropping patterns. Seed breeders now recognize the advantages of long-accepted local varieties and take into consideration the unique conditions and requirements of each rice zone. Emphasis on adoption of imported seed has given way to adaptive research aimed at "tailoring" varieties to the multiple seasons and zones of Bangladesh.

Each rice zone presents a unique challenge to the rice breeder . To ensure ripening of the boro rice harvest, photo-period insensitivity is necessary as the daylight hours lengthen in the spring. Because there is little risk of flooding, the short-stemmed varieties can make optimum use of fertilizer to support high yields. However, because boro rice varieties demand a great deal of water, their expanded use requires functioning irrigation programs. This presents a dilemma for seed research priorities; cultivators have long preferred drought-tolerant seed because they could not be certain that their fields would be reached by public irrigation projects.

The aus and aman are often sown together in the late spring. The aus is harvested as the flood waters rise; and the aman is left to be harvested as the waters recede, the weather grows cooler, and the days shorten. This intercropping is a traditional mechanism for reducing the risk of crop failure from pest attack and from unseasonal changes in flood water levels. With the introduction of new seed, this intercropping practice is being de-emphasized in favor of new aus and aman transplanted varieties that are pest resistant and able to elongate as flood waters rise. Unlike boro varieties, the new aman seed need to retain their photo-period sensitivity. Should a late monsoon indicate that the flood waters will be late in rising, cultivators can delay their aman plantings with the assurance that the crop can be harvested as the days grow shorter.

A first BRRI selection of an original IRRI line, Chandina BR1 for the boro, is proving to be more rapidly accepted than the older imported IR8 because it has a shorter growing season and because its shorter stem prevents lodging.

Mala BR2, a second BRRI selection of an IRRI line, is a long-stem boro variety suitable for the country's many flood-prone, low-lying areas. Flood resistance remains a challenge. IR442 is an improvement on the older IR20; it can endure up to six days of total submergence caused by a rapidly advancing flood, and can elongate ahead of less dramatic rises. This new strain is the first to combine high yields with the ability to elongate. The boro and aman rice seasons can now be characterized by a number of new strains adapted to the seasonal and zonal conditions within Bangladesh. New varieties tailored for the aus have been slow in coming, partly because the durable qualities of local varieties have given stiff competition to plant breeders. Breeders and agronomists are also learning that cultivators are growing their own improved local varieties, such as the aman Pajam, which are forcing a more restrictive definition of the new seed.

BRRI is now field-testing its own lines of high-yielding rice. Two that show early promise of acceptance are Biplob (BR3 - "Revolution"), which yields up to four tons per acre and is versatile as a three-season variety, and Mukti (BR5 - "Freedom"), a boro variety that combines high yields with the desired taste of traditional varieties.

New varieties now cover nearly two million acres of the approximately 22 million which are devoted to rice. Much of the boro rice acreage is presently planted to these new varieties; rapid coverage was made possible by expanded irrigation. However, the coverage of new aus and aman varieties is only 5% of their respective acreages; the capricious monsoon continues to control these twin seasons and slow the introduction of new seed.

Although the new boro rice has been the most successful, its acceptance may be arrested by the cost of irrigation. Winter lands are increasingly devoted to the more nutritious, less thirsty wheat and other dry-land crops. Research is supporting this winter season diversification, as well as the exploitation of another rice zone of Bangladesh - the hazardous deep-water areas. The unique ecological world of deep-water rice will test breeders' ability to develop high-yielding strains for monsoon floods which normally run between three and six feet deep. Some native low-yielding strains can withstand as much as twenty feet of water. Because the silt-laden flood waters provide natural fertilization and irrigation, and because competition from other crops is virtually nil, deep-water paddy has an impressive potential.

The Bangladesh rice culture is a complex mosaic; domestic research and extension institutions face a long-term responsibility. Because the economy is not based upon a mono-crop culture, this complexity represents safety. The mosaic of crop conditions over a twelve-month growing season provides strength against droughts, pests, and floods, and, therefore, resiliency for the model's technological base.

NOTES - APPENDIX A

(A-1) The references in this appendix to specific seed types are drawn from materials published by the Bangladesh Rice Research Institute.

(A-2) The British were the first to introduce new crop varieties of wheat and sorghum to Bengal before the 1947 Partition. According to Dalrymple ("Development and Spread of High-Yielding Varieties of Wheat and Rice in the Less-Developed Nations," USDA, August 1976), the common ancestor of current IRRI rice varieties is Peta, which originated, in part, from Bengal in 1941. The successes of IRRI's new rice varieties in Bangladesh have been matched by new wheat varieties from the Centro Internacional de Mejoramiento de Maiz Y Trigo (CIMMYT) in Chilpancingo outside Mexico City.

(A-3) The reader may be familiar with the subcontinental terms of _rabi_, "winter crop season,"and _kharif_, "summer crop season." Official documents of the Bangladesh Government use the term _rabi_ to refer to dry-land winter crops, such as oils and pulses. The terms _boro_, _aus_, and _aman_ generally (but not always) refer to the rice crop. Cultivators describe their crop seasons by the months of the Bengali calendar.

APPENDIX B

THE QUALITY OF RURAL LIFE

The emphasis upon agricultural production, as explained in Chapters 3 and 4, is not intended to exclude other requirements for development. The following three subjects are necessary aspects, although they are secondary to the priority given to production.

Nutrition and Health

Malnutrition is endemic to Bangladesh. Poor diets enervate laborers and render the population vulnerable to disease. In a country where so many are malnourished, poor health, poor nutrition, and low income are inseparable problems that are not amenable to single curative solutions.

Since the target group is the population as a whole, the lack of financial and human resources rules out reliance on western approaches to nutrition and health problems. Special foods delivered to people in relief camps have been equated with nutritional well-being. Although these foods are vital in times of disaster, such programs typify an approach that is far too costly to be replicated. The immediate food quality challenge, like that of food quantity, is making the best use of available supplies. Poor distribution and misuse of available land contribute as much to malnutrition as does insufficient food quantity. Seen in these terms, well-being for the poor depends on their increased productivity; only with the creation of rural purchasing power can hunger be alleviated. Medical indicators suggest that when harvests are good, nutritional deficiencies become less prevalent, food supplies and incomes increase, and diets expand and diversify. With poor harvests, diets shrink, the food selection narrows, and severe malnutrition reappears. (1) With stagnant agricultural trends, these problems are widespread and chronic. Bangladesh has rice, pulses, fish, edible oils, vegetables, and fruits, the preventive foundation to ensure improved diets and health. Traditional high-cost curative approaches consume public resources for those few with money and influence, and so these approaches nullify the chance for national coverage of a cost-effective alternative. In brief, it is my thesis that health and nutritional improvements will follow from the model's primary emphasis upon broad-based agricultural development. (2) (Institutional aspects of health and nutritional systems are discussed in Chapter 9.)

Women - Onlookers or Participants in Development?

I admit to an early misconception that the female half of the population naturally benefits from overall growth. (3) I now recognize a few of the problems that a male-dominated society causes and the economic advantages to be gained from female participation in achieving developmental objectives. The resource constraint necessitates a perspective that asks what functions women can perform more efficiently than men. Several are clear.

Males consume the best and the most from the family khana (kitchen) in Bangladesh as they do in many societies. Improved nutritional well-being for women and children will depend upon women's exposure to the world outside their own baris (homes). (4) Female education within non-formal and agricultural extension systems represents a cost-effective approach to nutritional improvement. The same approach applies to population control. In Muslim Bangladesh, the male's, and grandparents', desire for sons leads to the husband's domination of the decision of most couples regarding family size. (The exclusion of females from public life in Bangladesh is so complete that one foreigner quipped that it appeared men had learned to reproduce themselves.) So whether the objective is the small family norm or nutritional well-being, cost-effective approaches to an improved quality of life must include female family members. It is increasinlgy evident, though poorly substantiated as yet, that female participation in all of the country's decisions is essential for development.

Agricultural employment for women may grow with the expanded use of the new seed. However, mechanization tends to displace female labor. The pedal thresher and pregerminated seed drill are two examples of "appropriate" technologies that are capital "cheap" but displace women's work at home and in the field. This seemingly callous attitude toward physical labor is elaborated on in Chapter 6. Mechanization of even small steps and processes needs to be evaluated in the social context in which it is introduced. Expanding employment opportunities for women outside the home will, according to population experts, contribute to increased acceptance of the small family norm. (5) Parental recognition of the unmarried daughter's potential economic contribution to the family could be a factor in deferring marriage until a later date. The government is now promoting female participation in several kinds of development programs. Women's involvement in the processing and fabrication firms of market-town growth, and the innumerable services, must prove to be a short step away from purdha. (6)

Education for Development

Much of this book could be written entirely in terms of the contribution of education to the development process or, even more broadly, in terms of education's contribution to cultural normals and aspirations. Again, I refer to the contributions of others. (7) In Chapter 2 I stated there are not enough teachers available to educate the growing numbers of school-age children. Cost-effective educational techniques, with curricula relevant for a rural and agricultural population, is a new frontier which has been mentioned by only a few. All facets of our model depend upon millions of people having a wide range of practical skills; an educational revolution is as badly needed now as the technological seed revolution was in the 1960s. Because acceptance of the barefoot doctor says as much as societal as a medical changes in other countries, the social and aspirational milieu in rural Bangladesh must also learn to accept and sustain low-cost social services.

NOTES - APPENDIX B

(B-1) The occurrence of these nutritional changes has been noted in clinical reports by Dr. Colin McCord of Johns Hopkins University for the Thana Health Center in Companyganj Thana, Noakhali District.

(B-2) Work by Dr. McCord supports this thesis, as does the thana health approach pioneered by Dr. Zafrullah Chowdhury in Savar Thana, Dacca District. A critical assessment of the Government's health plans is contained in Oscar Gish's "Consultancy to the Bangladesh Ministry of Health," Dacca: July 1976, p. 9.

(B-3) We are indebted to the Ford Foundation office in Bangladesh for educating the government and foreign community to the role of women. Khushi Kabir, Ayesha Abed, and Marty Chen, Rural Women in Bangladesh: Exploding Some Myths, Dacca: The Ford Foundation, May 1976; Aloma A. Mascarenhas "A Report on Rural Women of Bangladesh," Dacca: USAID, 2nd Edition, March 1976, (with bibliography); Women for Women Research and Study Group, Women for Women - Bangladesh 1975 a collection of eleven essays, Dacca: University Press Limited, 1975, p. 246; The Bangladesh Rural Advancement Committee (BRAC), "Report on Functional Education Programme for Destitute Women in Jamalput (June - November 1975)," Dacca; and Susan F. Alamgir, "Profile of Bangladesh Women - Selected Aspects of Women's Roles and Status in Bangladesh," Dacca: AID, June 1977.

(B-4) Khana and bari are approximately translated as the family kitchen and the family home, respectively.

(B-5) This thesis is discussed in "The Policy Relevance of Recent Social Research on Fertility," Smithsonian Institution Staff Report, September 1974, pp. 20-23.

(B-6) The literal Persian meaning is "a curtain" which screens women from the view of men. When non-family males enter the bari women remain secluded in back rooms. When women venture out to urban areas they wear a burka, which is a tent-like fabric extension of purdah.

(B-7) Philip H. Coombs and Manzoor Ahmed, "Thoughts on Educational Strategy for Rural Development in Bangladesh," Dacca: The Ford Foundation, November 1973.

5 Food as a Development Resource

ONE COUNTRY, TWO FOOD WORLDS

The development of Bangladesh is fundamentally tied to rice, to its production and its price. Because millions of people live close to subsistence the supply and price of rice are crucial to individual well-being. 60% of the gross domestic product depends upon rice paddy. Furthermore, the equitable growth model is predicated on broad participation in the process of agricultural modernization; its vehicle is the new rice seed technology. In short, rice production is synonymous with well-being and development.

Bangladesh is off to a bad start; the new country inherited two separate food worlds, along with a legacy of focusing intensely on one and neglecting the other. The government pays the utmost attention to the urban food ration system which is sustained by foreign food aid, yet ignores the potential contribution which its rural citizens could make to the food supply and to development itself.

My purpose here is to analyze the penalties which have accrued because of the separation of these two food worlds. They must be integrated; their continued separate and unequal treatment ensures under-priced food for the urban centers and a stagnant rural economy. The political emphasis given to the ration system and the planning priority given to crop production do not add up to an integrated development strategy. I first describe the urban food system, then the agricultural wealth of the country-side; finally I suggest a proposal for the unification of these two systems which would ensure that food becomes a development resource.

THE FOOD RATION SYSTEM SERVES THE URBAN CENTERS

The system that now assures food for the urban centers developed as a result of famines that have swept the subcontinent for centuries. The famine

Table 5.1
Foodgrain Production, Imports, and Per Capita Supplies in Bangladesh

Fiscal Year	Population mid-year (millions)	Domestic (a) Production (millions of long tons)	Imports (millions of long tons)	Per Capita Availabilities (lbs. per year)	
				Without Imports	With Imports
1960	53.9	7.66	.46	318	338
1961	55.3	7.47	.58	303	326
1962	56.8	7.52	.54	297	318
1963	58.4	8.00	.77	307	336
1964	59.9	9.56	.49	358	376
1965	61.6	9.33	.34	339	352
1966	63.8	9.33	.89	328	359
1967	65.1	8.53	1.08	294	331
1968	66.9	9.95	1.02	333	367
1969	68.5	10.13	1.12	331	368
1970	70.8	10.73	1.55	340	389
1971	72.4	9.97	1.28	309	348
1972	73.4	8.89	1.77	271	325
1973	75.1	9.01	2.78	269	352
1974	77.4	10.65	1.64	308	356
1975	78.6	10.10	2.26	288	352
1976	81.0	11.51	1.47	318	359
1977	83.4	11.25	.78	302	323

Sources: USAID, and Food Department, Bangladesh Government

Note: (a) Calculated net of 10% for seed and loss

Table 5.2. Distribution of Foodgrain Through Bangladesh Government's Ration System (in thousands of long tons)

Category	1972	%	1973	%	1974	%	1975	%	1976	%	1977	%
Statutory - major cities	354	14	478	23	533	31	407	23	283	22	468	26
Modified - other cities and towns	1,435	59	1,138	55	556	32	626	35	252	19	395	22
Relief - free distribution	466	18	91	4	116	7	90	5	172	13	26	1
Food for Work	[a] -		[a] -		[a] -		[a] -		68	5	203	11
Priorities - military, police, hospitals	-		-		91	5	109	6	85	7	114	6
	283[b]	11	371[b]	18								
Government Employees - country-wide	-		-		224	13	294	16	177	14	305	17
Large Employers - factories	-		-		80	5	106	6	58	4	82	5
Open Market Sales	[c] -		[c] -		[c] -		[c] -		49	4	27	1
Private Flour Mills					110	6	133	7	137	10	168	9
Government Flour Mills					24	1	24	1	24	2	28	2
Total	2,538	100	2,079	100	1,733	100	1,789	100	1,306	100	1,816	100

Source: Ministry of Food, Bangladesh Government.

Notes: A long ton equals 2240 lbs. Columns may not add exactly because of rounding.

(a) Food-For-Work was started in the fall of 1974 but until April, 1976 was included in the Relief category.
(b) These quantities for 1972 and 1973 refer to all other ration categories.
(c) Open Market Sales have occurred since 1972 for the disposal of spoiled grain. In May, 1976, these sales were identified separately, and are being used on occasion to effect price stabilization.

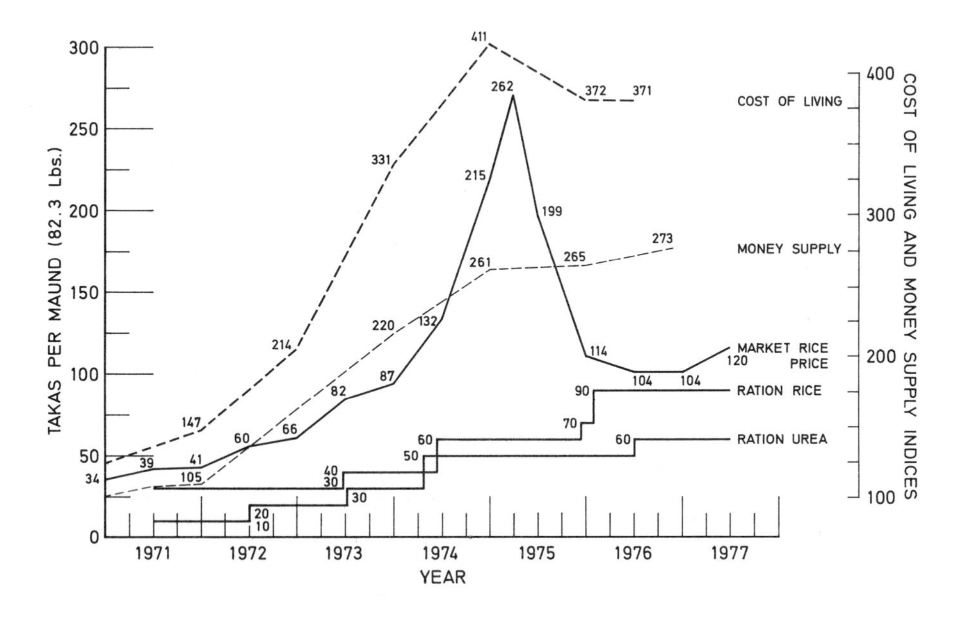

Fig. 5.1. Selected Prices in Bangladesh

Sources: Food Department and Statistical Division, Ministry of Planning, Bangladesh Government.

Note: Data are an approximation of price relationships for the rural population. Cost of living index is for Dacca middle class as no index is available for rural areas. Money supply is currency in circulation plus demand deposits. (For both indices FY 1970 = 100.) The rice price is the average of 57 towns. Ration rice price refers to the subsidized price of the ration system. The subsidized ration urea price is fixed at each thana fertilizer warehouse.

of 1943 left an indelible scar on the minds of the Bengali people. After an estimated 1.5 million people died and 40 million were left destitute by the famine, the British set up a public food-ration system to feed the poor. (1) Ever since the mid-1940s this ration system has been expanded with imported food; and, with each passing year, a system originally designed for destitute people increasingly feeds an urban population with steady incomes.

Food imports have totaled over 10 million tons in the six years since independence, yet these additional food supplies have only stabilized the per capita food availabilities of this growing population. Without these imports, a slight downward trend in per capita supplies is apparent from Table 5.1. (2) Reliance upon imported food is increasing while domestic production falls behind population growth. Are these trends causally associated? It is this suspected relationship that gives rise to my concern that the two food worlds of Bangladesh interact with each other in ways that constrain agricultural development.

The country's ration system begins at its ports on the Bay of Bengal. From Chittagong and Khulna harbors imported rice and wheat are shipped by rail to public warehouses throughout the country. The Ministry of Food supplies food to individuals on a weekly and bi-monthly basis through ration shops and public organizations. The recipients of these rations broadly compose urban Bangladesh and include, according to official categories, "Statutory" recipients in the six largest cities, government and factory workers, priorities (hospital personnel, police, and the military), and other urban consumers through flour mills. "Modified" recipients are in the country's smaller cities and towns. The Ministry of Relief distributes food to the destitute and to rural laborers through the "Relief" and "Food For Work" respectively. Table 5.2 describes the quantities of grains distributed through the system's 10 ration categories. (3) In addition to rice and wheat, ration card holders and public organizations obtain edible oil and, occasionally, sugar, salt, soap, and kerosene. The "Relief" category for the destitute is the one source of free public food. The ration rice price illustrated in Fig. 5.1 applies to most of the other ration categories.

In a country as poor as Bangladesh, it is inevitable that a system of urban privileges would cause serious repercussions. Two that affect the model directly include the inequitable method of determining the food deficit, and the system's disincentive effect on effort.

In order to anticipate the needs of the ration system the government calculates the food gap each year. The total domestic grain production is subtracted from the total per capita requirement to obtain the gap. The per capita grain requirement is estimated on the basis of 15.5 ounces per day for the population as a whole, which increases by 2.5 million people each year, or some 400,000 tons of grain. (4) Table 5.3 illustrates the quantities of imported and domestically-procured foodgrain that, when combined, supply the system's sales, termed "offtakes." However, this analysis has a major flaw; little provision is made for the distribution of these grains on the basis of need. In a country where so many are so poor, lack of purchasing power must be taken into account in any aggregated analysis of the food deficit. (5) The deficit is real enough but it remains unmet. Approximately 80% of the ration-supplied food serves those with cash in towns and cities. The food gap, calculated in the name of the poor, serves the middle class. (6)

Table 5.3

Public Foodgrain Stock, Import, Procurement, and Offtake Quantities (in thousands of long tons)

Fiscal Year	Opening Stock	Imports	Procurement	Offtakes
1972[a]	279	1,278	10	1,086
1973	359	2,780	16	2,618
1974	301	1,640	71	1,728
1975	217	2,256	138	1,757
1976	749	1,469	410	1,669
1977	897	780	313	1,473
1978	442	1,786[b]	623[b]	1,910[b]

Source: Food Department, Bangladesh Government.

Note: (a) For period January-June, 1972.
(b) Estimate.

The second shortcoming of the ration system is that it discourages effort, effort by the government to promote agricultural development, and effort by cultivators, through the mechanism of price, to invest in the new seed technology. It is not food aid per se that causes these twin disincentives, but the institutions within which, and for which, this food is utilized. The consequences of these disincentives, when seen in the framework of the equitable growth model, may cause the suspension of the developmental processes.

Much has been written about the possible disincentives that large food imports can have on an agrarian economy. I will examine the macroagricultural disincentives of these food imports and leave a discussion of related agricultural problems to later chapters. (7)

I will not detail the ways in which the ready availability of food aid reduces the political and administrative priority given to agricultural production. Suffice it to say that the numbers of official food aid requests made to food donors reveal the government's dependence on foreign food assistance. There is little evidence of a corresponding commitment at a high level in the government to domestic agricultural programs.

The market effect of food aid on domestic agricultural production has two broad aspects. First, the sheer magnitude of foreign food aid, as compared with the size of the urban population, suggests the adverse impact it has on domestic markets and, indirectly, on domestic cultivators. In the last six years imports have averaged 1.88 million tons per year, which is enough food, at 15.5 ounces a day, to feed 12 million people. Urban Bangladesh, towns of over 5,000 people, is estimated to contain only 7 to 8 million people. It is therefore apparent that rationed food literally blankets the economy and enables many, generally the middle class, to eat more than 15.5 ounces per day. (8) This food, sold at less than prevailing market prices, sharply curtails the size of the grain market for domestic cultivators, thereby preventing their incomes from growing as rapidly as they might in the absence of such a system.

Second, the negative effect of food aid is accentuated by the way in which it is priced and distributed. Most of the food is distributed to those with income, to those who are able to purchase their foodgrain from the market. The resource transfer from urban consumers to rural producers does not take place because of the availability of a cheaper source of food. During FY 1975, an inflationary year, this hypothetical transfer of money from urban consumers to domestic grain traders and producers would have amounted to two to three times the agricultural proportions of the FY 1975 Annual Development Plan. (9) With the rice price decline in 1975 and 1976, the potential magnitude of this transfer has declined sharply; the problem remains, however. The income transfer that could be taking place every year in support of agricultural prices could be much higher than it is at present if ration subsidies and coverage were curtailed. The model's market-based growth linkages remain theoretical because of the way in which imported food is priced and distributed. If the ration system served those in need, as it was originally intended, this disincentive effect of food aid would be insignificant. (10)

Reliance on imported food has bred still greater reliance in other ways. With good domestic harvests, market prices fall and ration sales slacken as consumers switch to the preferred domestic kinds of rice, wheat, and edible oil. The ration system only generates takas to the extent that its prices are lower than those prevailing on the market. (11) The upshot of this is that expanded harvests and low grain prices are not viewed by all with equal elation. The urban enclave, which relies on both foreign-financed food and takas, is caught in a web of dependence.

The negative effects of food aid in Bangladesh are not being offset by the positive uses to which food aid could be utilized. As we have seen in Chapters 2 and 4, the government is not expanding employment in any sector of the economy, except for Food for Work. Nor are public food stocks managed in a way which would prevent urban grain prices from rising above some predetermined level during periods of seasonally high prices and occasional poor harvests. The primary developmental benefits of food imports are going untapped.

However distorted in purpose the ration system may appear to an outsider, its importance to the urban elite must not be underestimated. Food security looms large in their minds. The ration system is really not a system at all, but a conduit through which available food is moved to supply urban consumers and to raise revenue. While the penalties of this political reality are obvious for agricultural development and for the well-being of the poor, altering this system requires acknowledgment of the system's political basis.

GOLDEN PADDY FOR THE RURAL POOR?

Reality gives the lie to one's visual impression; fields that change endlessly from green to gold and back to green every few months produce one of the world's poorest crops. What can be said of the rural population's struggles to sustain itself on these low yields in the face of ample urban food grain supplies?

The summer _aman_, which yields the single largest rice harvest of the year, sets the overall food supply and price conditions for many months. Still, its trend growth rate is below 2% a year. The newer winter rice and wheat crops, which are synonymous with the new seed technology in Bangladesh, show remarkable growth rates of 15 and 11%, respectively (see Table 5.4). However, since these crops were started recently on small production bases and as their rates of expansion are not being sustained, they do not push the long-term trend for all foodgrains above 2% a year. A decade after the introduction of the new seed, population growth still surpasses foodgrain production. (12)

In Chapter 4, I explained that the new seed technology is the key to production increases for the rural population. If employment and income growth are to occur, the new seed technology must be adopted. Progress can be questioned. According to a planning baseline, the new seed covered 2.4 million acres in FY 1970. The goal for new seed use in FY 1974 was 4.8 million acres, and the _Five-Year Plan_ target by the end of FY 1978 was 9.4 million acres. These numbers were revised downward by a series of Agricultural Task Force surveys conducted between 1974 and 1977. During FY 1975 and FY 1976 the total new seed acreage is estimated to have been no more than 1.7 million acres, or less than 8% of the total rice acreage. (13) Under the HYV (High-Yielding Varieties) Schemes started by the Ministry of Agriculture in the late 1960s, there was a natural tendency to exaggerate actual achievements. What has yet to be determined is whether these inflated numbers are to be explained by over-enthusiastic reporting, by definitional changes, which do explain a portion of this revision, or by the actual curtailment of new seed use itself. The implications of the first two possibilities are hardly as serious as those of the last. I also note that, according to government statistics, the yields of the new seed varieties have fallen. Between the years FY 1967 and FY 1975, the transplanted _aman_ yield fell approximately 33%; for _aus_, 30%; and for _boro_, 34%. (14) The association of these acreage and yield shortfalls with the scale of the ration system is indicative of the relationship between urban dependence on foreign food and agricultural stagnation.

This food production picture becomes even more sobering when examined at the village level. Several processes interact to explain the impoverishment of cultivators and laborers. All cultivators together sell roughly a quarter of the annual paddy crop in local village, or _hat_, markets in order to buy other necessities and to pay rents and debts. (15) However, two-thirds of this

Table 5.4 Foodgrain Production in Bangladesh in millions of long tons

	1960-61	1965-66	1970-71	1971-72	1972-73	1973-74	1974-75	1975-76	1976-77	1977-78 (est.)
Rice										
Aus (spring)	2.41	2.92	2.86	2.34	2.27	2.80	2.86	3.23	3.0	3.1
Aman (summer)	5.41	6.80	5.91	5.70	5.59	6.70	6.00	7.04	6.9	7.4
Boro (winter)	.45	.62	2.19	1.74	2.07	2.22	2.25	2.29	1.6	2.5
Subtotal	8.27	10.34	10.97	9.77	9.93	11.72	11.11	12.56	11.5	13.0
Wheat (winter)	.03	.04	.11	.11	.09	.11	.11	.23	.3	.4
Total	8.30	10.38	11.08	9.88	10.02	11.83	11.22	12.79	11.8	13.4

Source: Ministry of Agriculture, Bangladesh Government.

marketed grain is purchased by poorer people because their incomes are meager, and because debts and other needs prevent them from storing as much grain as they may have produced or earned. The poorest cultivators and agricultural laborers seek wage work much of the year and, therefore, depend heavily upon the local market for their grain. Yet when small grain purchasers are delayed until well after each harvest, prices are invariably higher. This is one of the vicious cycles of poverty. In comparing the early 1970s with 1976 and 1977, the higher costs of fertilizer and non-farm goods and lower rice prices have caused a further deterioration in the economic condition of more and more cultivators (see Fig. 5.1).

The bleak food outlook for the small villages of Bangladesh has recently been dramatized by estimates of the number of months each farm family is self-sufficient in grain. In a study of Pabna district, only 10% of the households produced enough grain for them to be self-sufficient for a full year. In a national sample survey, only 4% of the farm families were found to produce grain surpluses. (16)

The negative implications of foreign food dependence for the model's growth linkages become apparent. In humanitarian terms, these food imports have not caused per capita food supplies to improve. As for development, these "humanitarian" imports are discouraging agricultural production and the linkages on which growth depends.

In a way there is a parallel in these two food worlds. Cultivators and laborers turn to their fields in order to survive; the government turns to outsiders. The countryside yields its rice and jute and is penalized by having to compete with subsidized foreign aid food in its own market. The gap in these two food systems remains and is symbolic of the continuing acceptance of urban maintenance in the name of "humanitarian" food aid. Past opportunities for job and income growth are now lost; the "humanitarian" cost of this dual food system cannot be easily ignored.

FAMINE IN RANGPUR IN 1974

The gulf between these two food worlds became tragically apparent in the fall of 1974. Famine and the resulting deaths from starvation are tragic in their own right; together, they dramatize the shortcomings of present food policies, shortcomings that bode ill for the future. (17)

The districts of Mymensingh and Rangpur straddle the Brahmaputra River as it flows from India into Bangladesh. Each fall villagers reoccupy the fertile lands along this river and plant their crops on each foot of soil as it is released from the water. In the spring of 1974, the flood waters were earlier and higher than usual, and forced a retreat further and faster than was expected. People were pushed from their shacks and forced to leave their crops unharvested. The waters receded late that year and compounded earlier losses by not freeing the land in time for it to be planted with winter crops. Following on the deteriorating economic conditions of 1973 and 1974, the summer flood proved devastating for many; for some it broke their ties to the land permanently. Villagers were forced to sell their animals, their homes, their planting seed, and finally their fields. People camped at the door of the Land Registry Office in the town of Rangpur in order to sell their land. (18) By September and October of 1974 towns in Rangpur and Mymensingh were swamped with destitute people. The price of rice rose from 150 takas per maund (82.3 lbs.) in January of 1974 to between 300 and 400 takas per maund in places in the northwest during October and November. Even wealthy Muslim families, who usually could be counted on for assistance, were affected and gave less generously. This dearth of alms-giving is such an important indicator of shortages in Bangladesh that one term for famine, durvickha, denotes "when alms are scarce." Public works and relief programs had been curtailed since independence, and the value of their remaining expenditures was cut sharply by inflation. Because of their lack of purchasing power and very high prices, the destitute suffered out of all proportion to the amount of food in the country.

The government's response to the 1974 flood and subsequent famine was determined in part by steps it was forced to take in late 1973. The Bangladesh government committed a large proportion of its own foreign exchange for imported food because it perceived that the aman harvest of 1973-74 would be poor and that donor food assistance would be inadequate to supply the ration system. (19) By early 1974 a foreign exchange crisis, precipitated largely by these commercial food purchases, became sufficiently severe to cause a temporary freezing of private imports. By mid-summer of 1974 it became apparent that the annual monsoon flooding was abnormally high and would cause as much damage and crop loss as had first been claimed. A foreign exchange appeal by a cash-short government was converted into an international relief appeal as hundreds of thousands of people were driven from their homes and fields.

The steady "pauperization of the masses," that had intensified following independence, was capped by the flood. (20) It is this pauperization, not the flood itself, that caused the extreme hardship. No invisible hand feeds the poor. There is no automatic mechanism to unite hungry people with the food within their reach. The following sketches of the northwest by Nizam Uddin Ahmed contrast sharply with the rice-green country through which the destitute drifted. (21)

> Next year, the Union Chairman said, the number of landless farmers will increase because of new births as well as because many small farm owners in the current year have already sold their land to survive. He said a small farmer becomes landless within two years, for he would sell his cows in the first year, and then he would sell his land to pay off debts and to buy food the following year. His opinion was that unless something drastic was done to save small farmers there will be an even bigger famine in 1975... .
>
> Before Liberation the villagers were able to support their families somehow by working in fields and as day laborers but price hike and unemployment have forced them out of their villages in search of employment and food... .
>
> The Union Chairman stated that five persons had committed suicide in his union only the day before by taking endrine (liquid

> pesticide) as they were unable to withstand starvation any longer. All the people accepting rotis (flat bread) [from the relief kitchens] were observed to be quite deserving while children of lower age group who cannot be termed as anything else but skeletons were suffering more from dangerous malnutrition... .
>
> We witnessed three dead bodies on this road quite uncovered and naked, with aluminum mugs and worn out plates beside them... . We gathered that the dead bodies were unidentified and possibly had come from far-off places in search of food but had died being unable to get any ... .
>
> The Railway Station Master told us that the dead bodies would have to be buried without any ceremony or burial clothes (eleven yards of burial cloth per person are required by Muslim law) as the needed yards of any third class cloth would now cost minimum 110 takas, and he did not know of any persons who could pay him for burying these unidentified dead persons. The Station Master reported that in the beginning he was able to collect donations for burying dead persons who would breathe their last in his railway station but as soon as it became a normal burying affair of four to six persons a day, nobody cared to give any more donations ... .

Droves of destitute people filled the streets of Rangpur in early September. Their plight moved local merchants to draw on their own ration supplies in order to establish gruel kitchens. At about the same time the army also started distributing its ration-supplied food in hard-hit areas along the Right Embankment bordering the Brahmaputra river. Union officials struggled with their pitiful "Relief" allocations. By the end of September the Bangladesh Government announced that gruel kitchens would be opened in each of the country's unions and that 11,000 tons of grain per month would be allocated for the destitute. In all 5,862 gruel kitchens were opened, and "Relief" and "Food For Work" allocations climbed from 1,500 tons to 31,200 tons per month by October. Although foodgrain arrivals in-country were down sharply in September (to only 29,000 tons) and October (to 76,000 tons), offtakes remained high and there was some belt-tightening within the "Modified" and "Flour Mill" categories. The "Relief" offtake for the country as a whole was increased from 1% to 21% during the worst two months of the famine in October and November. By December, as the destitute found work harvesting the new aman crop, these kitchens were closed and "Relief" offtakes were curtailed to 6% of total fund offtakes by January.

Despite these steps, upwards of 30,000 people starved to death in Rangpur and Mymensingh, and another 10,000 died of cholera and related diarrheal diseases; some believe that the casualties were three or four times higher than these official figures. How many people actually died in villages across Bangladesh will remain unknown. (22) Hundreds of thousands drifted into towns and over 300,000 flooded Dacca's streets, where thousands died. (23)

The government had ample evidence in late 1973 and early 1974 that the law and order situation was desperate, and that prices were placing food out of reach of the poor. Still, the relief response was late and poorly focused. The early allocation of food for people affected by the flood could have been accomplished with relatively small amounts of grain. If 2,000 tons of grain had been promptly allocated to the northwest, starvation could have been prevented. Even in the early weeks of the summer's flood it was apparent that the real crisis lay ahead; prices would rise still higher and the market would supply little food. New crops had to be planted, and the destitute had to be put to work. (24) Appeals for relief supplies did give way to the promotion of wheat planting and food for work. By late fall of 1974, it became clear that the floods had once again contributed to a normal aman harvest. The juxtaposition of destitute people next to golden fields belonging to others was as revealing as the actual deaths were pathetic. No single factor is as damning of the man-made character of this famine as the fact that the price of old 1973 aman rice, which was ample in private stocks, started to fall in late 1974 to make room for the new aman harvest just coming in. (25) This was not the last famine in Bengal, only the latest.

MISMANAGED ABUNDANCE IN 1976

In late 1975 and in 1976 a food crisis of a different kind unfolded. It was evident that the gulf between the two food worlds remained, and that agricultural development would still bear the penalties.

In the aftermath of 1974's starvation deaths, low food imports, and low public food stocks, it was to be expected that a high level of food imports would be encouraged during the following year. In addition to these large supplies, the 1975 aman proved to be normal and the government was able to procure 410,000 tons during FY 1976. Other steps slowed the inflation to a standstill: during the first six months of 1975 the one hundred taka note was demonetized, the taka was devalued, credit was tightened, and the border was policed.

As a consequence of high food imports, good crops, and monetary changes, the price of rice fell sharply between April and November of 1975, from 262 takas per maund to a low of 102 takas per maund, and then remained relatively stable throughout 1976 and 1977 (see Fig. 5.1). Paddy and wheat prices fell to as low as 18 to 40 takas per maund as these crops were harvested. In the towns and cities the price advantage of ration commodities also fell and ration sales slowed, causing public food stocks to remain far higher than had been projected. (26) The relative attractiveness of public food supplies was reduced further during this period by upward ration price adjustments. Ration and market prices were now in close proximity for the first time in years (see Fig. 5.1). By late 1975 it became apparent that this food bounty would begin to impair other programs. High public grain stocks left little space for an aggressive procurement program. Some grain was stored in the open, and minor spoilage occurred in crowded stocks. To reduce these high stocks and the risk of spoilage, as well as to increase revenues, the government expanded the coverage of the ration system, pressured government employees to purchase their allotments, and lowered the price of rationed edible oil. In the face of ample private stocks, these public actions ensured that market prices remained low, possibly too low, for many months.

"Thus, within a period of less than two years, the fertilizer grain price ratio to which the farmer had become accustomed over the preceding decade has deteriorated by a factor of two to three times." (27) In 1976, Chambers of Commerce complained of poor business and blamed low agricultural prices. New seed use remained far below official estimates and during FY 1977 fertilizer sales and the use of irrigation pumps fell below targets. By 1977, there was talk in official circles of "reflating" the economy.

Despite these concerns, there was ample food for the middle class. Enormouspublic food stocks, and their politically motivated sale in a small urban market, caused a low rice price to stay low. Again agriculture was penalized. Having described the recent frailties of these two food worlds, I now suggest a proposal for their unification.

FOOD AS A DEVELOPMENT RESOURCE - A PROPOSAL

In the short space of three years, Bangladesh has endured precarious variations in its food supplies and prices. During these crises, and between them, the government has not used its ration system to serve development. Instead, domestic crop forecasts, ration system "needs," and stock estimates are interpreted liberally to give emple scope for imported food. What was to have been a program for feeding the destitute in the 1940s has now become a permanent urban welfare system that impedes developmental objectives. Agriculture is stagnating. The poor are left out of one food system and struggle to eke out a living in the other.

Food priorities must be reordered. The size of the rural population, the economy's agrarian base, and the fact that so many live at subsistence levels, demand that the government commit itself to more favorable agricultural prices and policies. The agricultural development strategies of the 1960s, which will be described in later chapters, are playing their limited role. The administration of agricultural input supplies must now be balanced by attention to purchasing power and food consumption.

This objective can be distilled down to the age-old choice between expensive food and cheap food. Bangladesh has few options. A dual pricing policy is prohibitively expensive. The government does not have the resources both to procure grain on a significant scale and to sell it at a subsidized price. Also, it would be inhumane to promote foodgrain exports as a price maintenance technique when so few would benefit from this process. The choice is, therefore, between cheap and expensive food for the economy as a whole. Accordingly, my proposal rests upon the acceptance of a fundamental proposition; the government can rely on its own agrarian resources to feed its population. A relatively higher food price and a high-level commitment to agricultural programs are keys. (28)

Food imports should complement and stabilize a reliance upon the countryside; they cannot be allowed to displace it. The basic mechanism for ensuring the incorporation of imported food with this shift to an agriculturally-led growth strategy is a public price-stabilization scheme. In large cities public food stocks should be sold when grain prices rise above a predetermined level, and these public sales should be curtailed when market prices moderate. They should not continue to flow regardless of prevailing market prices. In time, several of the system's ration categories should be terminated and, with compensatory salary adjustments, the recipients should rely on the private market and public open-market sales for their grain. Depending upon what tactic appears most feasible, ration coverage can be curtailed with or without accompanying reductions in food subsidies. Market grain prices should be higher than the 1976 and 1977 levels of Fig. 5.1, but a return to 1973-74 levels must be prevented because extreme food prices act to brake employment-creating processes. In this formulation, the urban population would continue to benefit from most of the imported food, but they would pay a higher price. (29)

The price-stabilization scheme should also extend a price floor to cultivators. Through public purchases, the government has implemented a floor price for rice and wheat in secondary rural markets. The primary objective of these procurement drives should be the effective maintenance of a price floor in small rural markets. (30) The achievement of tonnage targets to maintain the ration system should become a secondary objective because public stocks per se are less expensively built up with concessional food imports. There is a second reason for deemphasizing the public procurement system. Despite the small size of Bangladesh, the administrative difficulties involved in local procurement rule out implementing an effective price floor at the farm-gate, or even village-market level. This administrative reality should force recognition that production levels and the private grain trade determine the overall price trend throughout the year. The government procurement program can only complement this trend, and then only in a limited way. As public off takes become increasingly limited to open-market sales, domestic production and marketing incentives will expand to ensure more favorable farm-gate prices. (31)

A market-oriented food system by itself does little to serve the needs of the poor. The primary vehicle for their welfare, over the longer term, is a strategy of agricultural development. However, when food shortages occur, the government should initiate food-for-work projects and, in extreme situations open gruel kitchens. Food resources should be targeted on a needs basis to conserve food stocks, and to prevent erosion of the institutional discipline of ongoing development programs. These humanitarian programs provide an important nutritional floor to the uses of food for development.

Disaster-prone Bangladesh requires ample food reserves to meet frequent and unexpected demands upon her food system. A foodgrain reserve and sales analysis for a multi-purpose public food system requires a food stock level of 600-800,000 MT for the present population. (32) Any stock recommendation must be tempered by normal stock and storage costs, costs that are made higher by a hot, humid climate. Because food conditions can change dramatically in Bangladesh with little warning, the government needs a much stronger food management and analysis capability to implement and protect a multi-faceted public food policy.

In review, higher agricultural prices are essential for an equitable growth strategy. Reliance on open-market sales will encourage higher market prices for cultivators at the same time that humanitarian and urban food requirements are being met. With higher harvest prices, increasing crop production, and expanding employment, the per capita demand for food will grow. Food imports can then serve the economy well for food will have become a development resource.

It cannot be overemphasized that the unification of the two food worlds in Bangladesh is primarily a matter of government perspective. The ration system's present infrastructure can serve the mechanical requirements of a price-stabilization scheme. Agricultural input systems are largely in place, and the new seed technology is widely understood. Why should agriculture be allowed to falter while food is imported from half-way around the world? In the time it takes for foreign food to be ordered and delivered, another crop can be grown.

There is a natural tendency to view a proposal for change with hesitation. The presumption by many both in and out of govenrment is that the present ration system is adequate. It clearly is not. Whether the system's purpose has been political pacification, revenue generation, or even food for the poor, the two crises reviewed earlier show that the present system ill serves developmental and humanitarian requirements. Altering this old system, which favors a few, to guarantee food production and development will ensure food security for all.

Should domestic crops fail, public stocks will be available at moderated prices for those who can afford to pay, and they can be distributed to those who cannot. If food imports are unavailable because of crop failures and emergencies elsewhere, the bridge between increased production and broad-based increases in purchasing power will already have been built.

A CONCLUDING THOUGHT

The stage is again set for another dramatic performance. Whether it will be a famine, a period of mismanaged abundance, or some other waste of lives and resources, one thing is certain: the government is not managing its food resources on behalf of the country as a whole. Man-made problems must give way to man-made solutions.

The foregoing proposal is now understood by the government, and a few of its elements are being implemented. Happily several good harvests since independence have allowed the government some breathing space. Nonetheless, food shortages in the future will traumatize the government as they have in the past, causing a cessation of further modifications in the ration system.

Accordingly, this food proposal requires one additional thought. The dependable supply of cheap food has a grip on the urban mind that is difficult for an outsider to appreciate. Fear of what would happen if the monsoon was to fail, fear of the machinations of private traders, and fear of urban unrest prevent greater reliance upon the market. Until urban food security is guaranteed without qualification, food for development may remain a slogan. Perhaps food-surplus countries should guarantee provision of a minmum public food stock to the government, and should do so in exchange for policies designated to unify the two food worlds. A minimum stock of between

600,000 and 800,000 tons is a manageable amount for the donors, and it is sufficient to serve the multiple uses of food spelled out in this proposal. Until a sense of security is ensured for the urban elite, the macroagricultural requirements of the model will remain elusive.

NOTES

(1) For a brief analysis of this famine, in comparison to one in India, see Alan Berg, "Famine Contained - Notes and Lessons from the Bihar Experience," Washington, D. C.: Brookings, 1971, p. 114. According to unofficial estimates, during the Bengal Famine of 1943 between 3 and 4 million people starved to death.

(2) Statistical series such as those presented in Tables 5.1 through 5.4 should be read with caution. Because the exact population is not known and data on crop production are unreliable, the kind of precision suggested by these numbers is spurious. Nevertheless, definitional consistency year by year may provide accurate trends.

(3) The "Statutory" category provides nearly a pound of grain per person per day (and varying amounts of other food commodities) in the large cities of Dacca-Narayanganj, Chittagong, Khulna, Rajshahi, and Rangamati. Other urban categories receive the same quantities. The "Modified" category supplies one half the "Statutory" allocation per card. No official numbers are available on the numbers of ration recipients, their income, or geographic distribution. The "Statutory" category is estimated to have 2 to 3 million recipients; "Modified," another 2 to 3 million; "Priorities," around 800,000; and "Government" and "Large Employers," another 2 million. The actual allocation per ration card varies from month to month according to supplies in stock.

(4) For the ration gap calculation, a per capita amount larger than 15.5 ounces creates a larger total import requirement. An analysis by Chen suggests that the physiological foodgrain need is approximately 13.2 ounces per day, and when nutritional and cooking losses are included, this requirement becomes 14.4 to 14.6 ounces per day. Lincoln Chen, "An Analysis of Per Capita Foodgrain Availability, Consumption and Requirements in Bangladesh: A Systematic Approach to Food Planning," The Bangladesh Development Studies, Vol. III No. 2, April 1975, pp. 93-126.

(5) In conventional economic terms, food consumption is a function of income. This relationship must be qualified in the case of a poor agrarian economy because here income is largely a function of food produced. A monetized treatment can easily veil extreme and involuntary variations in purchasing power and nutritional well-being.

(6) Other factors have also conspired to direct the distribution of ration food to those with purchasing power. Before independence, international grain prices, domestic rice prices, and ration prices were low and not dissimilar, but the days of 15 to 20 takas per maund (82.3 lbs.) of rice are gone. Between

independence and late 1974 the domestic rice price increased six times. During this period, when international wheat and rice prices rose to around $300 and $600 per ton, respectively, and domestic market prices were still higher, the government continued to supply wheat and rice through the ration system at the taka equivalent of $169 and $203, respectively. As a consequence of these extreme price differences, it was advantageous for everyone with access to these ration foods to divert handfuls and even truck loads to the open market. Ration cards were forged in abundance, and by January of 1975 newspaper accounts estimated that one-third of the cards in Dacca were fake. Other kinds of abuses were also rampant. The effect of these market opportunities was to heighten the importance of purchasing power to obtain rationed commodities. During 1975 these extreme price conditions abated, and during 1976 and on into 1977 the market rice price stabilized at around 105 to 130 takas per maund, as illustrated in Fig. 5.1

(7) There has been considerable discussion in the literature of the possible disincentive effects of PL 480 Title I. To summarize, it is agreed that U.S. PL 480 Title I imports cause a disincentive to domestic agricultural production. What is at issue is the magnitude of benefits associated with the increased supply of this wage good. In general terms, Title I is said to have contributed to both Indian and to Korean development because it was imported during expansionary periods in the development of the urban-industrial sectors of these two economies. Mellor points out that Title I enabled India to expand urban employment during the 1960s at a rate of 6% a year (1976, p. 136). For an additional analysis of the Indian case, see Paul J. Isenman and H. W. Singer, "Food Aid: Disincentive Effects and Their Policy Implications," Economic Development and Cultural Change, Vol. 25 No. 2, January 1977, pp. 205-237. For an analysis of the Korean case, see Sang Gee Kim, "The Impact of PL 480 Shipments on Prices and Domestic Production of Foodgrains in Korea," in the Agricultural Development Council, Inc., Economic Theory and Practice in the Asian Setting - The Economics of Agriculture, Vol. III, pp. 155-173.

(8) The expenditure data in the Statistical Year Book of Bangladesh, pp. 283-84, indicate that per capita foodgrain consumption rises with income to a level of 22 ounces per day. The poorest quartile, however, consumes 12 ounces of grain per day.

(9) This potential transfer in FY 1975 has been estimated on the basis of the difference between the prevailing market and ration grain prices, and the offtakes sold through the ration system. No upward adjustment in this transfer has been made to take account of demand and supply elasticities. Although the price elasticity of demand for grain among most ration recipients is low and suggests that the potential transfer would be higher with a termination of the ration system, the amount of grain in private stocks and being smuggled out of the country during the 1973 - '74 period was said to be very high, though difficult to estimate.

(10) For a discussion of this point with respect to the Indian fair-price shops, see U. K. Srivastava, et al., Food Aid and International Economic Growth, Ames: The Iowa State University Press, 1975, Chapter 2, "Price Disincentive Effect in Recipient Countries," pp. 37-63.

(11) The ration system is both a financial boon and an economic sink. When the government purchases grain internationally and procures domestically with its own resources, a financial loss is incurred because c.i.f. and domestic procurement prices are above ration prices. For food financed on grant and concessional terms, however, there is a net financial gain. The loss in this case is an economic one because domestic revenues are deliberately foregone in order to ensure the supply of low-priced food commodities for the cities. Although the value of food imported on less than commercial terms is tallied at its c.i.f. cost in the balance of payments, it is sold below this price and, therefore, does not generate (or recover) a taka equivalent of its international value. These "losses" can be seen as a measure of the perceived political risk of urban unrest. With the fall in international commodity prices since 1974, and as the government continues to raise its ration prices, this economic loss is gradually being reduced (see Chapter 2, Table 2.3 and Chapter 5, Fig. 5.1). The economic "loss" incurred from the sale of rice, wheat, and edible oil has been calculated to be: $122 million in FY 1973, $216 million in FY 1974, and $53 million in FY 1975. In total for these years, revenues foregone have represented approximately 38% of the combined Annual Development Plans. From USAID Staff, "The Subsidy Burden of the Bangladesh Government's Food Ration System," Dacca: January 2, 1976.

(12) According to Raisuddin Ahmed (October 1976, p. 17) between FY 1961 and FY 1974 rice production for the country as a whole grew by 1.9%. According to his May 1976 study, boro rice grew by 14.9% and wheat by 11% between FY 1961 and FY 1974 on relatively small bases (pp. 21-22). By way of comparison, in Comilla Kotwali Thana, agricultural production grew by 4.2% from the years 1961 to 1972. Quazi M. A. Malek, "Rice Cultivation In Comilla Kotwali Thana," Dacca: Bangladesh Institute of Development Economics, December 1973.

(13) From Ministry of Agriculture, "HYV Task Force Reports 1974-75 and 1975-76," December 1976, and "HYV Aman Task Force 1976," January 1977. The transplanted (HYV) aman acreage has been revised downward from 1.7 million acres to as little as 500,000 acres. A senior agricultural advisor has estimated that in FY 1976 the new seed was adopted on 400,000 acres of aus 500,000 of aman, and 800,000 of boro; the FY 1977 estimate may be even lower. The FY 1977 HYV wheat coverage is estimated to be 300-400,000 acres. Because of this overestimation, because the new seed have in part displaced acreage devoted to other more nutritious crops, and because of the land, irrigation and credit practices described in the following chapters, I discount the "advances" that may have been made to date in new seed use.

(14) Statistical Year Book of Bangladesh - 1975, pp. 96-97.

(15) Farruk has estimated that 10% of the annual rice production entered the commercial grain trade during the 1960s, and that the public share of this market, the ration system, varied from 20 to 54% between 1955 and 1967. 1972, p. 20.

(16) John Thorp, 1976, and a study by Ahmadullah Miah, "Problems of Rural Development: Some Household Level Indicators," Dacca, IRDP, October 1976, p. 62.

(17) See Ali Akbar's early and detailed account in his "1974 Famine in Bangladesh," Rajshahi University (draft) November 1975. Also see Bruce Currey, "Mapping of Areas Liable to Famine in Bangladesh," Dacca: Johns Hopkins (draft), 1976.

(18) The sharp increase in land sales is documented by Ali Akbar, p. 58. The relationship between farm size and risk of death has been documented by a report on Companyganj Thana, Noakhali District in 1975. For those without land the crude death rate for the year was 35.8 per thousand; for those with more than three acres the rate fell to 12.2 per thousand. Infant and child mortality showed a similarly dramatic, inverse, relationship with family farm size. Colin McCord, November 1976, Table II.

(19) According to Emma Rothschild (The New York Times, January 10-11, 1977) U.S. PL 480 food shipments to Bangladesh were delayed or curtailed because U.S. grain prices were high and grain supplies were short. U.S. political interests lay elsewhere, and Bangladesh was found to be trading jute with Cuba, contrary to a PL 480 provision which stipulates that recipient countries may not trade with North Vietnam and Cuba.

Trip reports and newspaper accounts of the period make it clear that smuggling to India also explained food shortages. The proximity, or rather embrace, of the Indian border around Bangladesh, coupled with high incentives to smuggle during 1973 and 1974, severely taxed the country's ability to feed itself. Landless laborers and poor cultivators had to compete for food not only among themselves but with "foreigners." My concern warrants repeating. That is, purchasing power and not proximity to grain ensures that the rural poor feed themselves. Food production has been growing at less than 2% per year and population has been rising at the rate of 3%; therefore, smuggling of only 1% of the annual crop per year, 120,000 tons, cuts into an already low per capita food supply. Conservative estimates have placed the normal pre-independence grain flows to India at between 300,000 and 400,000 tons. During 1973 and 1974 the level was said to be two to three times higher.

(20) Ali Akbar p. 9.

(21) These quotations are drawn from field trip reports dated January 11, September 30, and October 10, 1974.

(22) In estimating the numbers of starvation deaths in 1974, the period of time is identified together with the specific population at risk, and the rate of excess mortality, or, the rate over and above that which is considered normal at that time of year. The time period was August through November of 1974 for three subdivisions of Rangpur and one subdivision of Mymensingh. The total population at risk was estimated to be 1.9 million people. W.H.O. doctors estimated that the death rate had almost tripled for the time period. Taken together, these factors indicate an estimated 16,000 deaths from starvation. It is impossible to ascertain a specific cause of death because caloric starvation renders a population vulnerable to many diseases. Cholera deaths in Rangpur ranged between 3,000 and 10,000 during the same period. Deaths from starvation in Dacca and in other parts of Bangladesh during

these months were at least 2,000 to 3,000. Official famine deaths have been estimated to be 27,000, but may actually be as high as 100,000. From USAID Staff, "Estimating Starvation Deaths in Bangladesh," Dacca, November 26, 1974.

(23) In Dacca the burial service of the philanthropic Muslim society Anjuman Mufidul Islam keeps records of its work over the years. The numbers of unclaimed bodies buried by this society varied directly with the price of rice during the years 1973-1976; 3328 were buried in 1974, while the figure for 1975 was 7274.

(24) Conditions that conspire to create starvation and recommendations for remedying these conditions were documented by the British a hundred years ago during the Indian famine of 1868-69. Unfortunately, in 1974 this experience was recalled too late and with too little energy. Bengal Famine Code, Revised Edition of 1913, pp. 1-17, and the Famine Manual of 1941, pp. 1-13, reprinted by the National Institute of Public Administration, Dacca, June 1967.

(25) USAID Staff, "Rice Situation in Dacca," November 12, 1974.

(26) For an account of this food glut, see Donald F. McHenry and Kai Bird, "Food Bungle In Bangladesh," Foreign Policy, Summer 1977, pp. 72-88.

(27) Economist Intelligence Unit Ltd., Fertilizer Marketing and Distribution Study, Volume I, January 1977, p. 71.

(28) From USAID Staff, "Bangladesh Food Management Policies - A Proposal for the Establishment of an Analytical Cell within the Government," Dacca, March 9, 1976.

(29) Because of institutional rigidities analyzed in the following chapters, food production may not be very responsive to higher agricultural prices. In the short term, higher urban rice prices may only provide windfalls to traders and to wealthy farmers without ensuring crop increases or broader rural participation in agricultural growth.

A grain price stabilization scheme, used in many countries including India, Indonesia, and the Philippines, is described for Bangladesh in USAID Staff, "Open Market Foodgrain Sales - Mechanics and Related Aspects of an Integrated Food System," Dacca, April 29, 1976.

Experience in East Asian countries suggests that the public sale of food, of up to 25% of the marketed grain trade, is adequate leverage for moderating urban grain prices. As the Bangladesh ration system supplies well over 50% of the urban market, its leverage should be curtailed.

In determining a price range within which a price stabilization scheme should operate to effect higher market prices of grains, at least two analytical approaches may be used. On the one hand, cost of production analyses, for which the government should recognize actual credit and tenure costs to tenants, would provide an a priori approximation of what constitutes favorable agricultural prices. On the other hand, agricultural production and input sales data are a useful check on this first approach.

A relatively narrow price range, between open market and procurement prices, should be avoided because stock and management costs to the public stabilization scheme would be high, because private grain traders need an adequate price spread within which to function, and because private grain traders have been shown to be efficient.

(30) In addition to these objectives, the Bangladesh Government is concerned with others. For example, food policy analyses have to encompass jute procurement and export targets, the effect of foodgrain price on sugar, edible oil, and tobacco production, the relative incentives for local compared with new seed production, and the effects of a higher wage bill on domestic manufacturing and exports.

(31) USAID Staff, "Food Procurement in Bangladesh - Note for Discussion," Dacca (draft), October 13, 1976.

Improved farm level storage is often claimed to be the only method by which cultivators can withhold their crops at harvest in order to sell them later at more favorable prices. In my view, the storage problem has been miscast. Farmers must sell grain, regardless of their physical capacity to store it, to pay for non-farm purchases and rent and debt obligations.

(32) A methodology for calculating storage reserves is included in USAID Staff, "Open Market Foodgrain Sales .....," April 29,1976.

6 The Impact of the New Seed – Reverberations From the Field

THE RELEVANCE OF THE NEW SEED

The potentially most significant technical change now taking place in the rural areas of the subcontinent is the introduction of the new high-yielding seed varieties. This "green revolution" was introduced in Bangladesh in the 1960s with new varieties of rice. These are now being joined to new, higher-yielding varieties of other crops such as jute, wheat, edible oils, pulses, and vegetables. With the new seed technology scarce land and capital can be utilized more intensively than had been thought possible. Crop yields should double and triple, and farm income should expand at similar rates.

Even though these new seed varieties require chemical fertilizers, irrigation, pesticides, credit, and technical knowledge, they are less costly per unit of production than traditional varieties. Since yield and income increases outstrip production costs sufficiently to reduce the average total cost per unit of harvest, feeding the population should become less expensive. The new seed can also put massive numbers of people to work. The same land can employ many more people than it has in the past. These new varieties offer a solution that is, in theory, equal to the scale of the production and employment problems outlined in our earlier chapters. Furthermore, the new seed can be planted on the country's millions of small farms because these varieties and their requisite inputs are highly divisible. No other technical opportunity can claim this degree of appropriateness. In brief, there are no technical reasons why the new seed cannot be central to our model.

However, despite the new seed's apparent appropriateness, the adoption rate of the new rice seed has been slow. The macroagricultural conditions discussed in Chapter 5 explain part of this, but we must also examine the cultivator's world.

The new rice seed from Los Baños and the new wheat seed from Chilpancingo have been transplanted to the fields of Bangladesh, but their advantages are not thoroughly understood in this new institutional milieu.

Inadequate suppliers of agricultural inputs and other development problems do hamper the adoption of the new varieties, but I see these problems are being secondary. (1) Instead, I will show that the new seed varieties interact with existing economic traditions in such a way as to threaten their relevance to the equitable growth model. While the new varieties are profitable, they do not provide the benefits to laborers and tenant cultivators originally envisioned. Laborers are not enjoying the added income made possible by larger harvests, nor is the demand for labor keeping pace with its supply. The condition of the rural poor continues to deteriorate despite the promise of the new seed.

My concern for a seed product appropriate to labor-rich Bangladesh necessarily raises the subject of an appropriate institutional process. If the new seed technology is not the technological breakthrough it is widely heralded to be, what then can be said of the process that has provided the country with these varieties? By drawing upon evidence from the field, I examine those institutional forces that determine and sustain technological choices for agriculture. I will explain why the new seed technology of the 1960s and 1970s may prove to be as inappropriate to the needs of Bangladesh as the farm machinery which was introduced years earlier.

EVIDENCE FROM THE FIELD

In evaluating the new seed, it is useful to compare its heralded technological potential with recent field evidence. Technology can be defined as a mechanical or organizational technique for the production of a good or service; any improvement in technique implies that existing resources contribute to a greater supply of this product or service. A new seed technology implies that the quantity of agricultural labor, land, and capital originally applied to traditional seed varieties will now produce higher yields. Here, the technological change is embodied within an input, the seed itself, which is a form of capital. As a consequence of this technical change, the average cost of the output falls; that is, food grain becomes cheaper. (2) Ruttan sums up the conventional expectation of the new seed technology:

> There are few growth dividends to be realized by simple resource reallocation within farms, communities, or regions in the absence of technical change embodied in less expensive and more productive inputs. Only as the constraints on growth imposed by primary reliance on indigenous inputs - inputs produced primarily within the agricultural sector - are released by new factors whose productivity is augmented by the embodiment of new technology is it possible for agriculture to become an efficient source of growth in a modernizing economy. (3)

According to Mellor, "Increased agricultural production, based on cost-decreasing technological change, can make large net additions to national income and place that income in the hands of the cultivator classes, who tend to spend a substantial proportion of it on nonagricultural commodities." (4)

This seed technology creates employment expansion and is the link to other growth processes.

A reduction in food costs is only half of the technical windfall. In comparison with local seed varieties, the new seed requires more man-days of work to apply fertilizer, to weed, and to harvest the larger yields. In switching to the new seed, the man-day requirements, according to official estimates, increase from 71 man-days to 117 for the boro rice crop, and from 58 to 77 man-days of work for the aman crop. As a general rule, the government estimates that 52 man-days of work are required to grow local rice varieties, while new rice varieties require 97 man-days. With the use of ideal levels of fertilizer and other inputs, these requirements can range upward to between 110 and 120 man-days. These added days of physical work assure laborers a substantial increase in agricultural employment. (5) The expansion of agricultural production will also create off-farm jobs and the food to feed an enlarged labor force. The model described in Chapter 4 is clearly based upon the wide acceptance of the new seed technology. However, this ideal conception of the way the new seed will generate growth is not substantiated by field experience.

For centuries, the rice crop has been a gift of the annual monsoon rains. The timing and amount of each monsoon determines the generosity of each summer's aus and aman harvests; the land has traditionally lain fallow during the dry winters. Crop production under monsoon conditions is risky and low-yielding, but, aside from the cost of labor, virtually free. The new seed varieties, however, are imported products that depend upon agricultural inputs foreign to this traditional world. The cultivator is expected to purchase fertilizer and water control that heretofore had arrived gratis with each silt-laden monsoon flood. For this reason, recent field evidence indicates that producton costs do not fall with the use of the new seed. Table 6.1 illustrates the fact that production costs per pound of rice, wheat and jute remain approximately the same; yields one and two times larger (line A) require similarly larger investments (line C). Chemical fertilizers replace natural, flood-born nutrients, and irrigation equipment replaces the annual monsoon. Test-plot yields, free of risks and budget limits, produce yields four and five times larger than the traditional levels of Table 6.1, line A. In the field, however, under monsoon conditions, what has been heralded as a major technological breakthrough for agriculture, is in fact an expensive innovation. These yield increases have their price. (The methods by which these data were gathered and compiled, and qualifications of their interpretation are discussed in the Note to Table 6.1.)

The summary data of Table 6.1 indicate that cultivators have reason for questioning the added costs and benefits of the new seed. Fertilizer-response data lead us to the same conclusion. Although new rice varieties are more responsive per pound of fertilizer than are local rice varieties, this difference is not as large as one would expect. According to trial data of the Bangladesh Soil Fertility and Soil Testing Institute, the yield response per pound of fertilizer for new varieties, in comparison with traditional varieties, is only 20 to 30% higher. (6) Stated in terms of price, the ratios of increased harvest value to fertilizer cost also illustrate that local and new seed varieties are not that dissimilar. For new rice varieties the value of the added harvest is

Table 6.1 The Effects of Switching from Traditional to New Seed Varieties

		Rice Aus[(a)]	Aman[(a)]	Boro[(a)]	New Boro to New Wheat	Jute
A. Yield (tons per acre)						
	T	.56	.56	.60	N 1.68	.56
	N	1.12	1.31	1.68	.75	1.12
% Change in Yield		100	133	181	-.56	100
B. Total Cost (cents per lb.)						
	T	1.8	3.0	2.2	2.7	1.7
	N	1.7	2.1	2.7	2.6	1.5
C. Production Cost/Revenues ($ per acre)	T	22/40	39/70	29/75	N 100/210	21/80
	N	43/90	60/163	100/210	44/107	36/180
%Change in Profit		33	118	-31	30	42
D. Man-days per Crop Acre						
	T	53	53	44	N 93	50
	N	99	88	93	55	80
% Change in Labor		87	66	111	-41	60
E. Percent Return to Labor with Increased Yield		31	20	19	20	10
F. Elasticity of Employment Change to Yield Change (Percent)		87	50	61	73	60

Source: Calculated from USAID Staff Surveys "Cost of Production of Transplanted Aman Paddy per Acre," January 20, 1976; "Cost of Production of Boro Paddy and Wheat Cultivation per Acre," March 19, 1976; and "Cost of Production of Aus Paddy and Jute Cultivation per Acre," August 4, 1976.

Notes: These data are drawn from interviews with cultivators who had recently shifted to new varieties. This sample, of between 20 and 30 interviews for each of the five seed types, is not representative of the country as a whole. The cultivators are treated as owner-operators, and are assumed to be using their own land and capital; no costs for these are included. Agricultural inputs are priced at 1976 ration prices. Because of these assumptions (addressed in the following chapters), the cost and profit data of line C are atypical.

In addition, these case studies are not strictly comparable because the field interviews were conducted in different areas of Bangladesh over several seasons and for varying qualities of land. Family and hired labor are valued at between 5 and 8 takas per day, depending on the case and time; harvest paddy is valued at 70 takas per maund (82.3 lbs); wheat, at 80 takas per maund; and jute, at 80-90 takas per maund. The prevailing exchange rate is Tk. 15 = U.S. $1.00. One metric ton equals 2204 pounds.

(a) Aus - spring, Aman - summer, and Boro - winter rice.

T = Traditional seed varieties, N = New varieties.

seven times the cost of the fertilizer, while for local rice varieties, and for new varieties of wheat, this ratio ranges between five and six to one. (7)

The similarity of local and new varieties, from the cultivators' point of view, is again suggested by data on the use of fertilizer by seed type. More pounds of fertilizer are applied per acre to new varieties than to traditional varieties. However, because local varieties cover a far greater area than do the new seed, and for the cost reasons cited above, the total amounts applied to local varieties are high. For example, in 1975-76, 36,000 tons of fertilizer were applied to local aus varieties, in comparison to 54,000 tons applied to new aus varieties. For transplanted aman, local varieties receive 58,000 tons and new varieties 72,000 tons. The payoff for fertilizer use is clearer with respect to the boro crop; local varieties received 32,000 tons while the new boro received 140,000 tons. (8) We suspect that these data overstate the proportion of chemical fertilizers applied to the new seed for, as explained in Chapter 5, the new seed acreage has been grossly overestimated.

From these data, based upon yields far beneath the new seeds' potential, I conclude that the new seed varieties do not yet represent a cost-reducing technological change. From the cultivator's point of view, the relative costs and benefits of these varieties, in comparison with traditional varieties, explain why they are not being accepted rapidly. This slow rate of new seed use may have serious consequences for an agriculturally-based development model.

LABOR'S SHARE - MORE FIELD EVIDENCE

The technical and cost characteristics of the new seed provide a partial explanation for their slow acceptance. For a fuller understanding, cultivator income from the use of the new seed must also be examined. Under conditions in which so many laborers own no land and very little capital, the relative demand for land, labor, and capital created by the new seed is important. Which factors of production enjoy the highest returns in the use of the new seed? The technical requirement that more man-days of work are needed to grow the new seed may disguise a low return to labor. This prospect would cause us to question the relevance of the new seed; according to the model, laborers, both as laborers and rural consumers, must share in the new harvests.

According to recent field data, the added man-days of work entailed in the use of the new seed do not increase in proportion to yield growth; compare line A with line D of Table 6.1. Furthermore, the 90 to 120 man-days of work promised by seed research institutions and government plans fall short under actual field conditions. When the physical labor requirements of the new seed are translated into income, the prospects for labor become even more discouraging. Table 6.1, line E, shows that labor income, as a share in the increased harvest, ranges between 19 and 31%. (9) The other shares of the harvests are for land and capital payments, which may or may not accrue to the cultivator. Landless cultivating families and hired laborers do not benefit in proportion to the new yield increases; the new seed varieties are capital- and land-intensive, and the owners of credit and land benefit accordingly. The implications of this are severe in a rural economy where most of the land is cultivated by landless tenants. In those countries where cultivators own their own land and have ready access to credit, this emphasis on labor's share would have little importance for development policy.

The link, therefore, between the new seed and improved welfare for the rural poor is weak. Crop production and employment targets of government plans are not likely to be realized. Landless laborers are not going to find much additional work on farmers' fields. Stated in quantitative terms, the elasticity of employment created with respect to growth in crop yields is certainly less than the 75% assumed in the first Five-Year Plan. That is to say, when the yield doubles because of a switch to the new seed, on-farm employment grows by only 50 to 87%, according to the field data in Table 6.1, line F. For the principal aman and boro crops, the employment increases are 50 and 61%, respectively. Data from Clay and Khan suggest an even lower employment elasticity of between 13 and 57% with a switch from traditional to the new seed. (10) Whether measured in terms of man-days of work or wage income, it is clear that laborers do not share significantly in the new seed technology. There is an important reason for this, and it concerns the real agricultural wage rate, another indirect indicator of rural well-being. The index of Table 6.2 illustrates that real wages have been declining for the last 25 years. The 1950-1975 series described in this table, when calculated forward to 1977, suggests a further drop of 25%. This declining index reflects population growth and severe competition for jobs. It is apparent that rural wage income, even with the advent of the new seed, is purchasing a deteriorating level of subsistence for millions of agricultural laborers. (11) While man-days of work increase with new seed use, the labor market is swamped by another overriding factor.

This evidence, together with the labor-force growth rate discussed in Chapter 4 and the trend in the agricultural growth rate discussed in Chapter 5, presents a grim picture. Should foodgrain production continue to limp along at a growth rate of only 2% a year, and should on-farm employment creation grow at half this rate, or even less as suggested by the range of employment elasticities, only a small proportion of the nearly one million entrants to the labor force will find work in agriculture. As Clay and Khan have pointed out, "The conventional treatment in development planning of employment and the under-employment problem is to tack an employment projection on to the production plan." (12) Individual well-being cannot be an "add on" to an equitable growth model. Because the new varieties are the only known technological foundaton for the model, the processes that have generated this new technology must be questioned.

Table 6.2 Bangladesh Real Agricultural Wage Index

	Money Wage in takas/day	Cost of Living Index	Real Wage Index
1950	1.62	76.2	100
1955	1.32	68.6	90
1960	1.95	94.9	97
1965	2.34	105.4	104
1970	2.98	132.8	105
1971	3.15	...	
1972	3.93	246.4	75
1973	5.59	351.5	75
1974	8.04	565.2	67
1975(a)	9.42	735.6	60

Source: A.R. Kahn, 1977, p. 151.

Note: (a) Data for first half of year only

TECHNOLOGICAL CHANGE - WHO BENEFITS?

Field evidence calls the new seed's relevance for the model into question. Although technical problems have been solved and these new varieties have been successfully introduced, their wide acceptance is in doubt. What are the processes that will improve the acceptance rate of this technological choice in the future? Before ways can be suggested for ensuring the continuance of the new seed revolution, I review the processes that have determined the selection of the new seed in Bangladesh.

The theory of induced technological change postulates that new techniques of mechanization and economic organization will be stimulated and reinforced by the relative domestic supply of land, labor, and capital. Economic growth, ensured *inter alia* by technological change, conserves scarce resources and uses abundant ones. A technical change is also likely to make more efficient use of inputs, aside from whether the factor proportions change. Each technical change, therefore, represents the co-terminus of two processes: the alteration of factor ratios to take advantage of the relatively more abundant factors, and greater efficiency in the use of existing resources. Technological change opens new opportunities for growth and also rations and rewards the relatively scarce factors of production. It is assumed in this theoretical case that domestic market prices accurately reflect relative factor supplies, and that domestic institutions are responsive to domestic factor endowment in their search for economic efficiency. (13) For Bangladesh, for example, domestic prices and research are assumed to generate techniques that reflect the relative abundance of labor over capital.

We can evaluate the recent history of technological change in Bangladesh's agricultural strategies against this brief theoretical sketch. The production strategy of the 1940s and 1950s emphasized agricultural extension work, and the introduction of irrigation and ploughing equipment. The farmer was to be made more knowledgable and more productive. This public sector priority, based largely on the successful agricultural experience in the west, assumed that farmers were ignorant of efficient techniques and that the traditional plough and bullock constrained production increases. These assumptions were entirely in keeping with western economic legacies discussed in Chapters 2 and 3.

During the 1960s a new technological orientation was introduced by the government. The constraint upon crop production was seen to be land, not the cultivator's knowledge; the new seed represented a land-augmenting technological change. Yields per acre, not per man, began to receive priority.

In drawing attention to these two technological developments, I emphasize that both were induced exogenously by the government, which, in turn, drew upon foreign advice and financing. Neither technology was developed or demanded by the cultivators themselves. (14) Nor, at the time, did either technology represent a domestic research product. Because of their size and cost, tractors have proven to be entirely inappropriate for small-farm agriculture; and modern irrigation equipment, as we will see in Chapter 8, is utilized primarily by the owners of land and capital. In Chapter 5 we reviewed the macroagricultural reasons for the low rate of agricultural growth. In the remainder of Chapter 6, and in following chapters, we will examine the consequences of these technological choices for equitable growth.

The new seed varieties represent a technology that exploits the factor endowment of Bangladesh. They are also highly divisible for a mosaic of very small farms. Still, it is one thing to make the conceptual case for the new seed and quite another to design processes that can effect its adoption. Seed research continues to obtain its support from a few governmental sources; its rural constituency is not in evidence, however. No domestic interest group is calling for agricultural research to develop lower-cost seed varieties which use more labor. What is the explanation?

From our earlier discussion of the country's economic legacies, we know that its technological choices are largely imported. The capital-intensive biases of foreign models permeate the Bangladesh economy and its plans. Development planning and policies do not reflect the path that would be suggested by the theory of induced technical change. Credit and equipment are cheap. In the face of massive unemployment and a declining real wage, little progress has been made to administratively direct technical choices, or to lessen control of the private sector in order to induce more capital-conserving processes. This capital-intensive bias, rooted in a colonial past, now finds substantial domestic support. Urban and rural vested interests gain a great deal from what is, in effect, a dual price system. The vast array of subsidies on food and agricultural inputs of one private system are enjoyed by those who have access to public resources. Cultivators and laborers pay higher market prices for resources in the other system. As I will show in the following chapters this dual price structure is institutionalized for agriculture; the owners of land and the participants in rural development programs, not the cultivators and laborers, enjoy the subsidies on agricultural inputs. The gains of increased production are not being shared with cultivators and agricultural laborers. As a consequence of this dual-price legacy, the demands of labor are not voiced; there is no labor-intensive constituency. Capital is not perceived to be in short supply, nor is its price high, for those who have access to public systems. In short, the processes that would induce labor-intensive changes are overwhelmed by older, exogenous process. Ruttan sums up the dilemma: "A distorted incentive system will have the effect of biasing the direction of technical change in a non-optimal direction and dampening the productivity of resources devoted to the development and diffusion of new technology." (15)

Instead of assuming that technical choices reflect the domestic resource endowment, we should ask "Technological change - Who benefits?" The induced technical change thesis finds its footing here, for it is the power of the urban elite that determines policy and price, and not the domestic resource endowment per se. Economic legacies are resilient, and they continue to bias decisions in favor of imported, largely capital-intensive solutions. Reliance upon imported food, for example, has reduced the need for the ruling elite to emphasize domestic food production. Accordingly, the new seed's potential income stream and its land-augmenting, labor-using character are not seen as sources of national growth or of improved rural well-being. As a consequence, the new seed and the adaptive research needed to ensure its relevance to the field finds little indigenous support.

The induced technology thesis posits that a technologically derived source of new income will draw local institutional support. Whether these institutions are already in existence or evolve in a new form, such domestic backing is the measure of successful technological adoption. However, the legacies that prevent support from being given to appropriate products also act to squelch appropriate processes. A new source of income does not necessarily induce its own domestic alliance. (16) Vested interests cling to imported food at the cost of domestic agricultural stagnation. However, this does not completely explain the failure to exploit the new seed; the traditions of land tenure, irrigation, and rural institutions have also prevented the new seed from becoming a self-sustaining process. Before turning to these traditions in later chapters, I offer some suggestions, which would have to be administratively induced, for directing agricultural research along an appropriate growth path.

ENSURING THE USE OF THE NEW SEED

The field evidence reviewed here could lead other countries to the conclusion that both foodgrain and employment growth should be sought through technologies other than that of the new seed. No other technological option appears relevant to the massive problems of Bangladesh. Altered policies and increased public investments are required; the new seed revolution cannot be allowed to falter. Ruttan identifies the central prescription:

> It seems clear that the development of a continuous stream of new technology, which alters production opportunities to conform to long term trends in factor and product prices, is key to the success in achieving relatively rapid rates of agricultural productivity and output growth in any country. An important element in the success of such a strategy appears to be a system of market and non-market institutions which accurately reflect the economic implications of factor endowments to agricultural producers, to public institutions, and to private industry. (17)

The heart of such a system for Bangladesh is the set of policy recommendations for food and agriculture outlined in Chapter 5. Until the urban ration system is toppled from its present position, agriculture will continue to stagnate. Several other steps can be added to this discussion on macroagricultural policies. For example, the public price-maintenance program for grain must purchase only the new seed varieties. The present practice of giving priority to local varieties serves the food preference of the urban elite; it does not augment demand for the new seed. In addition to creating more favorable terms of trade for the new seed, administered changes can alter the priorities of seed research institutions. Research must be undertaken which can effect decreases in the unit-cost of the new seed under actual field conditions, increases in man-days of work per acre, and preservation, if not enhancement, of labor's share in each harvest. On the basis of our field evidence, we know that there is a more demanding role for adaptive seed research than was first envisioned by seed breeders and planners.

In seeking to speed the new seed's acceptance, we must recognize that the many desirable policies needed for a dynamic agriculture are not likely to be implemented in rapid succession. The terms of trade will not turn rapidly in agricuture's favor; land tenure relationships will not be altered quickly; the annual floods will not be controlled in this century. For these reasons and others, the country's agricultural potential may not be increased for decades to come; average yields will not soon reach four and five tons per acre. However, the new seed must be accepted now; cultivators and laborers cannot wait for better times. The agricultural labor force continues to grow. Accordingly, the following research objectives are necessarily short-term, in lieu of what must ultimately become a heavily capitalized agricultural system. (18)

Because public programs are not succeeding in making fields suitable for the demanding conditions of the new seed, the resiliency of the traditional varieties is being retained. Research emphasis is being placed upon drought and flood-resistant varieties because grandly-designed irrigation and flood protection schemes are seldom effective. New varieties of deep-water rice, for example, capitalize on river-borne sources of nutrients and irrigation and yield two to three times more than traditional levels. Reliance upon the monsoon is certainly not costless, but it also has its benefits.

The largest cash cost for cultivators, and for many the only cost, is the purchase of chemical fertilizer. (19) Yet many areas of Bangladesh are awash every summer with silt-laden flood waters that deposit natural nutrients in significant levels per acre. (20) Seed researchers should recognize the value of these free nutrients when recommending doses of chemical fertilizers to cultivators in these areas.

Cash expenditures for modern inputs can be reduced in other ways. It has recently been found that the rices of Bangladesh are sufficiently free from pest attacks to allow the discontinuation of preventive application of chemical pesticides for most rice varieties and seasons. (21) The cultivator can make one less cash purchase.

The switch that is occurring from new boro rice varieties to new wheat varieties is evidence that the high cash requirement of the new rice is a serious burden. After independence, the Ministry of Agriculture started promoting new wheat varieties and, as a result, land previously planted to irrigated rice, as well as fallow land and some under dry land crops, began being converted to wheat. With this switch, irrigation and fertilizer costs fall, as do yields, and the need for hired labor is cut by two-thirds. These savings are significant for the farmer-owner who cultivates his own land and for the tenant who has to borrow money, although the adverse production and employment consequences for the seed-based growth model are clear, as can be seen in Table 6.1, fourth column.

Labor's share of the new harvests must be ensured by increasing the days of work per crop, the number of crops per year, and by restraining the level of non-wage cash expenditures for agricultural inputs until off-farm employment opportunities expand dramatically. Fortuitously, agriculture in Bangladesh is already very labor-intensive. The planting and harvesting of traditional and new crops continue to be done entirely by hand and with bullock power. As these twin steps, conducted twice a year in many areas, remain the principal sources of employment in rural Bangladesh, it is important that the mechanization of agricultural steps not be encouraged until the social costs of labor displacement have been evaluated.

Periods of high labor demand recur during the same weeks of the crop year in Bangladesh, causing labor shortages and seasonal wage hikes. As the necessity of paying high wages will in time lead farmers to invest in planting and harvesting equipment, the man-days of labor required per crop will fall. For many hired laborers, employment during these peak periods represents much of their annual cash income. Cutting these job opportunities, if only for a few days or weeks in the year, can have a disproportionately serious effect on their total wage income. Because total days of work in a year may be falling, the declining real wage of Table 6.2 may be more serious than is suggested by the index. Mechanization can, therefore, have immediate impact on annual employment and real wage earnings. However, a policy position on mechanization is not easily established.

While machines may be introduced as a convenience, they may also be necessary to ensure the cultivation of two or three crops per year.

Mechanization undertaken solely to relieve the drudgery of work is self-defeating from the point of view of national employment creation; yet it is obvious that mechanization can ensure added employment through yield and multi-cropping increases. The trade-off between mechanization costs and higher yields per acre must be evaluated in terms of the equipment's marginal contribution to yield, multi-cropping, and man-days of work per crop year. Although the model's employment objective requires the expansion of on-farm jobs, the emphasis here is upon the need for evaluation rather than the impostion of preconceived conclusions. The choices of mechanization are difficult to resolve a priori without field evaluations under actual conditions. A few examples serve to illustrate the complexity of the problem.

Increased multi-cropping is possible with better bred bullocks and improved implements, as well as with mechanical tillers and tractors. The first of these ploughing methods may be sufficient to prepare the soil during the dry season for a second and third crop. Because irrigation is generally required for rice cultivation in the winter, we will assume its availability for softening the dry soil before ploughing with bullocks. Tillers and tractors are far more costly than bullocks and may not be as efficient as the combination of bullocks and irrigation equipment. Alternatively, the winter season may be left to dry land crops. No research is being conducted on these types of cropping-system questions, nor is the new small-scale equipment being evaluated. (22) This new, "appropriate" equipment from the International Rice Research Institute in the Philippines and from Japan, is being used in several areas of Bangladesh. IRRI's pre-germinated rice-seed drill, which plants several rows of sprouted rice seed simultaneously, is inexpensive but sharply reduces the demand for labor during the planting season when wages are traditionally high. Labor costs are reduced and yields may be higher , but seasonal unemployment rises. The economic consequences of this seemingly "appropriate" piece of equipment have not been quantified. (23)

To preserve labor's share in the face of pressures to mechanize, we can continue to look to the plant breeder. A wider selection of high-yielding, short-duration crop varieties, tailored to the several zones and seasons of Bangladesh, will increase and spread the man-days of work more evenly across the year. This will break up the few short periods of high wages and spread overhead costs over more crops each year. (24)

Despite these guidelines, I am not optimistic that appropriate seed-breeding and mechanization choices can have a significant impact upon the lives of landless cultivators. In the face of population growth and the existing distribution of land and credit, these guidelines hold little promise for improving the well-being of the poor. I do not foresee the birth of a labor-biased agricultural constituency, or even technological or market-induced institutional changes supportive of the model's new seed base. As the next chapter illustrates, the new seed varieties are altering tenure patterns in ways which appear to be reinforcing the preexisting distribution of land and income.

We cannot rely on the administration of research policy to effect rural well-being. While seed research institutions are expanding new seed varieties, better varieties by themselves offer little return to labor. The same can be said of an appropriate mechanization policy for agriculture. The issue must be squarely faced; in the absence of an aggressive agricultural strategy and a sharp reduction in population growth, broad access to the new harvests depend upon radically altered institutions of land, credit, and price. It is equally as obvious that the responsibility for inducing appropriate processes and products in the future, changes relevant to rural Bangladesh, falls to those outside the traditional structure.

NOTES

(1) For analyses of agricultural development problems in the subcontinent, see Mellor, 1966 and 1976.

(2) This simple definition of technological change is made complex when relative prices are altered, technological rigidities are recognized, and changes are embodied in one or more of the inputs, as in the case of the new seed. For a description of the origins and variations of the new technology in Bangladesh, see the appendix to Chapter 4 entitled, "New Rice for Old - The Challenge."

(3) Ruttan, "Induced Technical and Institutional Change and the Future of Agriculture," ADC, December 1973, pp. 1 and 2.

(4) Mellor, 1976, p. 14

(5) These man-day estimates are drawn from The Economist Intelligence Unit, Ltd. (EIU), Bangladesh Fertilizer Marketing and Distribution Study, Volume I, Table 33, January 1977, p. 78; the First Five-Year Plan, p. 159, and the FY 1973 ADP, p. 189.

(6) EIU, Ibid., p. 74.

(7) Ibid., p. 73. These high-value ratios indicate that the returns of both new and old varieties are high and that fertilizer use rates are below optimal levels. Yet in Chapter 5 we saw that overall crop-production growth rates are low. The apparent inconsistency, between cultivator profitability and overall crop production growth rates, is explained by costs of credit and land, which are either ignored or underestimated in simplified farm analyses. These cost factors are analyzed in the following chapters.

(8) Ibid., p. 98.

(9) Similar low labor shares have been found in other studies. The return to labor, according to Clay, was found to be 26% with the introduction of tubewells in Bihar, and it increased to 31% after the farm owner had repaid the tubewell loan. See Edward J. Clay, "The Impact of Tubewell Irrigation on Employment and Incomes in the Kosi Region, Bihar, India," ADC Staff Conference, Sri Lanka, February 1975, p. 75. In a study of India, the return to labor ranged between 2 and 12%. John W. Mellor and Uma J. Lele (1972), p. 6.

(10) Clay and Khan, October 1977, pp. 26-28.

(11) Competition for jobs and land is causing real labor and cultivator payments to deteriorate. This competition is also causing traditional forms of payment to change from a share to a fixed-rate basis. Moreover, labor payments vary directly with the price of rice, another indicator of the degree of competitiveness. In 1976, for example, the price of rice fell significantly and nominal wages declined. The points are discussed in Chapter 7.

(12) Clay and Khan, op. cit., p. 4.

(13) For a discussion of the induced technology thesis and its analysis in light of the historic Japanese and United States' agricultural technology experience, see Yujiro Hayami and Vernon W. Ruttan, Agricultural Development: An Institutional Perspective, Baltimore: Johns Hopkins University Press, 1971.

(14) An exception to this statement is the development of improved local rice varieties, such as Pajam, of unknown acreage. These varieties have evolved by farmer selection in response to agronomic and economic conditions.

(15) Ruttan, op. cit., p. 7.

(16) I am not suggesting that the new seed varieties are not profitable, but that, as shown in later chapters, profit is more closely associated with the control of agricultural inputs (including the "control" of laborers and tenants) than with output maximization.

(17) Ruttan, op. cit., p. 7.

(18) In the future, agricultural investments may not include the optimal use of chemical fertilizers and pesticides recommended by present agronomic trials. If not curtailed by credit constraints, environmental restrictions must restrain the pounds of chemical put on each crop, two or three times a year, for two-thirds of Bangladesh.

(19) EIU, op. cit., p. 80.

(20) See the Proceedings . . . on Deep-Water Rice, 1975, and, particularly, the articles by S. M. Hasanuzzaman, "Cultivation of Deep-water Rice in Bangladesh," pp. 137-147, and by Animesh Chandra Roy, "Soil Characteristics and Fertilizer Response in the Cultivation of Deep-water Rice in Bangladesh," pp. 148-162.

(21) See the Bangladesh Rice Research Institute, "Recommendations for the Control of Pests and Diseases of Rice in Bangladesh - A Position Paper," June 1976, p. 6. This report, based on the work of David Catling and his associates, states that the aman crop is the only one of the three annual rice crops that requires a preventive pesticide routine. Therefore, except for the aman, all rice crop applications can be made on a corrective basis. The degree to which this happens depends on whether cultivators heed the advice of extension agents, and on the Ministry of Agriculture's surveillance and corrective capability.

(22) Evaluations of mechanical agricultural equipment have not included economic and social considerations. For example, imported tractors were promoted in Comilla district in the 1960s as a means of ensuring the profitability and attractiveness of the Comilla Cooperative Model to its members. Yet the multiple subsidies and their consequences which have

been enjoyed by these tractor cooperatives have been ignored by engineering evaluations. A comprehensive evaluation of bullock and tractor use in Bangladesh should include, among other things, an analysis of the Muslim practice of sacrificing the strongest bullocks at the annual Eid festival.

(23) The Bangladesh Government sponsored an appropriate agricultural technologies workshop in early 1975. See Proceedings . . . on Appropriate Agricultural Technology, 1975. Following this 1975 conference the Ministry of Agriculture established an Appropriate Agricultural Technology cell within the Bangladesh Agricultural Research Council.

(24) In addition to seed research and mechanization policies, input and output price relationships bear directly on production costs and labor's share. In the preceding chapter the case was made for higher harvest prices and for larger flows of public resources into agriculture. Higher prices for farm products would, inter alia, enable further subsidy reductions on agricultural inputs. However, safe generalizations about the desirability of subsidy reductions are difficult to make. On the one hand, lower subsidies both increase cash production costs and reduce labor's relative share in the harvest. Seen in these terms, the case for an across-the-board reduction in subsidies can be questioned. On the other hand, because of the declining trend in rural wages and tenure terms, and because Bangladeshi farmers enjoy one of the lowest nutrient/paddy price ratios in Asia (EIU, op. cit., p. 71), the reduction of subsidies reduces windfalls to the land-owning elite and, through larger, price induced, input supplies, causes prevailing market prices for inputs to decline. Both of these conditions benefit poorer cultivators. In any event, the efficiency and equity effects of a subsidy reduction should be studied on a case-by-case basis. From USAID Staff, "The Pricing of Agricultural Inputs in Bangladesh," Dacca: September 1973.

7 "83% of the Farm Area Is Cultivated by the Owners Themselves"

The above statement from the Bangladesh First Five-Year Plan is a myth. (1) This country, long known for its millions of small farmers, is, in fact, cultivated by tenants. What accounts for this myth, and, more importantly, what accounts for the predominance of tenant farms? What impact is tenant farming having upon the acceptance of the new seed technology? In the preceding chapters we have alluded to the fact that most cultivators of Bangladesh do not own the land they work. What implications does this have for the country?

The family or owner-operated farm, as it is often called, has been widely heralded in the western world as embodying the fundamental relationship between man and land that is required to translate individual initiative into agricultural development. Does this norm describe Bangladesh? In this chapter, the cultivators' legal and actual ties to the land, and how these help to explain the slow acceptance of the new seed and the low overall crop production growth rate, are examined. This analysis will also show why millions of people have already left the land and why more will follow. All but a very few of these people face destitution.

> There is already a large degree of tension over land, income and opportunity in Bangladesh today which will be increased substantially if the population doubles and tries to work the land under the same general set of institutions and conditions as exist today. (2)

Few recognize this growing tension. During the 1960s, the green revolution was acclaimed as a technological breakthrough that would reduce, if not supersede, the need for basic institutional reforms such as those for land and credit. It was suggested by some that production and employment increases generated by the new seed would obviate the need for a redistribution of land. (3) However, the attractiveness of this prescription evaporates when the technical possibilities of the new seed are examined in their institutional context. An analysis of actual tenure patterns in

Bangladesh provides the necessary institutional basis for land and tenure reforms which are recommended in the last section.

It is necessary to trace the history of tenure relationships in Bangladesh in order to predict their consequences for the model. The land legislation of this region not only predates modern Bangladesh, but even the arrival of the British East India Company. Now, centuries later, this historic tenure pattern is an impediment to agricultural development.

THE ZAMINDARI LAND SYSTEM OF GREATER BENGAL

For centuries the economic relationship of the ruler to the ruled in the subcontinent has been governed by the right of revenue collection. (4) Under Moghul rule, villages in the subcontinent were administered according to ancient Muslim laws of government and revenue responsibility. The Moghul Raj in Delhi had the right to collect revenue, a share of the grain harvest, but did not claim rights to the land itself.

The British East India Company was granted the privilege of revenue collection, called zamindari rights, for Calcutta and two other villages in 1698. The Nawab of Bengal negotiated this first zamindari right for 1500 rupees, "it being the best money that ever was spent for so great a privilege." (5) Sixty-seven years later, in 1765, the Raj in Delhi granted an extension of this revenue collection privilege to all of Bangal, Bihar, and Orissa. Revenue "farming" was to prove to be as important as the Company's commerce and administration in shaping the future of the region.

The grant from Delhi laid the legal foundation for what was to have been beneficent rule. Lord Cornwallis, then Governor-General of India, drew upon his knowledge of the landlord-tenant relationship in Great Britain for an administrative model for the control of British India. This model assigned responsibilities to the landlord that included a secure and progressive environment for the tenant's agricultural husbandry. The local landlords of Moghul India, or zamindars, recognized this British administrative necessity, and so explained the existing relationship with their own tenants in terms with which Lord Cornwallis could sympathize. Cornwallis' decision to embrace the existing tenure pattern, instead of requiring the development of an entirely new system of rural administration, appeared to be a matter of good judgment. The loyalty of the local zamindars to the British Crown was assured, in return for secure revenue and anticipated good husbandry. Native landlords changed masters - the Moghul Raj was replaced by the Crown - but the actual system of lord and cultivator remained unaltered.

The Permanent Settlement Act of 1793

For almost a century (1698-1793) the East India Company experimented with several methods of revenue collection, but revenue administration proved to be slow and difficult. The Permanent Settlement Act of 1793, which was the result of this experimentation, established an annual revenue sum of 26.8 million rupees to be collected in perpetuity from the local zamindars, in exchange for hereditary rights to the settlement areas of Bengal, Bihar, and Orissa. (Bangladesh is a portion of what was formerly eastern Bengal.) The Company thereby ensured itself a fixed annual revenue payment, without exception or delay, and the zamindars secured a right to their estates. The actual cultivators remained tenants with no status in law and subject to rents imposed by their zamindars.

When the Act was promulgated in 1793 there were 443 large estates that collected 47 million rupees from their rent-paying cultivators. The excess over the annual amount that was due the Company is explained by the fact that zamindari payments had to be on time. Many estates changed hands for non-payment and, as a consequence, a system of sub-zamindari interests evolved to reduce this risk of default; these intermediary landlords were called taluks. This process of subinfeudation divided the revenue burden, the risk, and even the control of land and paved the way for tier upon tier of intermediary rent-receiving interests between the Company and the zamindars on the one hand, and the actual cultivators, or raiyats, on the other. Each tier, at the cost of its own maintenance, ensured the revenue payment to the Company. Often there were four to twenty intermediaries between the zamindar and the raiyat; and sometimes there were tiers below the raiyat, for even he found it profitable to sub-let to sharecroppers, under-raiyats, and to landless cultivators.

The zamindari revenue for the Company was fixed from 1793 until India's independence in 1947. Land rents, however, were not fixed, despite legislative efforts to protect cultivators. As a consequence, the means for financing estates, both vast and small, was assured. Based on rents in effect in the late 1940s, the raiyats and under-raiyats paid between 120 and 220 million rupees in the name of ensuring the 26.8 million rupees to the Crown. (6)

Subsequent Land Legislation

Legislation succeeding the Settlement Act of 1793 sought to secure tenure, fix rents, and to define "cultivator." The Rent Act of 1859, one of many pieces of land legislation, conferred "occupancy rights" upon farmers who had cultivated their lands continuously for 12 years. The purpose of this Act was to enable tenants cultivating under zamindars to become occupancy tenants, and thereby gain the status of small zamindar-cultivators. However, because sharecroppers, (borgadars), were not recognized as tenants, and most cultivators were regarded as agricultural laborers, few cultivators actually gained a zamindari relationship to the Company. Nor did their status change when the British Government took direct control of the country after a mutiny of Indian soldiers in 1857-58. Contrary to the intention of the Rent Act, intermediary, non-cultivating classes were encouraged to grow. The statutory definition of "cultivator" explains why this happened; an occupancy tenant or cultivator was defined as a farmer "who primarily acquired lands for the purpose of cultivation with his own labour or by his hired labour." Cultivation by the "cultivator," or even his residence in the village, was no longer required and, in fact, was seldom practiced. This legal definition of cultivator, which was designed to accommodate the British indigo manufacturers of the time, laid the legal foundation for the growth of non-cultivating interests in land. Other legal clauses strengthened this foundation; for example, the Rent Act and subsequent legislation enabled the hypothecation of land and standing crops. The vagaries of the monsoons and inevitable poor harvests gradually forced poor farmers and cultivators into the hands of the moneyed elite; land and crops were exchanged for survival.

Contrary to the original intention of Lord Cornwallis and the pledges of his native aristocratic lords, little investment actually took place in rural infrastructure and conditions were not improved for the cultivators. This fundamental fault of the zamindari system of Bengal was noted as long ago as 1809: "Lord Cornwallis's system was commended in Lord Wellesley's time for some of its parts, which we now acknowledge to be the most defective. Surely you will not say it has no defects. The one I chiefly alluded to was its leaving the ryots (cultivators) at the mercy of the zemindars... The Zemindars of Lower Bengal, the landed propriety established by Lord Cornwallis, have the worst reputation as landlords, and appeared to have frequently deserved it." (7) Abdullah is more generous in his assessment of the zamindari system, stating "that they also had some contribution to maintaining a certain level of cultural and social decentralization is also undeniable." (8)

The burden of this "cultural decentralization" went unnoticed for a long time. Not until 1940 did the Floud Commission, in its investigation of land tenure practices, estimate that some 12.4% of the actual cultivators were sharecroppers and 18.6% of the farm labor force was landless. The impoverishment of many cultivators, in part a consequence of successive Acts, was slowly being recognized. The injustices perpetuated by two centuries of land legislation led to a Commission recommendation that the zamindari system be abolished. Until Bangladesh achieved independence, the Company and the Crown placed revenue stability before the well-being of the people.

By the 1940s, the multiplication of tiers had run its course; 73,000 separate estates in what is now Indian West Bengal and Bangladesh were paying revenue to the Crown. By then the raiyati farm had been reduced in size to an average of 1.85 acres; the under-raiyati farm, to .69 acres. (9) The zamindari estates of the Permanent Settlement (of Bengal, Bihar and Orissa) had been divided and redivided many times; Muslim inheritance laws and the fact that the population had quadrupled since 1698 had taken their toll.

The independent governments of Pakistan and India inherited legislation that had lost sight of the cultivator ploughing his field. In his place was a hierarchy of interests in land based upon revenue and rent responsibilities. M.A. Zaman sums up this legislative evasion well: "Granting such rights in a system where zamindari is profitable, the term 'cultivator' is loosely defined, institutional credit facilities are lacking, and land revenue is fixed but rent is not, only perpetuates a situation where the number of intermediary rent-receiving interests between the State and the actual cultivator increases over time." (10)

The State Acquisition and Tenancy Act of 1950

Following independence and partition of the subcontinent in 1947, the abolition of the zamindari system headed the list of social reforms. With the passage of the East Bengal State Acquisition and Tenancy Act in 1950 the new state of Pakistan became the direct owner of all lands and the direct receiver of revenue from cultivators in the new region called East Pakistan. The old raiyati cultivators were now to be called maliks. A ceiling of 100 bighas (33.3 acres) was placed on the malik's cultivated land, and all land in excess of this amount was to be redistributed by the state. For some, the 1950 Act represented a major restructuring of land ownership patterns. "These measures, which were completed about 1954-55, have created all over East Pakistan a vast body of small landed proprietors. In place of the landlords and the rent collectors and the tenants, we have simply six million farmer-proprietors." (11)

Others have suggested that there was no restructuring of tenure relationships, only a reaffirmation of the status quo. The clearest indication that no change occurred in the cultivator's status comes from the Act itself. The 1859 definition of cultivator was retained: the cultivating malik is one who "holds land by cultivating it either by himself or by members of his family or by servants or by borgadars or by or with the aid of hired labourers or with the aid of partners." The Act goes on to state that the malik does not sublet his land when he gives it on borga or sharecropping terms. Unlike the Rent Act of 1859, the 1950 Act did not permit the cultivating raiyats to acquire de jure rights by cultivating the land for a specified time period. In a preliminary draft the new Act contained protections for borgadars, but these were deleted in the final legislation.

The Act's implementation revealed other deficiences. Only 163,741 acres were confiscated by the first ceiling on farm holdings, and only a small percentage of this amount was actually redistributed. In 1961 the 100-bigha ceiling was raised to 375 bighas (125 acres) by President Ayub Khan in his bid to win rural support.

Actually, the greatest restructuring of the zamindari system was brought about by independence and partition rather than the Tenancy Act. Most of the largest estates were abandoned when thousands of Hindus fled to Calcutta. It could be said that the Act served to recognize a fait accompli, at least as far as these largest estates were concerned. Out of a total of the 2,237 largest estates in East Bengal, only 358 were owned by Muslims. The Act left hundreds of Muslim zamindars and talukdars untouched as few lower level intermediaries were legally abolished or even recognized.

The Act of 1950, legislated by the independent government of Pakistan, sanctified a new zamindari system in place of the old one. No changes were made in the definition of "cultivator" and, therefore, his position continued to deteriorate.

THE PEOPLE'S REPUBLIC AND THE PEOPLE'S LAND

The new government of Bangladesh also placed the abolition of the zamindari system high on its list for social reform. The new government's first land order exempted holdings of 25 bighas (8.3 acres) and less from the land tax. Receipts fell from 80 million rupees in 1971-72 to a little over 5 million takas in 1972-73. (12) A second order directed that the ceiling on family holdings be returned to the pre-1961 level of 100 bigha (33.3 acres). Under this order, 76,712 acres were expected to be released for the landless, but to date they have acquired only 33,300. (13)

Following the 1974 flood, another order was promulgated to restore lands to those who had been forced to sell under distressed circumstances. However, no land has been returned to date because the former owners do not have the money to repurchase.

A review of the most recent legislation reveals that the East India Company's land regulations, twice removed by independence, remain intact. No legislation has been enacted, or even drafted, that would require the farm owner to be the actual cultivator, assure tenants' rights in land, or otherwise marry labor and risk with productivity and reward.

Official recognition of the cultivator's actual status is avoided. Though not acknowledged in law, this recognition is beginning to arise from another source. Development programs and projects require feasibility studies, and these, in turn, require a much improved understanding of rural Bangladesh. (14) It is this combined work, started after independence in 1971 by institutions of government, research, and education, that is documenting the increasing poverty of rural tenants and laborers. Just as the Floud Commission prompted recognition of growing injustices, so may the present work force development programs to focus on the poor. Perhaps it can even force changes in the law itself; however, my optimism is guarded.

By and large, rural development programs still assume tht the cultivator is the actual owner of the land. Raiyats and maliks are the focus of these development efforts. The distribution of land by type of tenure is assumed to be correctly represented by the Agricultural Census of 1960 and by the Master Survey of 1967-68. These volumes claim that owners farm 59% of the land; other farmers own an additional 24%, and expand their acreage by renting another 14%; and only the remaining 3% of the land is farmed by landless tenants. (15) Therein lies the justification for the First Five-Year Plan's statement that "83% of the farm area is cultivated by the owners themselves." Our chapter's title retains its orthodoxy; the inertia of old definitions and data is formidable.

Nonetheless this official picture showed signs of wear in the 1960s, when 20% of the farm families were landless and 50% of all farmers cultivated only 17% of the land. The wealthiest 10% "cultivated" 36% of the land, while 64% of the farm families possessed holdings of less than three acres. (16)

This static picture of land use and distribution from the mid-1960s is suspect because it is based upon official definitions and because land sales are increasing, as can be seen in Table 7.1. During the flood of 1974, which seriously affected the region bounding the Brahmaputra River in the northwest, land registry offices recorded sharp increases in the transfer of title deeds. During 1973 the number of land transfers was 277,611 for Rangpur district; in 1974 the number increased to 399,054 deeds. In September and October of 1974, 61,000 and 45,000 titles, respectively, were recorded in the two subdivisions of Rangpur. (17) In a country of small plots and few total acres, these numbers are large.

Table 7.1 Land Sales in Bangladesh in 1969-70 and 1972-73

Farm Size Group (a)	Average Amount of Land Owned (in acres)	Percentage of Owned Land Sold	
		In 1969-70	In 1972-73
1	.53	53	60
2	1.66	17	18
3	3.48	14	16
4	7.46	7	8
5	19.58	4	4

Source: A.R. Kahn, 1977, p. 195.

Note: (a) The acreage size range of each group is not defined by Khan.

Rumors of land sales in 1974 were sufficiently alarming to cause the Ministry of Agriculture to survey the new deed records of the Ministry of Revenue. Within the 14 districts surveyed, it was discovered that 25% of the farmers with less than one acre sold well over half of their land in each of two periods: 1969-70 and 1972-73. The larger farmers sold progressively less.

In the late fall of 1974, a few of the between 200,000 and 300,000 impoverished people in Dacca were interviewed to learn more about their plight. The sample of 32 families is small, but it provides background data on a problem that otherwise might go unrecognized. (18) These families' original holdings which were inherited in the 1950s and 1960s, together with their post-flood land status, are summarized in Table 7.2. Eight of the 32 families had always been landless, 24 had held some land, and seven had owned more than two acres. With the 1974 flood, 11 more families became totally landless, and the 13 who still had land were forced to leave their villages to search for food.

Table 7.2 Loss of Land by 32 Families in Bangladesh

	Farm Size in Acres							
	(No land) 0	.5	≤ 1	≤ 2	≤ 3	≤ 4	≤ 5	5+
Numbers of Families owning each farm size:								
Pre-Independence	8	6	3	8	1	4	1	1
Summer 1974	19	7	5	1				

Source: USAID Staff, "Landlessness in Bangladesh - An Analysis of Interviews with 32 Families in Dacca," December 19, 1974.

Further conversation with these people revealed that their land holdings had been diminishing for a number of years. Floods, poor crops, and high prices had forced them to sell land in bits and pieces. In some cases they sold their land in one year, and, in succeeding years, their bullocks, their homes, and, finally, their utensils and farm implements. The transition had been from medium to small plots and then to sharecropping and landlessness. The final blow was the flood of 1974, which reduced these people to destitution.

The pain of the final sale of the final bit of land was evident on the face of one cultivator who was sitting on the floor of the Sub-Registrar's office in Chauddragram thana, Comilla district. The Sub-Registrar expressed the opinion that the cultivator was selling "with reluctance." (19)

These impressions lend support to the statistical evidence now available on the distribution of land in Bangladesh. Figure 7.1 illustrates the magnitude of the shift in holding patterns that has taken place between the 1960s and the late 1970s. The official data of the 1960s are badly out of date. While these two curves are not strictly comparable, real changes are occurring. We know from the Land Occupancy Study (LOS) that 10% of the farm households now control 50% of the cultivatable land; 33% of the rural households are without cultivatable land, while in 1967-68 only 20% were without land. Progressively, more families own smaller and smaller plots. And aside from the distribution of land, as the population has grown, the average farm size has fallen from 3.5 acres to 2.3; 80% of the farmers now have plots of less than three acres. (20)

These data and impressions do not disclose the breadth or dynamics of rural poverty. Research is not keeping pace with the deterioration in rural well-being. An ever smaller proportion of the population lives on the typical three-acre farm. We will show in the remainder of this chapter that the control of land and credit is the key to understanding this deterioration.

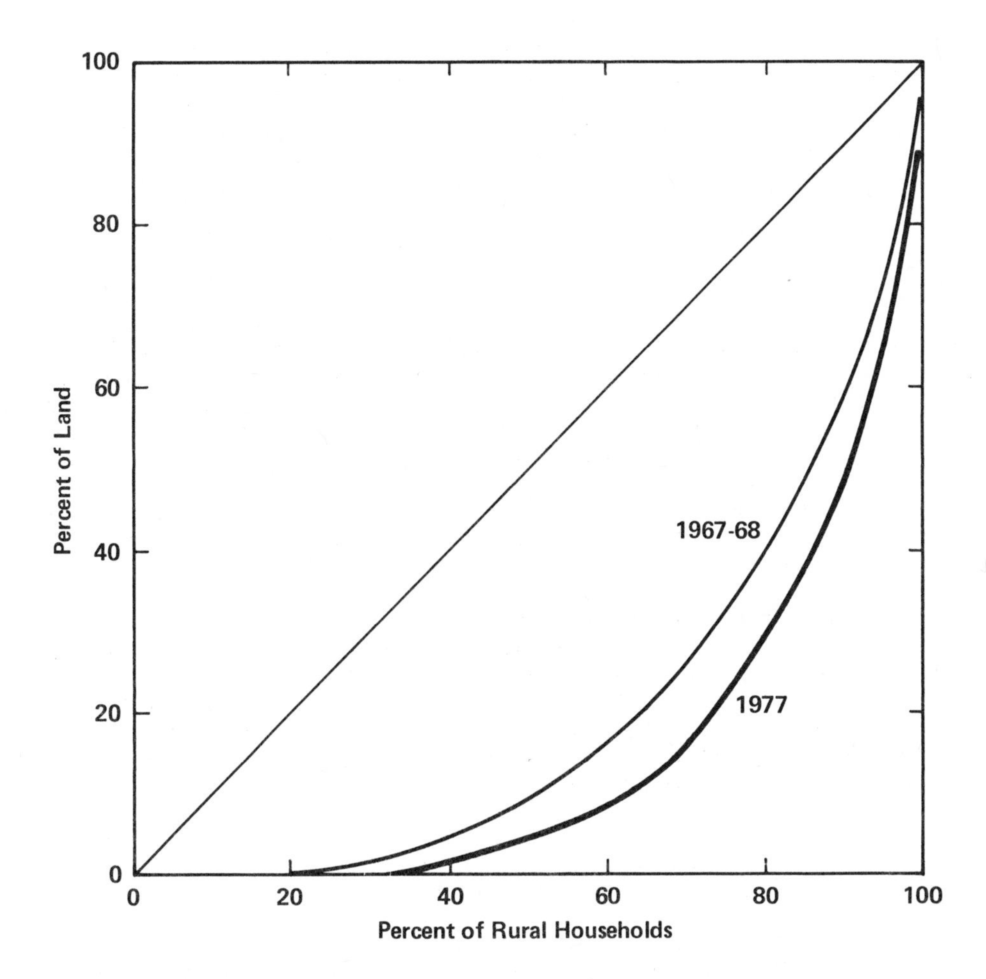

Fig. 7.1 Size Distribution of Land Holdings in Bangladesh

Source: Master Survey of Agriculture, 1967-68, Table I, and Januzzi and Peach, Table D-II.

Note: These curves reflect a changing distribution of land and improved data and definitions. The official data on the distribution of land in 1960, and again in 1967-68, show very little change, and so the two periods are shown as one curve. The data for the 1960s are not strictly comparable with those for 1977 because the former include total land owned and rented in, while the latter cover only owned, cultivated land. For this reason, caution should be used in comparing the two curves. A follow-up to the Land Occupancy Survey will be necessary to make an accurate assessment of changes in the distribution of holdings.

When public credit and modern agriculture inputs are injected into this rural economy, we find that these new resources are absorbed and distributed by the same set of institutional forces that control land. It is precisely this concern that focuses our attention upon tenure as a possible key explanatory factor affecting the prospect for agricultural modernization.

FUTURE CONSEQUENCES OF PAST LEGISLATION

I am not content to review the East India Company's impact upon this region's land legislation and let it go at that. The country's capacity to support 80 million people, soon to multiply to 160 million, depends fundamentally upon the conditions controlling the use of the new seed technology in a traditional tenure setting. In this section four hypotheses are offered that force an examination of the future. Can this land feed and employ its millions? An examination of future consequences of past legislation is obligatory, despite admittedly thin evidence on changing tenure patterns. I sense that the rural economy is being transfigured faster than it is being analyzed.

Recommendations on land and tenure reform will not be useful until there is a qualitative change in our understanding of rural dynamics. Official acceptance of official reports such as the Master Survey, does not serve this end. In a setting where half the population is already off the land, some tentative statements about cause and effect are needed to guide rural research, development programs, and land and tenure legislation. The following hypotheses have been suggested by field interviews and other reports and are tentatively examined in this light. (21)

I. Virtually all land in Bangladesh is farmed by landless laborers and tenants

In nearly 300 years, no land legislation changes have occurred that would swing the rewards of land ownership in favor of the cultivator. Added to the historic tiering of land's control is a population that is now six times larger than when merchants of the East India Company sailed up the Hoogly River to Calcutta. What is the result of these twin processes?

Prior to independence it was acknowledged that between 15 and 25% of the rural population did not own any agricultural land. It is unlikely that they were even cultivators in the sense of being responsible for the management of agricultural operations. Millions of people had to depend upon agricultural and rural service jobs, and some were destitute. Today, half the rural population is landless or near landless; village interviews suggest a range of between 40 and 60%. (22) What of the people remaining on the land?

Behind the labels of "owner," "owner-tenant," and "tenant" used in government publications, there is a literal maze of Bengali land-unit sizes and tenure patterns. Land sizes come in *bighas*, *kanis*, *gondas*, and *dhamas*;

tenant and sharecropping terms are borga, lagit, rehan, chukti, tebhaga, and phuran, to name a few. (23) Behind these local tenure terms is a pattern of relationships that bears testimony to the deteriorating position of the cultivator.

Recent field interviews with people from different geographical areas and different income levels suggest that approximately 10% of Bangladesh is farmed by owners and their families. (24) The proportion is not the 83% indicated by the Five-Year Plan. The remaining land is cultivated by people who own no fields and possibly not even their homesteads. From Tetulia to Teknaf, from one end of Bangladesh to the other, these cultivators predominate; they grow the crops of Bangladesh.

Owners of small farms are numerous, but they own and cultivate only a small proportion of all the land. Those with farms of more than three acres generally rent out all or a portion of their land under a wide variety of arrangements. Owners also rent land to each other and to tenants in order to consolidate their highly-fragmented holdings. Many owners may direct hired laborers, while other owners, preferring to live in the towns and cities, rent their land out on long-term arrangements.

As a general rule, most land is let out on a borga or sharecropping basis; the owner receives 50% of each harvest from his borgadar and does not share in the cost of fertilizer, water, or labor. The remaining land is farmed on various forms of annual cash leases (lagit) or on longer term usufructuary mortgages (rehan). Absentee landownership is becoming important as urban dwellers continue to buy land as an investment. Whatever the terms under which the landless cultivator obtains land, his production costs increase sharply when he pays his rent to the land owner. It is against this burden that he makes decisions about old and new crop varieties. The additional burden of credit is discussed under hypothesis II.

In addition to lending substantiation to our first hypothesis, the LOS includes data on the distribution of owned cultivatable land. This allows comparison of recent evidence with the Master Survey data from 1967-68, which is based on owned and rented in land. The recent data show that 10% of the households own 50% of the cultivatable land. Although this new evidence is not strictly comparable with Master Survey data (see Fig. 7.1 and Note), approximately 25% more land is now in large holdings. If the largest farms had been included in this most recent enumeration, the distribution of land would be skewed even further into the hands of a relatively few owners.

In short, the "small farmer" does not cultivate his own land. Instead, he oversees millions of tenants and landless laborers. Rather than being "small," in the sense of being poor, he represents the rural elite.

II. Credit is the key to the control of land. Tenants require credit to maintain access to land. Crop production and on-farm employment increases, made possible by the new seed technology, are in turn made possible by the control of credit and land.

It is useful to think of a hierarchy of factors that determine rural wealth. How important can the high-yielding varieties be in opening new avenues for income for more people when the distribution of those assets vital for the exploitation of the new seed is already firmly established? The control of credit may be more important than ownership of land in determining the beneficiaries of the new seed. The Act of 1859 legalized the mortgaging of land and crops to raise cash. During this period dadan, or earnest money, was paid by merchants as a form of advance credit to entice cultivators to grow indigo. These practices, in the face of agriculture's vulnerability to the monsoon floods, gradually made credit the key to the control of land and to survival. The use of credit for the purchase of modern agricultural inputs is a very recent phenomenon. Do field data support this perspective on credit? (25)

Hard times can be weathered by those with money, but the cultivators and the owners of small holdings may have to sell plots to feed their families. Debts can remain unsettled even though the last bit of land is sold and the destitute are forced to leave their villages. Of 32 distitute families interviewed in Dacca, 19 left their villages with debts settled but with no remaining assets, while 10 left unpaid debts. If they return to their villages, they will find their debts outstanding. The debtor-creditor relationship is more durable than that of land ownership itself. (26) For many poor people, the collapse into landlessness was gradual; and once their draft animals had been sold, for as little as $40 or $50, their creditworthiness evaporated.

The use of land is so integrally tied to credit that the two are not easily separated. Borga cultivation requires credit for inputs, and leases require cash payment in advance; both basic tenure arrangements require some cash for agricultural inputs. It is not unusual to find a borgadar (sharecropper) handing over an entire crop to the owner in order to pay the rent and to repay input loans. (27)

The rehan tenant arrangement, which involves cash in exchange for a long-term mortgage, is commonly used by poor owners to obtain money to buy agricultural inputs. During crises, several cash advances for food can equal the full value of the land; and a wealthier owner soon takes possession. Rehan represents a desperate effort to raise cash, but at the price of becoming inevitably and irrevocably landless. (28)

The control of credit and land determines who uses the new seed, and at what price. Public crop production programs benefit the landed because landowners hold the local administrative and developmental positions. They have the minimum acreage required for membership in such programs and they own the land. As increased yields flow into the hands of the landowners, so too, as we will show in Chapters 8 and 9, do agricultural inputs flow for their benefit. Even in the Comilla cooperatives (discussed at length in Chapter 9), land ownership of at least three acres has been used as a prerequisite to membership. Consequently, members of modern input programs "on lend," or re-lend, public resources to their cultivators at market rates of interest. (29) The new seed reinforces centuries of continuing land and credit traditions.

The interrelationship of credit and tenure under conditions of extreme population density can be further dramatized by describing the foregoing discussion in dynamic terms.

For the rural poor, a little cash reserve buys food during periods of seasonal unemployment. For cultivators, cash buys access to land. Cash, and the ability to borrow, ensures continuity.

Landless laborers have only their food needs to fulfill and are, therefore, willing to work for low wages. If they won't, others will. For landless cultivators and owners with small farms, an annual harvest income that falls short of providing the food they need forces them to search for off-farm work. It can lead them to incur further debts in order to obtain food and agricultural inputs, and it may force them to sell some land. For landless cultivators and owners of small farms alike, the burden of existing and added debts can easily absorb the increased production from their land, with and without use of the new seed, and their off-farm wage income. A decline in the sale price of grain can be as ruinous as a natural disaster.

Agricultural laborers and cultivators are, therefore, forced to work for wages below the level required to feed their families, to maintain their homesteads and farm implements, to feed their bullocks, and to buy inputs. (30) Their consumption needs act to erode their remaining assets and the slight chance of converting additional income into new assets. Because the numbers seeking work are so great and because there is a lack of institutional mechanisms to protect the poor, real wages are falling toward a literal subsistence level. As we will show, tenure terms are also being eroded by the competition for land.

Even landowners are caught in this squeeze between food needs and meager incomes. Because of population growth and the decline in the agricultural terms of trade, families with some land increasingly have to work for cash in the off-season in order to fulfill their annual consumption requirements, and they have to do this at wage rates set by those without assets. Accordingly, and this is my main point, cultivators and small farm owners face an erosion process from two directions: credit and agricultural inputs are obtained from the elite at market rates, while wage and tenure terms are set by poorer groups seeking work and land. More land changes hands; and more people become _de facto_ serfs. Those with six acres or more may be self-sufficient in food, and therefore need only worry about the division of land among their own family members. (31)

This institutional treatment of credit and tenure dynamics, when cast into the cost and share terms of the previous chapter, identifies an added burden on cultivators. Market rates of interest of no less than 100% per year, or approximately 50% per crop season, add another 17 to 23% to the cost of purchased inputs. At harvest, when the _borgadar_ hands over half his crop, his food costs double. (32)

The new seed technology may open avenues for income growth, but not to more people. The technical fact that the new seed can be grown in a "small farm" agricultural setting is, for Bangladesh, irrelevant. What is relevant is that old and new resources combine to further the concentration of power.

III. Tenure terms are deteriorating against cultivators because of increasing competition for land and because credit and the agricultural inputs related to the new seed are controlled by the landed elite. As a consequence, crop production and on-farm employment growth rates are low.

I have shown in previous chapters that food grain production in general and use of the new seed specifically have not begun to tax the agrarian potential of Bangladesh. Unfavorable harvest prices and the capital-intensive bias of the new seed explain much of this. Land tenure practices must also be understood. As most land is cropped under some form of tenancy, the terms for sharing inputs and outputs between owner and cultivator may be having an adverse impact on the acceptance rate of the new seed. What are the future consequences of existing, and I believe changing, tenure terms?

Because of the deep-seated credit and tenure traditions, we would expect to find that the new seed technology does not disturb existing economic relationships. However, because of population pressure, together with the opportunity for profit presented by the new seed, traditional forms of tenure are breaking down, and their terms are clearly deteriorating against cultivators.

A few field interviews are enough to reveal that the borga sharecropping arrangement, prevalent throughout Bangladesh, is increasingly giving way to more exploitative tenure terms. Under borga, the owner has traditionally shared in the risk of production, although not in its cost. Competition for land is causing a further separation of ownership and profit from physical work and possibly from input costs and risk as well. Conversations with villagers make these trends clear; new forms of tenure are beginning to emerge.

To take advantage of the new seed, owners are paying for the cash input requirements of their borgadars, but their price for this assistance is two-thirds of the crop. This arrangement, called tebhaga, is synonymous with the tenant's use of new seed varieties. In comparison with borga, tebhaga encourages fertilizer use and better management. (33) In a few areas, however, the demands of the new seed appear to weigh heavily on owners. Because boro rice requires irrigation and other modern inputs, some owners in Comilla district cease cultivation with their laborers during the winter months and give their land on borga. This shifts the cash, management, and half the risk burden to the cultivator for what is, as we have shown, a costly crop.

In Tangail and Mymensingh districts in the center of the country, borga farming is giving way to "owner-operated" farming, operated, that is, entirely with laborers. Costs and risks are now being undertaken by the owners who wish to realize the full profits of new seed cultivation. More fertilizer is being used. However, production increases are being achieved at the expense of borgadars, who are becoming landless laborers on what had been "their" land. (34) Yields may increase under owner management but employment may not. The new owner-manager, unlike the borgadar family, will employ a laborer only to the extent that added productivity covers his wage.

In addition to the greater prevalence of owner-managed farms, borga is also giving way to various forms of lease arrangements. In those cases where a landless cultivator or owner leases in land for an annual fixed cash payment, lagit, the terms of such an agreement may be more favorable to the cultivator. Annual, and particularly longer-term, leases give the cultivator an added incentive to use fertilizer. What is not clear is the prevalence of long-term usufructuary mortgages, rehan, where an owner, under duress, loans out his land for cash to a generally wealthier owner. Since the press of debts and food needs have forced him to lease his land in the first place, the poor landowner can seldom repay the loan and he ultimately "sells" out. This is the principal way land is transferred throughout the country. (35)

One may hypothesize that these changes in tenure patterns would take place even without the new seed. The increasing population density, underemployment, and the real wage decline suggest that competition is causing severe downward pressure on tenure terms, as well as upon wages. The share forms of wage and tenure payment may disappear completely. What can be said of the effect these changes are having on incentives to use the new seed?

A review of these new tenure patterns, first in conventional economic terms, and then in their institutional context, sheds some light on tenure's impact upon the new seed's acceptance. A _borgadar_ will not find it profitable to invest heavily in agricultural inputs because he bears the full cost and retains only half of the harvest. He will optimize his income at some level of fertilizer use, and so yield, beneath the level which would be profitable for an owner-cultivator himself. This line of economic reasoning favors the fixed-cost over the _borga_ arrangement because the tenant enjoys the entire harvest produced by his increased use of fertilizer and other inputs. This form of tenure is, therefore, said to be a more favorable one for the tenant, as well as one that would serve to boost agricultural production. (36) An institutional analysis forces us to consider a different conclusion.

Credit plays an important role in evaluating different forms of tenure. If, instead of extracting half the harvest in kind, owners charge cultivators market-determined interest rates for loans to pay for leases and inputs, it cannot be said _a priori_ that the cultivator is better off. The cultivator may be on a fixed-lease basis with his owner, but the terms of his loans are set by intense competition for credit and land. The cost of credit operates to press the cultivator's income toward subsistence. He has little choice but to work the land of the owner. To resist is to be pushed off the land. Accordingly, no form of tenancy may encourage new seed use. (37)

Field research is needed to document the erosion of tenure terms described here and to identify the impact of these terms on crop production and rural well-being. From our interviews we find that production may be increasing under the owner-manager form of tenure but at a price of servitude for the rural poor. This situation is unstable, if not explosive.

IV. The compression of people on the land is forcing them to change their conceptions of rural life. Both the landed and the landless feel trapped in the villages because upward and outward mobility is slowing to a standstill.

It is both remarkable and frightening that in the short space of four or five years village Bangladesh has become aware of its predicament. (38) In dozens of interviews we heard villagers speak of the coming crisis. The impact of population growth upon village life has entered their consciousness. They reflect on times when good land lay fallow. They see what is happening to their farms. "Soon there will be only enough land to bury our children." (39) Millions of people are living longer and millions more are being born. Where a few families could harvest the fish from the village tank some years ago, now three adult generations survive in each homestead to fish the same tank. Cooperation to maximize the pond's yield is impossible. (40) The peaceful village is gone.

Among the landed in village Bangladesh, family growth causes a division of homesteads and so is a source of constant instability. These families used to be able to count on industrial and civil service jobs for their educated sons; now their sons sit at home. The owners of land need not cultivate as they find so many willing to do it for them. Yet, with deteriorating real wages and tenure terms, they sense that traditional village relationships are being pressed to the limit. Landowners may be forcing greater production from their land but they are doing it at the expense of the rural poor. The village elite often live in fear. Absentee ownership is increasingly involuntary. (41)

Cultivating families struggle to obtain credit and to maintain cultivating rights to the land. Survival means debt. Village elders enforce repayment by indentured servitude and the mortgaging of crops. The laborers and cultivators are beginning to realize that their predicament is not caused by the hand of Allah but by their own people. Villagers are aware of the press of population on their land, and, with good reason, they do not see the new seed technology as the means for relieving their sense of entrapment. Tension may burst into conflict before a five-fold increase in rice yields can ease it.

INCENTIVES FOR CULTIVATORS

The Political Reality

Successful land reforms come all too frequently from authoritarian countries that are able to implement both the reform and an aggressive agricultural production upon which success depends. Subcontinental land reforms have been exercises in comparative statics because of lack of commitment to a real redistribution of land and to agricultural production. Bangladesh is no exception.

The urban middle class in Dacca and other cities and towns makes up less than 5% of the total population. This urban group of private business people, professionals, civil servants, and army members retains strong family ties with village Bangladesh and continues to buy land. Because of economic and political instability, there may be greater interest in land now than during the Pakistani period. Consequently, the enactment and implementation of land and tenancy reform legislation by the urban middle class is improbable; they have demonstrated their ability to nullify threatening legislation. Unpopular decisions can be put off since imported food ensures urban stability; a basic wage good is abundant for people who would otherwise have to become concerned with poor agricultural performance.

On the other hand, land reform may be possible. Attitudes are changing and functional definitions may be enforceable. There are landed interests who recognize the necessity for reform, and who may initiate it. Their motives may be the result of concern for the nation, anxiety over their own survival and a fear of rural unrest. Absentee owners may see that they have more to gain from agricultural modernization than from agricultural stagnation. Villagers, landed and landless alike, are voicing some of these issues. At the national level, there is some recognition that rural programs are failing because of the lack of public attention to favorable agricultural price and tenure relationships.

In the remaining sections of this chapter, I base my prescriptions for guiding land and tenure reform on the hope that evolutionary change is possible. It is only a hope.

Lessons and Advice From Others

Bangladesh has had a wealth of advice on the optimal size of an ideal farm under land reform. Some of these recommendations are reviewed here to indicate why attention to size per se, apart from other facets of the rural economy, is not very helpful.

The optimal farm-plot size is at the center of most reform discussions. A. R. Khan points to that 2.6 million acres would be freed under the present Master Survey landholding patterns if a size ceiling were to be placed at 7.5 acres. (42) M. A. Zaman suggests that a ceiling of 8 acres would affect 8% of the farm families with larger holdings, and that a ceiling as low as 5 acres would affect only 20% of the farm families. (43) On the basis of a maintenance level of family income, Zaman has calculated that 3 acres would be an adequate minimum; an FAO study places this minimum at 1.5 acres. (44) The Bangladesh Government recognizes that 800,000 acres would be freed if the present ceiling of 33 acres were enforced. In addition, 1.4 million acres of government, khash, land could be distributed. Zaman estimates, drawing on his own work and that of A. R. Khan, that as many as 3 to 4 million acres may be available for distribution from existing khash land and from additional land freed by a ceiling of 7.5 acres. Let us first examine what these farm-size options tell us of the prospects for reform, and then set the matter of farm size in a broader context.

These farm-size recommendations suggest that land is available for redistribution in significant amounts and in efficient sizes. It is inaccurate to claim, as some have done, that land is not available for redistribution because the country is already being cultivated by millions of small farm owners. The above-mentioned size recommendations have of necessity been based upon the Agricultural Census of 1960 and the Master Survey of 1967-68. We know from the Land Occupancy Survey that the size distribution of farms has been seriously underestimated. An accurate assessment of land ownership would make it clear that more land exists in holdings of 5, 50, and even 500 acres than anyone is ready to admit. Taking this into consideration, there may be enough land, in arithmetic terms, to turn the landless into farm owners.

A farm-size recommendation, without recognition of other economic factors, can be of little practical value. The dynamic aspects of the cultivator's economic life must be addressed. An efficient farm is a function of the available technology and of tenure terms. Given a family income norm, it is also a function of its income-producing capacity. Price changes shrink or expand the harvest in much the same way that technology can shrink or expand land's productivity. The owner's ability to retain his land, under the fluid conditions of Bangladesh, is also central to a reform program. It makes little sense to undertake the trying task of land redistribution when the factors that created the original maldistribution may not have been identified. These factors must also be addressed in a reform package.

In addition to the issue of farm size, authorities have recommended farm models other than the owner-cultivator one as being the optimum arrangement toward which reforms should work. Lucid analyses of the historic development of land tenure relationships in Bangladesh are available. But these analyses conclude too readily that cooperative farming is the only route to distributive justice. The recommendation for cooperative farming, a move from the feudal to the collective which bypasses the individual capitalistic form, glosses over political realities and the problems of cooperation in a society which historically has stressed individualism rather than cooperation. Cooperative pilot farms exist in Bangladesh but are a failure on both distributive and efficiency grounds. (45)

"Three-shares" is another cooperative farming arrangement being tried by private agencies in Bangladesh. It combines the land of the landowner with the labor of the landless to grow a high-yielding crop; credit, other inputs, and management are supplied by an outsider, and each receives a third of the harvest for his contribution. It is my view that the management requirement rules out this model's replication. (46)

The individual-owner model is in my judgment a necessary condition for economic growth. However, an immediate redistribution of land is improbable under present economic conditions. Similarly, a tenure reform to give incentive to cultivators has only a slightly better chance of being implemented. Nevertheless, because the cultivator as owner clearly enjoys most of the factor payments described in Chapter 6, and because the equitable growth model rests on private initiative and market-based growth linkages, the owner-operated farm is the ideal toward which the government should direct a reform.

Because official definitions and data have been taken at face value, it has been assumed by reform advocates that land redistribution would affect relatively few people. Accurate surveys would place considerably more land in the hands of the urban and rural elite. Resistance to reform will be widespread; millions of tenants are already beholden to them. Furthermore, it has been assumed for too long that the cultivator is the direct recipient of the government's crop production programs. Any reform which alters the traditional relationship between owner and cultivator may disrupt agricultural production and further erode the condition of the poor. Reform recommendations have to take cognizance of these basic realities. (47)

Stabilizing the Rural Economy

The first steps in a land and tenure reform program are the setting of higher food prices, which amounts to taxation of the cities, and the shifting of development resources into rural public investments; the political test has to be met here first. An altered food system, as prescribed in Chapter 5, will provide food-price stability and a humanitarian floor to protect the rural poor during a program of rural institutional change. However, higher food prices and an enhanced share of public and private resources for agriculture, if not immediately followed with land and tenure reforms, will provide a windfall to land owners at the expense of cultivators. If this were to happen neither cultivators nor the nation would enjoy the potential increases in production and employment per acre that would be possible with reform.

Land is security and power in a poor economy, and wide fluctuations in prices and political fortunes make it more valuable. New sources of income and forms of assets must be found. Giving more people rights to land and its production requires that others change or diversify their economic interests. Enlarging resource flows into agriculture for the new seed and rural infrastructure will generate the growth linkages described in Chapter 4, and thereby ease the sense of entrapment. Market towns must flourish. Rural credit should become widely accessible. Rural savings should be channeled to rural investments through formal banking institutions. (48)

Tenure and Land Reform

Land tenancy and land ownership reform principles that give first priority to agricultural incentives for increased production are proposed here. The relationship between owners and tenants must promote seed-based growth linkages. I suggest a two-part reform. The first part accepts the actual owner-cultivator relationship as it is, and presses for altered tenure terms. The second part focuses on the redistribution of land. The time interval between the two phases must be utilized to make progress on other price and institutional reforms.

The broad goal of an agrarian reform program must be increased production in terms of which altered tenure terms are explained and adjudicated. Public commitment to agriculture must be visible and vocal and must be backed by public resources and price changes. Public expression of new tenure terms, even without immediate enforcement, will set standards for a vital subject on which the government has never publicly taken a position.

It is now being recognized by a few public officials and an occasional member of the village elite that _borga_ terms may have to give way to a more equitable proportioning of the harvest and its costs. Because the _borga_ system is so prevalent, tenure reform should start with this institution. The government should recognize the growing village tension over land as an opportunity to state that the owner's share must be reduced from 50% to

40%, and even to 25%, as is the case in many Southeast and East Asian countries. (49) This shift must be accompanied by an equitable division of the costs as well. The decontrol of agricultural inputs, to be discussed in Chapters 8 and 9, will force owners to lower the rates to their cultivators for credit, fertilizer, and water. Progress on other economic reforms, such as food and price policy, will also cause the crop returns to cultivating families to grow. (50)

Governmental recommendations on lease terms should be approached with caution. The flat cost of a lease is preferable to a share arrangement from the cultivator's point of view, but in this rural institutional setting the lease arrangement may speed the process whereby owners of small farms lose their holdings. Broad access to formal credit programs must precede lease legislation, and is central to rural development. Expansion of savings and loan institutions also will serve the dual purpose of opening investment opportunities for the landed and checking their previously unchallenged control of rural resources.

While the many recommendations made in these chapters should slow the alienation of land, the government's land registry procedures should also act to check this process. Owners who are under pressure to sell their plots in order to raise cash should have the option of entering a formal credit institution. Under crisis conditions, these owners should be able to obtain relief food.

No distribution of private land can take place until the government has an accurate assessment of ownership by individual and by family. Cadastral surveys are making some progress but are subject to pre-existing definitions and evasive practices. At the outset of a tenure and land reform, these surveys must be expedited and the definitions must be made functional. A large rural cadre should be mobilized to conduct these surveys and to implement the first phase of reform. This mobilization will develop the field staff necessary to implement a radical distribution of land and to build social awareness.

Even prior to a redistribution of private land, khash lands should be divested. Six percent of all land, including that which was expropriated under prior reforms, is said to be publicly controlled. A reform based on two acre farms would be acceptable; the technical viability of a two-acre farm is amply demonstrated by the fact that at present the country is actually cultivated in far smaller fragments. More favorable prices and agricultural input supplies will greatly enlarge the value of this size farm. These khash lands should be legally transferred to the tenants who are currently cultivating them and to the owners of small plots. (51)

Char lands, which arise from silt deposits along the edges of many rivers and the Bay of Bengal, should also be transferred to their actual tenants. These "lands," which are owned and platted despite having been under water for years, should be redistributed by the government as they emerge.(52) While this would act to impose a land ceiling on the legal owners, the past non-productivity of this land and its continuing exposure to floods should lessen the political difficulty of establishing a new ceiling well below the present 33 acre limit.

The first phase of tenancy reform does not deal with the issues of the cultivator's legal rights to land, his security of tenure, or the redistribution of private land. Moving to a second phase depends fundamentally upon the success of share reforms while other institutional reforms are evolving across a broad front.

The Bangladesh Government should consider a sharp reduction in its land ceiling and the distribution of legal titles to the cultivators of Bangladesh. The political difficulties of such a move are manifest. If the land ceiling were reduced to 5 acres, 7.6 million acres would be available for redistribution. This would allow landless families to own a two-acre farm. Alternatively, the landless could be given one acre, and those families owning less than one acre could each receive an additional acre. If the size ceiling were reduced to two acres, 13.6 million acres would be released for redistribution under this plan. When land that has escaped registration is captured in future surveys, we estimate that an additional 500,000 to one million acres will be identified for distribution. Although such a sweeping reform would provide titles to a nation of tenants, other policy and program changes have to be made to improve rural conditions; a concentrated program must be undertaken to check population growth, and popular participation must be the byword of economic policy. (53)

Small farm units are viable in technical terms, and with concomitant reforms, particularly those of price and credit, the economic return to the family will increase significantly. Whether such small plots can achieve self-sufficiency will depend upon the success of a wide range of reforms. Rural family income will remain dependent upon traditional work and income-sharing mechanisms and upon rural works and market-town growth, which have been prescribed in earlier chapters.

During the second reform phase, additional measures are needed. What cultivators gain by reform should not be subsequently lost because of crop hypothecation, inheritance, and mortgage rights that, however well-intended, may adversely affect the new owner-cultivator. Also, land consolidation needs empirical and legislative examination to free the countryside of the serious dis-economies of fragmentation. (54) We do not address the compensation issue, a vital subject in its own right, except to urge that payment be tied to investments in market-town development.

The theoretical basis for a major redistribution of land is the reward of increased agricultural productivity for the rural population and the nation. Economic growth requires it. Only with a redistribution of land and broad access to credit and other inputs will the well-being of the rural population improve. As Chapters 6 and 7 make clear, laborers must have a claim on resources beyond that provided by their own toil. Resources are not available to base individual well-being upon welfarism and relief. In the absence of a land reform, the new seed technology holds little promise. Bangladesh is steadily becoming a nation of serfs.

NOTES

(1) Bangladesh Government, First Five-Year Plan, p. 84.

(2) A. Z. Obaidullah Khan, 1974, p. 6.

(3) See articles on India in USAID's Spring Review on "Land Reform in India," 1970, and on "Small Farmer Credit," 1973.

(4) The USAID mission in Dacca was alerted to the origins and extent of land tenancy in Bangladesh by Professor F. Tomasson Januzzi of the University of Texas at Austin. The historical review that follows is drawn from three separate studies: F. Tomasson Jannuzi, "Preliminary Report Concerning the Need for Further Research on the Hierarchy of Interests in Land in Bangladesh," Dacca: USAID, June 1976 (draft); M. A. Zaman, "Land Reform in Bangladesh to 1970," Madison: Land Tenure Center, February 1976, p. 51; and Abu Abdullah, "Land Reform and Agrarian Change in Bangladesh," The Bangladesh Development Studies, Vol. IV. No. 1, January 1976, pp. 67-114.

(5) Hobson-Jobson - A Glossary of Colloquial Anglo-Indian Words, 1903, p. 980.

(6) Assuming that all cultivation was performed by under-raiyats, a revenue burden of Rs .72 per acre actually cost the under-raiyat Rs. 5.6 per acre. Abdullah, op, cit., p. 70.

(7) Hobson-Jobson, p. 980.

(8) Abdullah, op. cit., p. 74.

(9) Ibid., p. 70.

(10) Zaman, op cit., p. 22.

(11) A. H. Khan, "Community and Agricultural Development in Pakistan," East Lansing: Michigan State University Asian Studies Center, January 1969, p. 16.

(12) M. A. Zaman, "Bangladesh: The Case for Further Land Reform," South Asian Review, Vol. VIII No. 2, January 1975, p. 109.

(13) From an article in the Bangladeshi newspaper Ganokantha, December 18, 1974.

(14) The post-independence bibliography of rural development research is now voluminous; many of the principal studies are listed in footnotes and in the bibliography.

(15) Bangladesh Government, Ministry of Agriculture, Master Survey of Agriculture 1967-68, p. 12.

(16) Ibid., pp. 9-10.

(17) Ali Akbar, p. 58.

(18) For a more detailed analysis of poor people, see A. Farouk, et al, "The Vagrants of Dacca City," Dacca: Dacca University, Bureau of Economic Research, 1976, p. 63.

(19) USAID Staff, "The Land Registry Office in Chauddagram Thana, Comilla District," July 12, 1976.

(20) Jannuzzi and Peach, LOS, Tables D-II and D-III.

(21) This section of Chapter 7 was prompted by Jannuzi's 1976 report (see note 4). After Jannuzi's visit to Dacca in 1976, the author and his assistant examined four hypotheses during field trips to several areas of Bangladesh. In 1977, Dr. A.K.M. Gulam Rabbani of the Statistical Division, Ministry of Planning, in conjunction with James Peach and Tom Jannuzi, designed, tested, and conducted a Land Occupancy Survey (LOS). A random sample survey of all districts was used to test an expanded form of the first hypothesis discussed in this section of the text. For the first time, a formal survey, the LOS, used functional definitions, and estimated proportions of landlessness and types of tenure. Although the LOS was completed prior to this book's publication, this section of the chapter is based largely upon interviews conducted by the author and his assistant.

(22) In estimating the degree of landlessness, official documents and most surveys rely upon household tabulations that are maintained by each union council. Although these lists determine taxes and the distribution of some public commodities and are presumably up-to-date, there is reason to both overcount and undercut the poor. I draw my estimate of landlessness from this source. The LOS, which did not rely upon union council tabulations, used three definitions of landless in its random sample survey: those without any land, those who may have household land, and those who have less than one-half an acre of arable land. Together, the three categories amount to nearly 50% of all rural households. LOS, p. 41 and Table D-III.

(23) In the land unit definitions, 3 bighas are equal to 1 acre, as are 2½ kanis, or 20 gondas, or approximately 8 dhamas. Many of these "standards" overlap in various regions. Acre and decimal (1/100th of an acre) are used throughout the country. I will cite just a few of the many sharecropping and lease arrangements. Borga is the basic sharecropping arrangement. Lagit and rehan are annual cash in advance and long term mortgage arrangements, respectively. Cultivators who farm on borga and lagit are called borgadars and lagitdars. Chukti is a cash lease in the Sylhet area, and tebhaga is a tenure form that gives one-third of the harvest to the cultivator, and two-thirds to the owner in exchange for his contribution of a substantial proportion of the input costs. Phuran, from the Rajshahi area, refers to a flat-rate lease for a single annual crop. These definitions are necessarily abbreviated; their full description would encompass the economies of each region within Bangladesh.

(24) On the basis of its national sample, the Land Occupancy Survey estimates that "only 10.5% of the cultivable acreage is tilled exclusively with family labor." LOS, p. 6. The remaining land is farmed by borgadars, by cultivators who lease land, and by laborers under the direction of owners. Until all land

is actually mapped by its owner, it is impossible to identify, on an interview basis, all land ownership because land is held under names of children and relatives, and under nonexistent names. Owners may not admit to holding more than the legal 33 acre limit, while tenants may claim to own some land. Absentee owners are, of course, not interviewed. As a result, some land escapes being tallied. This is recognized by the LOS, page 30. In our interviews, tenants and owners of small farms described their area's largest farmers as holding from 50 to several hundred acres.

(25) This section is based upon numerous field surveys conducted by the USAID staff (Program, Agriculture, and Capital Development Divisions) on tenure, credit, and fertilizer use during 1975-76.

(26) USAID Staff, "32 Families," December 19, 1974, op. cit.

(27) USAID Staff, "Trip Report and Notes on Chauddagram Thana, " July 13, and 16, 1976.

(28) If an owner of a small farm has to give up his own land to raise cash in order to buy food, he may obtain a rehan agreement. The new "tenant" on his land, generally a wealthy owner, may let it out on borga, and, as a consequence, the owner may end up cultivating his own land as a tenant. For discussions of rehan see USAID Staff, "Notes on Land Tenure Arrangements in Chauddagram Thana," July 28, 1976; "Rehan Bandhak (mortgage) Around the Country is Becoming More Prevalent," October 22, 1976; G. Wood in M. Ameerul Huq, editor, 1976, pp. 139-143, and LOS, p. 33.

(29) There is evidence that in Comilla district it was the "middle farm size" cooperative members, not the owners of the largest farms, who first accepted the new seed technology. The explanation for this may have to do with the possibility that "middle size" owners are more likely to be the actual cultivators, whereas the "larger" owners let out their land on borga.

(30) As noted in Chapter 6, the daily agricultural wage appears to vary directly and closely with the price of paddy. Clay (November 1976) has also found that changing forms of agricultural wage payments, from a share of the crop to a fixed wage basis, is causing real wages to fall.

(31) According to Muslim law, daughters inherit one-half of the share of the land that sons inherit. Widows inherit a small, fixed proportion of the total. In practice, however, the father's land is divided equally among the sons. Despite the prevalence of this practice, and the rapid growth in population, the LOS notes on page 72 that the divisive process of land inheritance does not function rapidly enough to prevent more and more land from gravitating into fewer hands.

(32) These costs of production analyses have immediate policy implications because each public procurement drive is preceded by a discussion of the "just (procurement) price." Official recognition that present procurement prices are inadequate is slow in coming, in part because the prevalence of high interest rates and tenancy is not willingly recognized. A calculation of these costs is in USAID Agricultural Inputs Project III, FY 1977 Dacca, pp. 29-33; and USAID Staff, "Cost of Production and Average Revenue of Borga Farms," April 18, 1977

(33) The USAID Staff, Agriculture Division, conducted numerous fertilizer-use surveys in 1976-77 and included questions on fertilizer use by tenure type.

(34) USAID Staff, "Field Trip Observations on Tenure," July 29, 1976, and LOS, p. 33.

(35) See note 28 on rehan. The supply of money is said to constrain the prelevance of rehan and lagit either because money is not available or because owners of small farms cannot obtain large loans from wealthy landowners and moneylenders. Borga farming would otherwise be disappearing faster than it is.

I have tried to avoid the term "moneylender." All wealthy villagers, landed and commercial alike, lend money to relatives and others on a wide range of interest rates and collateral requirements.

(36) For a diagrammatic analysis of both forms of tenure see M. Raquibuz Zaman, "Share-cropping and Economic Efficiency in Bangladesh," The Bangladesh Economic Review, Vol. I No. 2, April 1973, pp. 149-172.

(37) Borgadars are under increasing pressure to produce. Owners look for good cultivators and, in some cases, demand that they use fertilizer. Borga terms may also be stiffening. In one area we found that borgadars were bidding against each other with 200 taka "entrance fees" to secure land to share crop. LOS P. 42. Nonetheless, borga is giving way to other forms of tenure and owner management. See also LOS, pp. 6-7, 42.

(38) It is noteworthy that this four or five year time frame is not identified with independence. It is the author's impression that this awareness arose from the sharp increase in the price of rice that occurred in 1973-74. According to Clay, cultivators he interviewed noted that the shift to contract leases and to daily fixed wages began about 1971.

(39) USAID Staff, "Field Trip to the Northwest," August 29, 1976.

(40) Edward Glaeser of the USAID Staff cited this example in 1974 to explain failures in cooperative institution-building.

(41) USAID Staff, "Changing Social, Economic and Political Trends in Rural Bangladesh," July 14, 1976; and various other political reports and newspaper translations.

(42) A. R. Khan, 1972, pp. 138-139.

(43) M. A. Zaman, 1975, op. cit., pp. 103, 107.

(44) FAO, "Perspective Study of Agriculture Development for Bangladesh - Working Papers on Policies and Programs Regarding Agrarian Structure in Bangladesh," Rome: October 1974, pp. 4, 6.

(45) This recommendation is made by an FAO study (Ibid.), and by Alamgir and Abdullah of the Bangladesh Institute of Development Studies in their previously-noted articles. Brief analyses of the cooperative farming record are available in A. M. Muazzam Husain, "Co-operative Farming in Bangladesh," Report of the Workshop, Bangladesh Agricultural University, Mymensingh, April 1973, p. 20.

(46) The Catholic Relief Service, and the Faridpur Academy, directed by M. M. Abdullah, were two of the first groups to promote "three-share" cooperative pilots. This concept may have had its origins in the Tebhaga (Three Share) peasant movement in East Bengal in 1946-47 which called for two shares of the harvest for the cultivator and one for the landlord. These recent share pilots are discussed in USAID Staff, "The Plight of the Landless in Bangladesh," (draft) February 9, 1974.

(47) Approximately 25% of the annual foodgrain crop is sold at harvest in the rural markets of Bangladesh. Later, 50 to 67% of this amount is purchased back by poor rural laborers, cultivators, and owners of small farms. The grain in rural markets is supplied largely by owners of large farms, who harvest more than adequate amounts from their own fields and from rent and interest payments made in kind. Accordingly, a dramatic alteration of tenure patterns would disrupt the amount of marketed paddy and, possibly, the availability of food for the poor.

The adverse production effects of land reform is an old concern. For an analysis of the effects that arise because of changes from sharecropping to leaseholds and to ownership in the Philippines, see Duncan A. Harkin's, "Philippine Agrarian Reform in the Perspective of Three Years of Martial Law," Madison: Land Tenure Center, 1976, p. 30.

(48) A commercial bank officer acknowledged to the author that although some 50% of his bank's savings originated in villages and towns, only 1.5% of the bank's funds were lent in these areas.

(49) Bangladesh Government/FAO/UNDP Mission, Land Problems and Policies, Dacca: April 1977, pp. 22-23.

(50) A thorough-going tenure reform would prescribe tenure security, fixed lease terms, inheritance rights, and several other features. In the text I have posited that a tenure reform, as a first step toward a land reform, should focus upon altering the way input costs and harvests are shared. This narrow emphasis may have a greater chance of being implemented, and with greater promise of result in terms of the model's objectives and my wide-ranging prescriptions, than would emphasis upon tenure security or some other facet of tenure reform by itself. Having said this, I recognize that political resistance may cut short any tenure reform effort. Even discussion of the subject in the central government may cause the owner-manager arrangement to completely displace borga.

(51) Because most khash land has been pre-empted by the village elite, its redistribution will not be an easy matter. This point was made clear in an article describing such an attempt that resulted in murder. From "Obstructionist Rural Elite," Holiday, January 30, 1977.

(52) For a fascinating case study of a char land dispute, see Shapan Adnan and the Village Study Group, "Land, Power and Violence in Barisal Villages," Dacca, March 1976, p. 8.

(53) Even if a radical land reform is ruled out, any effort to improve production and rural well-being in this institutional milieu still requires

political and administrative commitment. I posit an alternative type of land reform to demonstrate this point. It is clear that traditional tenure forms are being displaced by the owner-manager model that, as I have pointed out, is creating a nation of serfs. Under such conditions, the government could stimulate food production on "large" farms by increasing food prices in the cities, and could tax this income stream by removing agricultural input subsidies and by taxing large-farm profits. The government could also apply labor legislation to the agricultural labor force and otherwise provide a food floor to the rural poor. Again, this "reform" would rely heavily upon political commitment and administrative capability. This concept of reform has been drawn from V. M. Dandekar and N. Rath, Poverty in India, Bombay: Indian School of Political Economy, 1971, p. 139

(54) The dis-economies of land fragmentation are significant and force attention to consolidation. M.A. Zaman, 1975, op. cit., p. 33n.

8 Water for Land's Development

Monsoon rains and mammoth rivers inundate the Bangladesh delta every year; during the summer there is far too much water, and during the winter there is far too little. This extreme variation is becoming an increasingly harsh fact of life. These annual floods can no longer be accepted with equanimity because of the press of population on the available land. These floods also pose intricate water-control problems for cultivators and for the government.

Water is vital to the new rice seed, and so to the model. Yield and cropping intensity increases require irrigation, which, in turn, requires that the government's water policies and programs be effective. However, a larger water program cannot be prescribed when past investments have contributed little to an expansion of irrigated acreage. Why have these efforts fallen short of their goal? (1)

Because the summer floods have always brought havoc in their wake, river control to protect the country's crops from flooding has been a logical prescription for decades. River embankment projects, which have received priority since the 1960s, have little increased crop production to show for their cost. Public irrigation programs have fared slightly better. Once again, we find that the country has suffered from the application of inappropriate concepts and programs. The former Pakistan government allocated vast resources in the name of improving production for its rural population. Foreign technical assistance generated dozens of studies and justified projects costing over 500 million dollars. Yet benefits calculated in the early 1960s remain elusive.

It is my purpose here to bring the issue of flood-control strategy into perspective by giving voice to the arguments of many individuals both in and out of government who have become disillusioned with the original strategy. Flood-control embankments and major irrigation schemes have come under increasing attack from technicians, as well as from the cultivators themselves. Project costs continue to climb with seemingly little regard for the trickle of benefits. It is time to recognize what cultivators have been doing to ensure water for their fields during the nearly two decades that the flood-control strategy has commanded public attention and resources. Two views, one technical and one from the field, argue for a more diversified water strategy for the future. We will review several major flood-control and irrigation projects, as well as some other irrigation techniques. We will also examine the ways in which cultivators have accommodated themselves to the ineffectiveness of the grand schemes that were designed to enlarge their harvests. The division of river water with India as symbolized by the Farakka Barrage, which diverts a portion of the Ganges to Calcutta, may also force the Bangladesh government to take a second look at its water strategy.

TIME AND THE RIVERS FLOWING

The English word "flood" is so laden with images of disaster that it impedes recognition of the advantages of normal flooding for the Bangladesh delta. The Bengali word for "flood" means "unwanted water;" this more clearly identifies floods in excess of normal levels as giving rise to damage. The normal monsoon rains and accompanying rise in three of the world's largest rivers - the Ganges and the Brahmaputra Rivers of the Himalayas and the Meghna from the Sylhet Basin within Bangladesh - are expected to flood millions of acres and to turn tens of thousands of villages into islands. Silt-laden waters are needed to irrigate the country's traditional rice crop.

A few generations ago the population was sparse, villages rested on the available high ground, and there was little need to farm the flood-prone lower lands. The monsoon rice crops fed the country. With population growth, villages and fields expanded not only to meet each other but to the edges of the rivers. Population growth has also dictated that cultivators "spread" their crops into the dry season, making irrigation a necessity. Until the 1960s, 90% of the dry winter lands remained fallow. Fields and villages now encroach upon lands that once belonged entirely to the rivers. The poorest cultivators have to cultivate the bottom, or char, land. They do so knowing that if their crops are out of phase with the floods they will lose their harvests to as much as 20 feet of water. This can happen when larger than normal amounts of water flood the land and when the water rises faster or earlier and falls later and slower than is usual. Eighty percent of the annual rains of some 84 inches fall during the five months from May through September, while the winter months, from November through March, receive only 6% of the total. Droughts can ruin dry-land winter crops. Both floods and droughts now have to be risked in order to grow enough food to maintain the population.

A statistical description of these rivers makes them appear even more formidable. The monsoon rains and Himalayan snow-melt drain 600,000 square miles of the Indian subcontinent through deltaic Bangladesh. The run-off of this vast area is funneled through a land representing less than 8% of the total drainage basin. (Of the 33 principal rivers in Bangladesh, 32 originate outside her boundaries.) In times of flood, these rivers peak far above their dry season flows. By the time the Ganges and Brahmaputra reach the Bengal Delta, they have become giant meandering streams in a land averaging 30 to

40 feet above sea level. The Ganges, or Padma as it is known locally, enters Bangladesh at an elevation of 34 feet, and the Brahmaputra, or Jamuna, enters from the north at an elevation of 50 feet; the rivers flow on to the Bay with a slope of five inches per mile. In flood, these rivers are so wide that their banks disappear for months.

Together, these rivers normally discharge 1.5 million cubic feet of water a second (cusec), placing them in a class with the Congo River which discharges an average of 1.4 million cusecs, the Mississippi which discharges 600,000 cusecs, and the Amazon which discharges an average of 3.5 million cusecs. At flood stage, however, the Bangladesh delta disgorges 5 million cusecs. Each year's normal high is 22 times the 225,000-cusec minimum flow of the winter months. This extreme variation represents only one of the challenges to water development.

An annual silt load of 2.4 billion tons places these rivers of Bangladesh in a category by themselves. In flood, these rivers normally cut two to three inches off one bank or the other, but under extreme conditions they can scour laterally half a mile in a season. Lateral movement not only destroys crops but erases earthen embankments and whole villages. The price which must be paid for this natural water and fertilizer supply is the continuing reshaping of the landscape, the silting up of canals and tanks, and the erosion of embankments designed to prevent lateral movement and flooding.

As each summer's flood approaches, questions are raised for which there are no answers. How much land will the water flood, where will it flood, and how soon? When should the crops be planted? Only 6% of the country is permanent river bed, and another 10% is flooded to some depth each year. Beyond this assurance, half of the country's 55,000 square miles are vulnerable to flooding; each year carves a different record. Since 14 million of the country's 21 million cultivatable acres are vulnerable to floods, some crop loss is unavoidable. In addition to the land that is inundated by the flooding rivers, some three million acres suffer saline intrusion from the Bay of Bengal.

For the cultivator and the water engineer these aggregated flood data have little meaning; the actual flooding of any particular piece of ground is of prime importance to them. Here the data are sketchy because surveys are still underway. Approximately 25% of the flood-prone area is flooded to a depth of up to one foot every year. Another 36% of the land is flooded regularly to a depth of between one and three feet. Fifteen percent of the flood-prone land is normally flooded to a depth of between three and six feet, and another 15% of the land along the rivers and in inland basins is normally flooded to depths in excess of six feet.

Because floods can arise from the rivers, from torrential monsoons, and from high water tables, as much as 90% of Bangladesh can be flooded at one time or another during a typical year.

Added to these challenges is a deficit of materials with which to control these flows. The Bangladesh delta is flat and entirely mud; there is neither rock with which to build dams and embankments nor sufficient geographic relief to create natural storage basins. This hydrological setting places great demands on both cultivators and seed research scientists and makes any attempt to control and otherwise guide the rivers extremely difficult.

Ideally, the same water-control system that irrigates fields in the dry season should not only protect them from summer floods but drain them when flooding occurs.

Water development in Bangladesh is without a doubt a severe test of ingenuity. There is very little acreage that has neither too much nor too little water, and much of the country suffers from both of these conditions. Containing these rivers within the traditional embankments of western flood-control projects is costly and possibly futile, given the scale of the rivers' flood peaks. Because of these difficulties, only 7% of the cultivatable land is irrigated at present. In contrast, India irrigates 26% of its cultivatable land; China has achieved a 69% target; and Pakistan irrigates 65% of its acreage. (2) The country's development depends upon the use of it hydrological riches. Currently cultivators are expected to pay certain costs and to endure uncertain harvests. With better yields and more crops per year, the stakes grow higher. Any agricultural strategy that hopes to bring improved livelihoods to millions of cultivators must solve this problem. Perhaps the answer to water development rests in the Bengali's definition of flood; flood waters may only be undesirable if they prove to be "unwanted." We will find in later sections that one solution to the water problem does reside within this cultural definition.

WHAT PRICE WATER CONTROL?

In the last few decades the rivers have become increasingly menacing. Human suffering has been severe at times, and crop losses have been frequent. It was inevitable that the control of these rivers would receive high priority from the government of East Pakistan; it saw the benefit which had accrued to West Pakistan after British engineers brought irrigation to its desert decades earlier. Following Indian independence and partition, West Pakistan benefited from even greater investments in water, in the form of giant dams. However, in East Pakistan development expenditures in general, and those for water in particular, remained far lower than in the West wing. Bengalee leaders perceived water control as a political issue as well as an economic necessity. Massive flood-control projects were seen as the only way to insure agricultural growth.

In 1957 a United Nations technical mission led by General J. A. Krug, a former head of the U.S. Army Corps of Engineers, recommended that the rivers be embanked and their channels improved. An equally important recommendation by the mission was the establishment of a separate water authority on the grounds that the existing bureaucracy was too rigid and slow. Further studies in 1963 by General John R. Hardin, and in 1964 by Professor J. TH. Thijsse concluded that the rivers had to be completely controlled. Professor Thijsse stated the ultimate objective precisely:

> The river flow is confined to a stable and fixed bed at all stages of discharge, allowing of efficient inland navigation. The water in the land between the rivers as well as between the rivers on the one

> hand and the sea on the other, is completely controlled. It is kept at the most favorable level. When there is too much, the surplus is evacuated. When the crops and the raising of cattle need more, the rivers supply the storage. (3)

This simple statement became the basis upon which tens of millions of dollars were spent for feasibility studies of the delta, and hundreds of millions were later spent for the projects themselves. The East Pakistan Water and Power Development Authority was set up in 1959 to handle flood control, drainage, and irrigation. The American firm of International Engineers, Inc. drew up a Master Plan that detailed a 20-year program of 51 major projects to cost, at the time, $3.2 billion. Flood protection for 12.1 million acres and irrigation for 7.9 million acres would be assured.

With singleminded attention, the Water Authority or Board strove to control the flooding in as much of the country as was technically possible. By July 1971, the Water Board could state that its first projects protected 2.5 million acres and that it was technically and economically feasible, according to the Master Plan, to extend this protection to 7 million acres by 1980. With Bangladesh's independence, the Water Board's ambitions grew along with the influx of foreign aid. The First Five-Year Plan was to have contained a Water Board request for over $600 million to finance 152 major and minor projects. For reasons that will become apparent in later sections, this allocation was cut to $407 million and the flood protection target was similarly curtailed.

Within the Water Board some emphasis was being given to the improvement of its pump and gravity irrigation systems because it was slowly being recognized that the link between flood control and benefits was irrigation for a new high-yielding crop in the dry season. Many of the Master Plan projects contain irrigation components that were to expand the Water Board's irrigation coverage from 122,000 to 463,000 acres during the First Five-Year Plan. Outside experts believe these numbers are exaggerated, and it appears that at the end of the five years the coverage will be no more than 200,000 acres. The 1973 irrigation benchmark was also deflated, from 122,000 to under 100,000 acres. (4)

The Master Plan has dominated the country's water strategy for nearly two decades yet, after the expenditure of over $550 million, its major projects irrigate less than four-tenths of 1% of the cultivatable land at a cost of over $6,000 per acre. Why did this imported advice cost so much and yield so little? The answers are found in an examination of two of these Master Plan projects.

The Ganges-Kobadak Project

The first of the 51 Master Plan proposals, and certainly the most controversial, is the Ganges-Kobadak (G-K) flood control, drainage, and irrigation project which was started in 1954. Located near the Indian border in the southwestern portion of what was then East Pakistan, this early project was to have irrigated 350,000 acres with a system of large canals filled with water pumped from the Ganges. The project was to have been divided into two phases, and the capital cost was estimated at $30 per acre. This climbed to $2200 for each acre that was actually irrigated under Phase I; in 20 years the cost went from $10.5 million to $130 million. By the mid-1970s, and ten years behind schedule, only 60,000 acres are being irrigated. Much of this irrigation water is being used for the existing monsoon aman crop instead of for new winter crops, which the project was originally calculated to benefit.

To enumerate G-K's shortcomings is to describe problems which have since been faced by all water projects. In the early years interministerial coordination was not thought necessary to assure profitable on-farm water use, and farmers were not organized. The new seed varieties had yet to be introduced, and irrigation and fertilizer were not always available at the farm level or even accepted by the farmers in the project's first years. The half mile inlet channel from the Ganges to the pump house silts readily, and, consequently, a dredge has to be retained in the channel. The pump house itself contains three giant 1,300-cusec pumps that are so sophisticated that installation and maintenance have proven to be very difficult; the three pumps have yet to function at the same time. (5)

Few lessons have been learned from this largest Master Plan project. The Water Board still does not call for coordination with the Ministries of Agriculture or Rural Development, nor does it require water-user organizations in all of its projects. Foreign experts have said that the Water Board "...has little interest and no expertise in who uses the water it develops." (6) Assuring on-farm water remains a problem in other major water projects, including Chandpur, the Buri-Teesta, the Coastal Embankment Project, and the Thakurgaon Tubewell Project in the northwest. Of these, the Coastal Embankment Project is noteworthy for its unique problems, which dramatize the shortage of fresh water during the winter dry-season.

The Coastal Embankments Project

The coastal area of Bangladesh presents a special water-control challenge. Valuable arable land is damaged by saline water that intrudes northerly each dry season. The Master Plan proposed a Coastal Embankments project to empolder 61 areas along the bay in order to protect homes and crops from saline water and storms. Between 1960 and the early 1970s over 2,000 miles of embankments were constructed, an important benefit in disaster-prone Bangladesh. However, the protection of life that was ensured by the polders should encompass the protection of livelihood. A growing population cannot exist on a land upon which productivity cannot also be enhanced. While the embankments protect homes and sometimes traditional crops against tidal bores and saline water, the project does not provide irrigation water nor cropping systems for the polders' population. As a consequence of the reduced flood-born siltation, the soil has hardened and aman rice yields have remained low and have even fallen in some areas. As in the Ganges-Kobadak project, the earthen and flood gate structures were built at a cost of $200 million, but, because the project was not approached from the cultivator's point of view, this costly infrastructure has not augmented crop production. Once again, expanded yields and an extended cropping season were promised, but as in the G-K area, the monsoon aman remains the mainstay along the Bay. (7)

By the end of the 1960s it became clear to some in the government that protection from the summer floods did little to tap the dry season's crop potential. The emphasis had to shift from flood control in the summer to irrigation in the winter.

The Thana Irrigation Program

It was not until the Thana Irrigation Program (TIP) was started in 1959 that a link was established between on-farm irrigation and a new crop. The Program's so-called "low-lift pumps" were soon irrigating an acreage larger than all the existing Master Plan projects combined and they continue to do so today. The small pump set, a diesel engine connected to a centrifugal pump, "lifts" water from low-lying ponds and canals and irrigates as much as 80 acres, the pump's ideal command area. For the first time an entire project is in the hands of those who can benefit from it. The pump set is small and mobile, and the two cusecs of water go directly to the fields. The pumps are utilized within a cooperative framework that is designed to group farmers around a large piece of imported equipment. Production loans are provided through these group cooperatives, and training is delivered through an extension program. TIP groups were organized across the country by the Agricultural Development Corporation (ADC) and they soon became responsible for most of the country's winter rice production. Both TIP and the Rural Works Program were conceived as parts of the Comilla model, discussed in Chapter 9, to provide an integrated and decentralized water development strategy, the antithesis of the heavily-centralized approach of the Water Board. (8)

In 1961, TIP irrigated 110,000 acres; a year later 500,000 acres; and, by 1977, over 1.4 million acres. The increase in winter rice production was similarly impressive. The public sector now has 36,000 pumps to field each winter season. The Program's irrigation ceiling, which can be achieved without permanently affecting the hydrological balance, is 45,000 pump units. In addition to pumps owned by TIP, some 5,000 pumps are now privately owned. When the Program reaches its technically determined ceiling and each pump irrigates a 50 acre command area, then 2.3 million acres will be irrigated by this technique alone.

Because the founders of the Program recognized that the low-lift pump would irrigate an area far larger than any one individual farm, the optimal acreage had to be pulled together so that each pump could be efficiently utilized. The two "equalizers" of the indivisible piece of equipment are the organization of farmers into cooperatives, to take advantage of the pump's physical irrigation capacity, and the provision of crop loans to overcome the input cost of the new seed technology. (9) Coming as it does on the heels of the Water Board's costly projects, TIP can hardly be faulted. Nevertheless, the problems it has encountered have also been the problems of water development in a minutely differentiated hydrological and institutional setting. The two "equalizers," cooperatives and loans, proved to have shortcomings that explain why the pumps' command areas have decreased over the years. (10) Despite admonitions from advisors to reduce the Program's subsidies, the continued provision of these subsidies is the principal reason that the command areas have shrunk. Because of his small financial investment in the pump, each manager can make an ample profit without using it at full capacity. Why managers do not press for greater coverage and still greater profit, an apparent anomaly, is explained in a later section.

TIP's inefficiencies are made worse by the Program's distributive effects. Recipients of TIP water are not members on an equal footing; as often as not cultivators buy water from the managers who control the pump cooperatives. The provision of credit is similarly dominated by the rural elite, as described in Chapters 7 and 9. In short, the "two equalizers" have functioned as unequalizers; TIP has expanded for the benefit of the landed elite at the expense of command-area performance and the actual cultivators.

The Thana Irrigation Program has provided an important lesson in the search for appropriate methods of irrigation. Land is being irrigated at a cost of $10 per acre as compared to the major irrigation projects which cost over 200 times as much. (11) The low-lift pump is exploiting an important surface water reserve. The country's rich hydrological diversity allows this search to continue in new directions.

Pumps and Tubewells

During the early 1960s, a third approach to irrigation was initiated; the exploitation of groundwater paralleled TIP's development of surface water. In the far northwest of what was then East Pakistan, in Thakurgaon thana, a deep tubewell project was started by the Water Board to exploit groundwater. Sixty-nine thousand acres were to be irrigated by large three and four-cusec tubewells, some 381 in all, electrified by overhead power lines. This project ultimately cost $28 million and four years after completion it irrigated less than a third of the projected acreage. Because the large scale equipment, pipes, and drilling rigs were imported, the cost per pump was approximately $75,000, which would place the cost of irrigating one acre at $412. The cost per acre actually irrigated would be several times higher than this projected figure if account was taken of the 100 idle pumps and the unirrigated but projected coverage. (12)

At the time, the technical appeal of large wells must have been attractive. It was thought that their high capital cost would soon be offset by their efficiency in providing volumes of water. However, the technical sophistication of the Western equipment overtaxed the technical staff's maintenance capacity from the beginning. In addition to cost, the project had a serious technical deficiency. The soil's porosity, shown to be extreme after the fact, called the use of irrigated rice, and so projected benefits, into question. Today, wheat is rapidly displacing rice as the winter crop in the area. As in its earlier flood control and irrigation projects, the Water Board paid little attention to cropping systems or to the organization of farmers.

Although its costs were high and its shortcomings well known, as in the case of the Ganges-Kobadak project, Thakurgaon did open the door to the exploitation of ground water in Bangladesh. Because the flood-control strategy had proved to be ruinously expensive and without significant benefit, and the low-lift pump program had almost fully tapped the potential surface watewr possibilities in the country, tubewells of all varieties and shapes soon became the new water-development frontier.

As the Thana Irrigation Program contrasted sharply with the Master Plan projects in the early 1960s, so the Comilla tubewell experience contrasted with the Thakurgaon project. Smaller, two-cusec tubewells, designed along the lines of successful tubewell programs in West Pakistan and China, were introduced by the Comilla Academy. Comilla's cooperative workshop, together with the Agricultural Development Corporation, trained well drillers, manufactured local hand-powered drilling rigs, and fabricated parts for a cooperative tubewell program in Comilla district. These wells were far cheaper than ones that relied entirely upon imported equipment and came to represent, albeit briefly, the best tradition in the adaptation of resources and manpower to costly problems. (13) The 236 wells drilled between 1962 and 1969, 211 of which operated, cost $6,000 to $7,000 each, or between $3,000 and $3,500 per cusec, a sharp cost cut from the parallel strategy in Thakurgaon. This experimentation was extinguished in the late 1960s because ADC's virtually complete subsidies for imported engines, pumps, and drilling equipment caused the suspension of private tubewell experimentation and manufacturing. It was not resumed until after independence. Why pay $7,000 for a private or cooperatie well when the ADV would provide one for only $63 a season. (14)

The exploitation of the country's groundwater resources was plotted in the 1960s, and elaborate public plans were drawn for thousands of wells of all sizes. It was not until after independence that these ambitious targets were tempered by the accumulating field experience that was slowly forcing its way into official consciousness.

OPPORTUNITY FOR REASSESSMENT

With Bangladesh Independence many technical people hoped that the new government would foster a more balanced approach to water development. The major projects had had enough time to show their weakness. Their very high costs, long gestation periods, and minimal contribution to increased production had fueled critics with ample field experience. By 1973 these projects had absorbed $550 million, and the cost overruns exceeded original estimates by a factor of three. The low-lift pump program had yielded results, and the large tubewell project in the northwest showed promise of groundwater, though not of pumping technique. What Thakurgaon had promised, the smaller Comilla wells had delivered.

The new country's First Five-Year Plan shifted planning priorities to include quick-yielding, labor-intensive irrigation schemes and an expansion of low-lift and tubewell techniques. However, the euphoria of independence soon dissipated; the lessons learned in the 1960s did not cause the hoped-for reassessment of the country's basic flood-control strategy. Annual plans and budgets soon revealed the durability of past ways and the frailty of new hopes. (15) Over half of the planned allocation for water development went toward flood control. (16) Bangladesh's Planning Commission did not have the competence or the staff to challenge the authority of the Water Board and its contractors. (17) Nor was it possible for foreign consultants who had learned the hard lessons of the 1960s to urge the redirection of project assistance.

The failure to achieve early irrigation targets remains evident, as does the poor food production record. Master Plan projects, even more costly now, remain largely unfinanced. A transition toward more effective irrigation systems is lengthening into years, despite ample evidence of the efficacy of alternative techniques. An opportunity for reassessment has, in reality, become an impasse. The country's water programs are severely disjointed; lack of leadership and coordination are delaying the day when the cultivators of Bangladesh can be assured of an effective public irrigation strategy.

Further Challenges to Orthodoxy

Lessons not learned by the Water Board in the 1960s were at least being picked up by the foreign donors in the 1970s. A few small projects were modified and received financing, but others did not. Two of the latter cases are noteworthy.

Following the construction of the Brahmaputra Right Embankment in the northwest in the 1960s, the Water Board sought financing for two flood control, drainage, and irrigation projects adjacent to the Embankment. The Kurigram area along the Indian border and the Belkuchi area along the Brahmaputra to the south were to be protected with embankments and drainage pumps and to be irrigated with large canal and tubewell systems. Because the flow of the Dudkumar River through the Kurigram area diminishes dramatically during the driest part of the year, going from 216,000 to 2,190 cusecs, water supplemental to that from the river had to be assured with tubewells. Consequently, a double irrigation system was required. On close analysis, the projected benefits did not warrant the cost of 50-year flood-peak embankments for both project areas. The major water-control features of Kurigram soon totalled more than $650 per acre, a cost apart from the institutions required to translate flood control and drainage into on-farm water supplies and increased crop production. The continuing westward migration of the Brahmaputra, particularly in the Belkuchi area, was also a factor in lowering the project's return. When the original Master Plan cost estimates were updated to the mid-1970s, it became apparent that the projects as originally conceived were uneconomical. The Water Board showed no interest in correcting the coordination and on-farm deficiencies of these projects or in seeking less costly alternatives. In fact, changes were "resisted vehemently." Foreign assistance was lost in the eleventh hour. (18)

After independence, the tubewell contribution to the irrigation target was increased substantially. The isolated experiences in Thakurgaon in the northwest and in Comilla in the east were soon spread across groundwater-rich Bangladesh. Nearly 400 deep wells in Thakurgaon grew to approximately 9,000 wells by 1976, and the 200 smaller Comilla wells grew to 5,000. Despite these gains, the First Five-Year Plan targets for both types of wells fell far short. Thirty-four thousand wells in all were to irrigate 1.4 million acres during the period; instead, 14,000 wells, 40% of the goal, have brought water to 75,000 acres, or to 5% of the projected acreage.

There are multiple reasons for these shortfalls, reasons similar to those that constrain the effective command-area coverage of Master Plan schemes. In addition, hydrological studies indicate that groundwater reserves may be less than originally estimated; the 9.5 million acre tubewell irrigation target may have to be curtailed. The major shortcoming of these imported irrigation techniques has been their inappropriateness to the country's institutional setting rather than the technical difficulty encountered in trying to adapt them to Bangladesh.

Public Irrigation and Equity - An Assessment

Sharing the water that each water project produces has proven to be a perplexing problem. Without irrigation, the new seed shows little advantage over the traditional varieties. Although water recipients receive complete capital subsidies and partial operating subsidies on irrigation equipment, these privileges have not caused public projects to be fully exploited. (19) Organizing cultivators around each source of water would be a challenge under any circumstance: plots are small, numerous, and scattered; cropping patterns are minutely differentiated; mechnical breakdowns occur frequently; and the publicly controlled supply of pump parts is made profitably scarce. Furthermore, there is no traditional village authority or community unit that coincides with, and, therefore, could organize, a technically efficient irrigation area. Irrigation coverage is also deliberately limited in order to avoid obligations to a great number of water users.

Subsidies themselves are a major deterrent to command-area expansion; the comparatively small cost of the pumps allows ample profit at a command area coverage below the technical optimum of each well. If the manager of a cooperative pushes for greater coverage when it is not financially necessary to do so, he risks dilution of control and he assumes responsibility for others' crops.

The argument that subsidies are needed to promote the acceptance of these innovations among small-farm owners has long since lost its validity. Water is in great demand among cultivators, who pay market-determined rates of from $15 to $20 per crop acre for water from public sources. The little well equipment available on the open market sells at a premium. Experience has shown that the provision of subsidized wells to groups, coupled with subsidized production credit, has encouraged a division between those who control and benefit and those who labor on the irrigated land. (20) In short, water subsidies operate contrary to their intended purpose by redistributing income and land upwards into the hands of the larger land owners, as Chapter 7 demonstrated.

In addition to these inefficiencies and inequities, the subsidies encourage the inefficient operation of the bureaucracies themselves. Little revenue is generated from recipients, and their views are not sought. Poor project performance is explained by the lack of outside financing. Should water groups be charged the full cost of irrigation, they would not pay for water that was not delivered. Subsidies insure that bureaucracies can remain safe from client criticism.

These institutional difficulties suggest that even the small tubewells may be too large for Bangladesh. A small well was considered in one project proposal; given its capital cost, however, its loan repayment schedule, realistic assumptions about its command area and water charges, and the revenue from two annual rice crops, the proposed well could not be financed by land owners with less than six acres. Because few farmers own this much acreage, and because the control of tubewells furthers inequities, the proposed project was terminated. (21)

The inappropriateness of these wells may also be indicated by the social tension surrounding their use. Wells of all sizes are being drilled with little thought of their demands on groundwater reserves. Those farmers with influence have public wells located on their land. Those who have neither influence nor wells are becoming intolerant of the arbitrary windfalls enjoyed by a few. In one deep tubewell project area, half of the nearly 300 wells have been sabotaged with bricks and bambo and still, a formal evaluation of this project is avoided. In a dry year when the larger, deeper wells dry up the shallow ones and surface water runs low, envy will turn to anger.

I conclude that this experience with imported techniques has led to a double tragedy. Field experience has yet to alter First Five-Year Plan allocations, and were it to do so the small scale techniques would remain out of the reach of most cultivators. Under the tenure conditions described in the previous chapter I doubt whether any amount of group organizing can ensure equitable access to public wells. Tubewells and low-lift pumps may already be straining the country's hydrological potential, and its social fabric.

Concessionally-financed food imports have filled the food gap for the cities, a gap created in part by ineffective water strategies. While neither this food nor the public irrigation strategies have benefited the vast majority of the cultivators, the latter have not been sitting idle. Their own contributions to water's development during this period may now hold greater promise for guiding future water priorities then have the imported preconceptions.

LESSONS FROM THE FIELD

Cultivators were wresting their livelihoods from this riverine world long before Western approaches were imported to control it. These cultivators were to benefit from Master Plan projects and imported tubewells. Their survival, in the face of these failures, must hold lessons for the public sector's water strategy. I believe that these lessons will come to represent enduring contributions to the country's agricultural growth. As Thomas points out, "the relative roles of the government and the farmer have now changed. The farmer is now the innovator and the force for the expansion of irrigation." (22)

No technological adaptation is more striking than the numbers of men physically lifting water onto their fields during the dry winter months. With the use of the swinging basket, a shechuni, and the doon, a boat-shaped trough attached to an overhead balance beam, water is lifted onto fields from rivers and canals. As the waters recede each season and the lift grows greater, men lift water up a bank a tier at a time to a bigha plot, one-third of an acre. This is costly in terms of labor and it is also risky, for the water often dries up, or is used up, before the crop can be harvested.

Bigha by bigha the land irrigated by these country methods is growing. At present one million acres are being irrigated in this manner, according to official estimates. (23) Country methods may be irrigating as much area as the Thana Irrigation Program and several times more land than that irrigated by the major projects and tubewells.

The cultivators' most recent innovation is the use of the hand pump, or "pitcher pump," as it is known in the West, to irrigate one and two-bigha plots. Though originally designed to supply villages with drinking water, some of these pumps have been stolen from their villages and pushed into neighboring fields. (24) Using the hand pump is brutal work but it enables family members to grow an additional food crop in the winter. A total capital cost of between $45 and $75 places these units within reach of far more cultivators than is possible with power pumps. The vastly increased supply of these pumps in the market, together with very high grain prices in 1973 and 1974 have been responsible for the fact that 35,000 of them are now in use.

Despite the obvious attractiveness of this hand-operated technique, it is not clear that it is an appropriate irrigation "solution." First, the food energy cost of manual operation is high and, though more foodgrain is produced than is consumed, the work output can be more efficiently supplied with small motors. Second, and more important, even this small scale of technology may be controlled by those with land and capital. Should this prove to be generally true, then, in this tenure-credit milieu, these "appropriate" hand pumps may be no different in the distribution of their benefits than the large imported deep wells in Thakurgaon. (25)

Although cultivators led the way with these innovations, several agencies are now redesigning these drinking water pumps expressly for irrigation. Experimentation is also underway with other forms of hand-powered, and foot-powered, pumping techniques; bicycles are being connected to centrifugal pumps. For the first time, outsiders are improving on techniques born of necessity, in the field. (26)

The imported pumps and tubewells first introduced in the 1960s are also being adapted to local conditions. In several districts low-lift pumps are often floated in boats from field to field to make more effective use of a fixed capital investment. The pumps are also used for "double pumping," similar to the country method of tiering described earlier, to lift water into tanks and impounded canals so that higher pumps can irrigate the fields. Villagers are starting to see the need for greater water reservoirs. Village ponds and canals are being re-excavated and dammed to capture monsoon water for dry-season irrigation.

The earlier Comilla experience with locally manufactured tubewells is now being revived. The private sector is finally being allowed access to imported parts and raw materials for domestic pump manufacture and well installation. As the public sector further liberalizes its control of irrigation equipment, the private sector will irrigate progressively more land. Comilla's contribution to appropriate techniques has not been lost.

The pressure of people on the land is finally forcing the government to look to the deep-water rice areas of Bangladesh as a source of foodgrain. What has been seen heretofore as wasted regions of unwanted flood water are now being appreciated for their potential. During an average monsoon, 19% of the country is flooded with more than six feet of water; yet these lands provide nearly 16% of the total annual harvest. (27) In a few areas rice grows in as much as 20 feet of water. As it is now clear that the major flood-control projects will not provide crop protection, these flooded regions must become increasingly productive under monsoon conditions. The yields of newer deep-water rice varieties are being increased from one-third of a ton per acre to a ton and a half.

Another approach to land and water development is simply to do without water, or at least to manage with less of it per crop acre. The flood control advocates of the 1950s and 1960s who justified their investments largely on the projected return of irrigated dry-season rice, so completely dominated the thinking of the time that other crop strategies were eclipsed. Despite this emphasis upon rice, wheat production, which requires one-half to two-thirds as much water, may in time surpass winter rice production. In fact, because wheat production costs are half those of rice, Bangladesh may be on the verge of a wheat revolution. (28) In addition to wheat, several agencies are experimenting with dozens of dry-land crops to provide a higher-value, more nutritionally diversified diet. (29) Traditional rice crops are also being examined in the search for greater productivity. Because of the risk of drought in the weeks immediately preceding and following the monsoon summer months, the six to seven million acres planted to traditional _aus_ and _aman_ rice varieties can be planted ,without benefit of irrigation, to new higher-yielding, drought-resistant varieties. This represents an increase of eleven million acres over the present one million acres planted to higher-yielding, rain-fed varieties.

In the past 30 years this region has been introduced to a wide range of irrigation technologies; imported and country methods have been fully tested. There has also been a greater diversification of cropping patterns. The monsoon _aman_ no longer rules the crop year, and irrigated _boro_ rice no longer dominates water planning. These irrigation and cropping options have developed in response to the region's hydrological and institutional complexity. Whether this rich experience, led by the cultivators themselves, will now be publicly directed and coordinated to exploit the land's productivity remains to be seen. (30)

This rich field experience developed despite many public flood-control and irrigation programs. Public commitment to an imported water strategy slowed but did not stop the cultivators' search for appropriate land and water techniques. We also know from our review of these public programs that the production benefits enjoyed by tenants and laborers were limited. The tenure and credit structure of Bangladesh prevents equitable participation in all irrigation techniques, including those thought to be labor-intensive.

The lesson of this field experience is not to seek even smaller, less expensive forms of irrigation technology. Instead, the analysis in Chapter 6 directs us to examine broad institutional forces that induce appropriate processes and products, including those governing water use. The policy changes that will encourage both the development of appropriate irrigation techniques and a more equitable sharing of the increased production include the altered price and tenure recommendations prescribed in earlier chapters. The new seed technology must be made appropriate to Bangladesh. This success requires, for example, that the Thana Irrigation Program be made to work on both efficiency and distributive grounds. The problems with the low-lift pump, as a pump, are not the same as those TIP shortfalls attributable to other economic institutions. The mechanical equipment can be made more appropriate; but, more importantly, the tenure, pricing, and organizational aspects of the rural economy must be altered so that the productivity of land and water can be vastly increased and more equitably shared. The model's employment and income-growth linkages depend on this.

FARAKKA AND THE FUTURE

Too little willingness to question the flood-control premise of the Master Plan has delayed the day when the country's water development programs will be effective and coordinated. In reviewing the evolution of these programs, I find that effective irrigation systems and the promotion of dry-land and deep-water crops have been detained by the preeminent attention given to the major rivers. India's Farakka Barrage may also keep the country's water strategy in suspense. (31) More is at stake than the 40,000 cusecs that India can divert from the Ganges for Calcutta during the low flow of the dry season. This diversion and the threat of others along the common border between Bangladesh and India may delay the day when a diversified land and water developement strategy will make its full contribution to agricultural growth. Farakka could speed achievement of this growth or slow it.

The Barrage, only 12 miles from the border of Bangladesh, became a sensitive subject long before its gates were lowered in 1975. If its 40,000 cusecs were to be diverted only during the monsoon floods, it would be a small proportion of the total seasonal flow and would help cut high flood peaks. However, because the Indians claim that this diversion must take place through the dry season when the Ganges flow falls under 100,000 cusecs, it jeopardizes the fulfillment of Bangladesh's irrigation targets. (32) Bangladesh would benefit from the coordinated use of this water, which would partially remove the peaks from the floods and insure water during the dry season; but India increasingly needs water to feed its millions, to rid the port of Calcutta of silt, and to maintain its cities and industries. A durable division of the river will be hard to achieve.

India's use of water will have a direct effect on the supply of surface water available in Bangladesh for country methods and low-lift pumps and, over the longer term, on groundwater reserves for tubewell development. With the reduction of fresh-water supplies during the dry season, salinity from the Bay will intrude earlier and further than it would otherwise. The Indians can claim that Bangladesh has little need for water during the dry season since it does not have an extensive dry-season irrigation system. This claim has validity; Bangladesh has devoted its resources to river control and flood protection, which contribute little to crop production.

In addition to diversions from the Ganges, India's irrigation needs are causing her to claim shares of other rivers' dry season flows. The Indians propose development of 200 of the 250-cusec dry season flow of the Khowai River in the northeast. The same may happen on the Muhuri, the Teesta, the Dudhkumar, and the Dharala Rivers.

In the winter there is not enough water for both countries, yet millions of cubic feet of water flow out to the Bay during each monsoon. The subcontinent has the terrain to store water, but it does not yet have the coordinational commitment or the resources necessary to realize this potential. India has proposed a Ganges-Cauvery link canal which would connect the Brahmaputra with the Ganges, and with the Cauvery River in southern India. While this link would reduce flood peaks for both countries, it would fill reservoirs that are inaccessible to Bangladesh. Instead of waiting for subcontinental agreement, Bangladesh could, as a partial solution to this problem, mobilize her people to re-excavate canals and tanks in order to store her own dry-season water.

Bangladesh faces a dilemma. Should it pursue the major water projects that are so costly and yield so little in order to lay legal claim to what would in effect be a diminishing winter river flow, or should it rely entirely upon the accommodating practices of cultivators? Can a balance be achieved between these two extremes? Clearly, a commitment to effective on-farm water management, to dry-land crops, and to deep-water paddy would soon result in increased yields and cropping intensities; no ten-year gestation period need be tolerated. (33) However, the bulk of the country's water development resources are still being allocated to Master Plan projects; a powerful domestic bureaucracy continues to use foreign and domestic resources in a manner which is out of proportion to their contribution to the country's development.

The Bangladesh Government may learn to accommodate itself to the extreme variations of this riverine world. Its cultivators have learned to adapt in order to survive. Farakka may force recognition that the country must do the same.

NOTES

(1) The basic data for this chapter are drawn from the First Five-Year Plan, Annual Plans, the International Engineering Company's Master Plan (December 1964), analyses by James M. Coleman, John W. Thomas, and Stephen F. Allison, and numerous other technical studies.

(2) USDA, The World Food Situation and Prospects to 1985, December 1974, p. 70.

(3) J. TH. Thijsse, "Report on Hydrology of East Pakistan - May-October 1964-65," p. 5.

(4) According to Bangladesh Agriculture in Statistics, p. 60, the Water Board's irrigation coverage in FY 1973 included: tubewells and low-lift pumps in the northwest, 27,390 acres; the Dacca-Narayanganj-Demra project, 10,878 acres; the Buri-Teesta, 1,146 acres; and the Ganges-Kobadak, 60,000 acres; for a total of 99, 414 acres.

(5) The problems of G-K have been enumerated by Thomas in "Development Institutions, Projects, and Aid in the Water Development Program of East Pakistan," (draft), Harvard: Development Advisory Service, March 1972, pp. 14-17.

(6) Princeton Lyman, 1971.

(7) River embankments create special problems of their own. Because monsoon rains and swollen streams can flood an inland area rapidly, flooding can occur behind embankments as well as on their river-sides. The control of individual embankment gates, which is generally in the hands of the Water Board, can become a very heated issue with local farmers. Because flood heights and velocities increase in confined channels, embankments can affect a river's course which, in turn, can hasten lateral erosion. Embankments also prevent silt-laden monsoon floods from spreading across the land and, for the same reason, saline intrusion flows more northerly each dry season than it otherwise would. The adverse consequences of embankments warrant comprehensive analysis. It could be argued that the flood peaks will always be too high, the silt load too great, and lateral erosion too frequent to justify embankment of the major rivers until upper riparian coordination with India, Nepal, and possibly China is assured.

(8) For descriptions of the Thana Irrigation Program and of tubewell developments of the 1960s and their controversies, I have drawn from Thomas (1976) and Stephen Allison, "Progress Towards Development of More Appropriate Technology for Land and Water Developement in Bangladesh," Dacca: World Bank, March 1974. Thomas gives special emphasis to the integration of TIP within the framework of thana-level planning of land and water resources in Bangladesh.

(9) From Princeton Lyman, 1971.

(10) Bangladesh Government, Statistical Year Book of Bangladesh 1975, p. 239. One study, drawing upon the number of low-lift pumps fielded and the

annual consumption of fuel, estimates that the actual command area per pump may be as low as seven acres.

(11) John Thomas, "Rural Development in East Pakistan," (draft), May 30, 1970, p. 15.

(12) John Thomas, op. cit., March 1972. Also USAID Staff, "Field Trip Report on Thakurgaon Irrigation Project," Dacca: June 30, 1976.

(13) The literature refers to "deep" and "shallow" tubewells. These two words loosely describe: large and small diameter well pipes; three to four cusecs of pumped water as contrasted with one quarter to one cusec; deep (200 to 400 feet) as opposed to "shallower" wells; and submergible turbines as contrasted with surface-mounted centrifugal pumps. Well-drilling techniques are also implied by these terms: imported mechanical rigs for deep tubewells; locally made hand-powered ones for the shallow wells.

(14) John W. Thomas, "The Development of Tubewell Irrigation in Bangladesh; An Analysis of Alternatives," (draft), Harvard Development Advisory Service, February 1972. Also in Timmer, 1975, pp. 31-67.

(15) See World Bank, Proposals for an Action Program - East Pakistan Agriculture and Water Development, The Water Program, Vol. III, July 17, 1970. Thomas and Lyman (op. cit.) identified the institutional and consultative relationships between foreign donors and an autonomous bureaucracy, the Water Board, that go a long way in explaining the difficulties in trying to alter water development priorities.

(16) Fifty-four percent of the First Five-Year Plan's water allocation is for flood control. p. 153.

(17) Bangladesh Government, Annual Development Plan - 1973-74, p. 53.

(18) USAID Staff memos of March 28, November 20, and December 11, 1975.

(19) The cost benefit analyses in the First Five-Year Plan and individual tubewell studies indicate that cooperative groups and large-farm owners can easily pay the full capital cost of these wells. Depending upon market prices and other assumptions, most medium-sized wells and low-lift pumps can be paid for in two to four crop seasons. In Comilla, according to Thomas (1972, p. 17), an $8,000 two-cusec tubewell could be purchased in one or two seasons. In 1977, a half-cusec well cost $1,200. According to the First Five-Year Plan (p. 150), the ratio of cost to benefit for a low-lift pump is 1 to 8.1; for a shallow tubewell, 1 to 6.6; for a deep tubewell, 1 to 5.1; and for large-scale irrigation projects, a more modest 1 to 4.1. Although these high ratios depend on optimal command areas and the supply of other inputs, they suggest that capital subsidies can be removed. The First Five-Year Plan states that a larger share of the annual operating costs is to be recovered from irrigation recipients, and that, despite its own evidence, capital costs are to remain fully subsidized. Low-lift pump users pay 23% of the annual operating costs; shallow tubewell users, 34%; and users of deep tubewells, only 14%. Water is free in Master Plan irrigation areas. To date, only minor decreases have been made in these operating subsidies.

(20) This argument is discussed and documented in Chapter 9. Recent evidence with respect to the control of deep tubewells is provided by M. Khalid Shams, "Land Ownership Pattern Among Deep Tubewell Allottees in Kashimpur ADE," BADC: December 1976.

(21) AID Staff, "Preliminary Report - Shallow Tubewell Project," Dacca, March 27, 1974.

(22) John W. Thomas, 1976, p. 6.

(23) According to the Statistical Year Book (p. 98) country methods irrigate 30% of the total irrigated area of 3.56 million acres, or approximately one million acres.

(24) The use of hand pumps for irrigating winter crops appeared to increase dramatically in 1975-76, although the number of these pumps in use prior to this dry season is not known. The economics of these pumps is described in the USAID Staff paper, "Field Report on Irrigation by Handpump Tubewells," Dacca, March 24, 1975. More recent surveys suggest that the pumps are being used increasingly for vegetables and wheat, and less for boro rice. USAID Staff, Capital Division, "Farmer Dealer Handpump Survey," Dacca, September 29, 1975. Also UNICEF, "Preliminary Report on Survey of Manually Operated Shallow Tubewell for Irrigation," Dacca, April 1976.

(25) The field evidence on this point is contradictory; one USAID study suggests that most hand pump tubewells are privately owned and operated, while a second one suggests that most are rented and operated by tenants.

(26) Much of this work has been encouraged by Stephen V. Allison op. cit., and by John Shawcross and W. K. Journey of UNICEF.

(27) Bangladesh Rice Research Institute, Proceedings .... on Deep-water Rice, 1974, pp. 1-24, 135-147.

(28) Wheat production increased from 120,000 metric tons in 1974-75 to as much as 300-400,000 tons the following year. In West Bengal wheat production grew 18 times in eight years, to 837,000 tons in 1974-75; a similar record may be achieved in Bangladesh. Stephen D. Biggs and Edward J. Clay, "Wheat in Bangladesh - An Economic Analysis of Past, Present and Future Developments," Dacca: The Ford Foundation, August 1975, p. 27; and the Government of West Bengal, Directorate of Agriculture, "Wheat 1975-76."

(29) Government research stations and several voluntary agencies have been working to introduce a wide range of winter vegetables and other crops. The work of the Mennonite Central Committee is noteworthy.

(30) Although technical flood-control studies dominate the feasibility-study literature, two alternative approaches are available. The World Bank and USAID have offered analytical methodologies for developing appropriate land and water systems in Bangladesh.

(31) For centuries Calcutta has been the only major city in this region of the subcontinent; it is central in every sense of the word. Before the 16th century the Ganges flowed past Calcutta but, as the major rivers of the Delta

moved eastward, this vital port began silting up. Now the smaller Hoogly River flows through Calcutta and needs continuous dredging to maintain the port's access to the Bay. In part, the Hoogly needs dredging because the Indian Government dammed a few of its tributaries for irrigation. In 1961 the Indians started construction of the 7229-foot Farakka Barrage across the Ganges north of Calcutta. Although the dam was completed in 1970, the gates were not closed until the winter of 1975-76. Then its 130 gates were lowered and 40,000 cusecs flowed down a feeder canal into the Bhagirathi-Hoogly Rivers toward Calcutta.

(32) In 1975-76 the Bangladesh Government claimed crop losses and salinity intrusion in its southwestern districts as a consequence of the Farakka's diversions. The value of the Ganges-Kobadak irrigation system depends upon a minimum river height in the Ganges; the pumps' efficiency falls rapidly to zero as the inlet water height drops towards 13 feet mean sea level. River flows below 20 feet mean sea level disrupt navigation, fishing patterns, fresh water supplies for the region's few factories, and groundwater reserves for tubewells. These common annual dry-season losses are further compounded by Farakka. In 1977, the two governments reached an interim agreement on a division of the dry-season flow past Farakka.

(33) The Bangladesh Government should consider founding an On-Farm Water Management Institute patterned after its existing seed research institutions. The purpose of the Institute would be to study and improve existing irrigation techniques utilized by cultivators and pump owners, to adapt imported irrigation equipment to local conditions, and to train agricultural extension agents in on-farm water management. This investment in experimentation and training, coupled with the public sector decontrol of irrigation equipment and parts, would lead to a much improved command area performance for existing and future irrigation investments.

9 Rural Institutions for a Resource-Poor Economy

Rural institutional strategies gained attention during the 1960s because agricultural development programs were not making a contribution toward improving the well-being of the rural poor. A few development planners, sensing a deterioration in the quality of rural life, designed the Comilla Academy and associated institution-building programs to encompass those who had been left out of the programs. Their intent was to provide organization and services to owners of small farms who otherwise might not participate in the expanded harvests. (1) Princeton Lyman has said that Comilla's "Integrated Rural Development Program ... in its own way ... is searching to create an institutional structure for rural Pakistan (now Bangladesh) that would make it possible, short of totalitarian means, for twice as many people as today to live and work productively on the scarce land of East Pakistan." (2) This rural structure is now partly in place in Bangladesh, yet its developmental objective remains elusive. Why, after nearly 20 years, is this so?

Too many authors and government officials have assumed that Comilla's programs can bring development to rural Bangladesh. The previous four chapters have been devoted to economic institutions that, in my view, explain why millions of people are not participating in agricultural growth. The consequences of these institutions for individual well-being must be understood and reversed; rural programs in themselves cannot enrich the rural poor. The emphasis in these earlier chapters on crop production must now be balanced by an evaluation of the rural programs of the 1960s that were designed to enlarge participation in rural development.

Space does not permit an evaluation of each rural program; there are too many. Instead I posit three principles drawn from accumulated experience that help to identify rural institutional strengths and weaknesses; these can be used as criteria for designing rural institutional processes that assure rural participation.

First, public developmental programs should be predicated on a three-tiered conception of rural delivery systems. The first, or bottom, tier represents the individual acting in his own self-interest in his political and economic environment - the village. The top tier of this rural delivery model represents ministerial systems that provide the policy and program guidance, resources, and technologies that encourage rural participation in public institutions. The middle or third tier, representing rural institutions as they are conventionally understood, serves as the nexus between program direction from the top and the participation of millions of people at the bottom.

The second principle of this institutional model is the full-cost pricing of public resources. Building on a thesis introduced in earlier chapters, I will show that direct public subsidies distort the evolution of institutional processes in a labor-rich, resource-poor economy.

The third principle is the provision of public resources on the basis of performance, demand, and need. A corollary of this third principle is an institutionally assured check and balance of public resource flows.

By use of these three principles I illustrate that the country's present rural institutions, like several of its economic policies, must be altered in order to make productive lives possible for a population which will double by the end of the century.

EFFECTIVE DELIVERY SYSTEMS

Before each of its three tiers is discussed in detail, the importance of the first principle can be illustrated by describing an approach to rural health that is now being explored by the Cholera Research Laboratory in Dacca. The government is replicating the curative, or hospital-patient model, to the thana level in the form of the Thana Health Center. Because this costly western approach is unlikely to bring health care to the rural population, the government and other agencies are exploring alternative measures. For years the Cholera Laboratory has offered treatment to cholera patients as a necessary humanitarian adjunct to its continuing research on cholera and other diarrheal diseases. Cholera is often in its advanced stages by the time its victim obtains hospitalization. Severe diarrhea, dehydration, and shock call for prompt treatment and hospitalization, which require doctors and nurses, bed space, and intravenous solutions, is costly. A curative approach that identifies the cholera victim at the very symptoms of the disease has been suggested for field experimentation. The existing medical infrastructure and private pharmacists can be motivated to provide instruction so that, at the first signs of diarrhea and lassitude, the victims will purchase premeasured packages of medicine for oral administration. This approach promises to cut the number of seriously ill cholera patients, who continue to require a large portion of the national health budget. (3)

Identifying and treating cholera at an early stage helps both the individual and the national health budget. The individual acts in his own self-interest. The middle tier, consisting of rural public clinics and, in this case, private practitioners and healers, provides the education and medicine to cure the individual; this tier also provides a referral service for hospitalization should more sophisticated curative attention be required. The top tier, requiring costly staffs, buildings, and equipment, provides medical research, training for medical personnel, and specialized hospitalization; and this does not need to be reproduced in every thana.

The Model Farmer program described in the appendix is another example of an appropriate delivery system which is being replicated for cultivator education. This program can be utilized to expand nutritional well-being, functional literacy, and a host of other services. This type of approach brings a qualitative change in public delivery and service techniques and holds hope for reaching the rural population. (4) As we have seen in Chapter 2, the quantitative expansion of largely western approaches to social services is not succeeding. Comilla's cooperative and thana development models represent a qualitative change in rural institutional strategy. In the nearly two decades since their conception, how have they fared?

Individuals and Their Villages - The Bottom Tier

The Comilla Academy conceived and tested programs for providing organization and resources to poor farmers. In the early 1960s the poor were seen to be the owners of small farms that had to be made more productive. The landless were poorer but few in number. In time, as account was taken of the numbers of landless laborers and landless cultivators, the "small" owner-cultivator -- Comilla's "small farmer" -- was pushed toward the top of the rural income ladder. Even the permanent laborer, attached to the landowning family, is not the lowest on the rung. Many day laborers are ashamed to admit they have fallen so low; and we now recognize that there are hundreds of thousands of destitute below the status of day laborer. Comilla's target group of poor proved to be a small, relatively well-off, proportion of the total rural population. (5)

Recent anthropological studies in Bangladesh have added to our understanding of the village and Comilla's village cooperative. Here again, we find that accepted nomenclature has not accurately described Comilla's relationship with individual farmers within their villages. A village cooperative is no more a village in the western sense than a small farm is relatively small. What has come to be known as a "village cooperative" is, in fact, a group of households within a village that recognizes a common basis of authority. Among these households, owners of small farms are not easily singled out. The elders of this "village" and its members, regardless of economic standing, act as a social unit. Therefore, while any one of a number of dichotomous labels, such as large and small, rich and poor, landed and landless, will describe economic relationships within these units, the terms do not define classes; the village is cohesive. (6) Having said this, I recognize that the internal injustices are real. One recent report has said it well: "The inequality, however, is made tolerable, the domination veiled, and the stratification obscured by kinship and quasi-kinship formalities in which dominance is legitimized through extra economic personalized sanctions." (7)

The relationship of villagers to rural programs like Comilla's cooperatives is also better understood. Some Comilla Academy reports suggest that the small farm owner cooperatives have successfully bypassed the village elite as they were designed to do. A recent study has found, however, that because cooperative members remained subordinate to the village elite in their traditional relationships and obligations, these traditional relationships prevail over attempts by outside programs to reach within the village. (8) Another study has carried this analysis further by documenting that the elite often have the support of their fellow villagers because the villagers appreciate that it takes persuasion and influence to obtain outside resources. (9) It is now generally recognized that Comilla's cooperatives were dominated by the influential villagers from the outset.

Professor Akhter Hameed Khan sensed the interplay of these village forces in the early 1960s. The cooperative had to become a movement that would endure in the face of economic and population pressures. He suggested that civil service personnel should guide the cooperative to check the influence of the village elite. Past lessons could not be ignored: the older union level cooperatives and the Thana Irrigation Program were recognized as the antithesis of cooperation and participation. Consequently, Comilla's administrative hierarchy was appointed from outside to bypass the powerful village elders, and farmers with small plots were obliged to participate in the new village cooperatives. Cooperative discipline and not commercial enterprise was to make the cooperatives economically viable. An emphasis upon economic enterprise, it was thought, would open the door to elite control. As we now know, that door was always open. (10)

This review of village cooperatives illustrates that bureaucratic intervention on behalf of equalitarian objectives has not been possible. The target group was miscast, the unity of the village was underestimated, and the strength of the civil service was overestimated. Owners of small farms cannot be reached easily because influential villagers control traditional resource flows and relationships. In a milieu free of social and economic checks on the elite, reaching the target group proved to be too great a challenge. (11)

Furthermore, the civil service was obliged to administer subsidized inputs. The termination of subsidies (argued in the following section) would remove windfalls that have handsomely rewarded the elite's domination of Comilla's programs. Profit and influence must spring from economic productivity, not from the control of inputs. The prescriptions of other chapters will help to create a wider range of productive activity, activity that will be rewarding to broader groups of people. Although I am not recommending acquiescence to the village elite under present resource policies, transforming static villages into dynamic ones will require the inclusion of the elite in rural growth processes. Stimulating these growth processes will require the alteration of many economic policies and traditions that are broader in scope than any single rural institution designed for one target group.

The Capital-Intensive Top Tier - Program Guidance, Services, and Technologies

Western social service standards require that villagers have the same teacher-student and doctor-patient ratios that city dwellers enjoy. However, the application of an urban standard to the country as a whole would be prohibitively expensive. In recognition of this cost, the Comilla Academy designed and tested the Thana Training and Development Center (the TTDC) as a more effective approach to rural development. Under this program all developmental ministries would be represented in each Thana Center. The appendix to this chapter describes these programs in some detail. Although Comilla's conceptual innovations were poorly implemented in the 1960s and early 1970s, the offices of this new Comilla experiment are now physically in place throughout the country.

Comilla's thana-based service center requires a different type of capital intensity. The budgetary savings achieved by not replicating buildings and staff at the village or union level must be expended on imaginative development programs to attract villagers and their representatives to the thana. If the TTDC is to function as originally envisioned, developmental messages, technical services, training programs, and technological innovations must be available at the thana. Agricultural extension messages for model farmers, instructions for new seed varieties, and lessons in family planning, rural health, and nutrition are being designed and packaged by central government agencies. Television and radio are being explored for their educational potential. The Comilla cooperatives promote the administration of crop loans and extension messages without losing the accounting discipline of a central bank and the crop production planning envisioned by central research centers. Yet the messages have grown weak; thana staffs are apathetic, and the packaging of attractive developmental messages via radio has not been forthcoming. (12) The capital-intensive top tier, the developmental ministries, is falling behind in its ability to sustain villager interest in the TTDC. The staff and informational demands of Comilla's programs have not kept pace with the program's expansion to all of the country's thanas. This new type of capital intensity, never fully understood by the line ministries, is being diluted in the push for thana coverage.

Ideally the creation of information by ministries should be guided in part by village acceptance at the bottom tier. Villager use, therefore, indicates ministerial success, and this success requires field testing of material created and promoted by the top tier. If villagers do not attend cooperative meetings, make little use of a new seed, and under-use a recommended fertilizer dose, this information must be fed back into the respective government agencies. The performance of the capital-intensive top tier should be judged and guided by village acceptance or nonacceptance of its messages. From our preceding chapters we know that villagers, and particularly cultivators, are judging this performance harshly.

Providing open access to guidance, resources, and technologies is a necessary governmental function in the early stages of agricultural development. However, by the late 1970s, when the new seed package is widely understood, governmental control over virtually all inputs should be sharply curtailed. The government is moving to liberalize its monopoly on the retail distribution of fertilizer and pesticide but complete decontrol of these inputs, and of irrigation equipment and parts, is still many years away. As control of these agricultural inputs is shifted to the private sector, thana officers should be retrained to administer thana planning and information processes.

The Rural Works Program usefully illustrates the specific benefits of the three-tiered approach. Some planners have recommended the detailed planning of earthen infrastructure in rural Bangladesh to promote integrated road and water development. The advantages are obvious yet the cost of this exercise at the national level would be immense, for it would require detailed technical knowledge of each village. Consequently, the ministerial tier of the government should concern itself only with regional planning and the specification of engineering standards required for small-scale canals and roads. The actual selection and location of these small-scale projects should be left to individual villages. Crop production and employment benefits of public works would be built into each village project by the use of standard labor-intensive designs and by the selective financing of socially-beneficial earthen projects. The TTDC is the middle tier, where final decisions are made and projects financed. The capital-intensive top tier - the source of design and financing - keeps its own costs down, ensures adherence to developmental criteria, and attracts villagers to production-oriented projects and to wage employment.

With minor variations, this is a restatement of the Rural Works Program's original principles. As in other Comilla programs, the original concept of Rural Works has long since been blurred. However, the concept in the face of a still larger population, remains clear and holds hope for rekindling the planning of public resources at the thana level.

Whether the developmental contributions of any of Comilla's programs can be rekindled depends on the successful implementation of recommendations made in these chapters. This is especially true of the Rural Works Program. Improving the efficiency of the Works Program is desirable; but until land and other resources are more equitably distributed, Rural Works laborers, whether paid in cash or kind, will continue to toil on projects that enhance the harvests of others no matter how efficiently their work may be organized.

The Integrative Middle Tier - Development Institutions at the Thana Level

The rural institutional literature has given heavy emphasis to the integrative middle-level thana tier, half-way between government and the people. To reemphasize the conceptual usefulness of this tiered Comilla concept and to expand where others have been brief, I have stressed the individual-village bottom tier of this model and the capital-intensive top tier. Nonetheless, the Thana Training and Development Center and accompanying thana programs need a closer assessment.

Because the TTDC is physically in place throughout the country and Comilla's cooperatives are in place in half of the country's thanas, they are seen as successful by most authors. However, the TTDC is functioning poorly, if at all. In the 1960s the TTDCs brought villagers and the government together in "easy and uneasy" contact. (13) Suspension of thana elections for most of the 1970s has prevented elected officials from functioning on the boards and committees of these developmental institutions, thereby making thana cooperation and planning virtually non-existent. Thana resource decisions are made largely on the basis of authority and influence; village elders and civil servants expect this to be the case. Symbolic of the new thana concept's further erosion is the movement of the old offices of administration and revenue into the newer buildings of the TTDC campuses. Those who attend TTDC programs for training and services are motivated largely by the payment of per diems and travel allowances. Farmer attendance at Thana Central Cooperative Association training meetings is low; villagers have no illusions about influencing decisions on resources allocated in their name. (14)

The three-tiered Comilla concept, as a concept, is sound but needs strengthening. The method of its administration, however, has blurred its value to the point of extinction. Focusing on a narrow target group and using subsidies for credit and for agricultural inputs have acted to steer costly public resources into the hands of the rural elite. When this three-tiered concept is allowed to function as it was originally formulated, it will ensure that market and administrative forces pull in the same direction to encourage participation in thana decisions and to join ministerial programs with village Bangladesh.

THE PRICING OF PUBLIC RESOURCES

Comilla's conception of how rural institutions function appears to have gone seriously astray in the area of resource pricing. Subsidies thwarted the cooperative's financial objectives and hindered implementation of the three-tiered rural delivery concept. It was assumed that the civil service could channel subsidized resources to small farm owners. Instead the rural elite co-opted these resources, financial performance deteriorated, and subsidies discouraged private investments. The strongest pricing statement that can be found in the early Comilla literature is that a larger share of the public costs would be shifted to cooperatives and their members as solvency improved. (15) As I will show, these public subsidies appear to have prevented the solvency they were designed to finance.

The Comilla cooperative model focuses on crop loans to assist poor farmers in their use of improved farming techniques. In previous chapters on the new seed and on tenure, the importance of credit has been emphasized by illustrating the way it determines access to the new seed, to water, and to land itself. Comilla's early emphasis on credit is reassuring in the light of these analyses, but at the same time Comilla planners and, more generally, central policy makers failed to anticipate the penalties that subsidization would bring. The provision of credit and other resources by the government to poor farmers, on terms far more favorable than those in the open market, led to the co-optation of these resources by the very group the Comilla model was designed to circumvent; neither wealthy farmers nor village traders could be bypassed. In effect, subsidies caused a gulf between Comilla's objectives and its achievements. I will discuss the cooperatives' loan performance and then turn to the use of subsidies for agricultural equipment. A review of the original justification for the introduction of these subsidies will conclude this section.

As acknowledged in Akhter Hameed Khan's candid Tour of 20 Thanas, the influential, and not the owners of small farms, soon dominated the village cooperatives' managing committees. (16) Through the guise of these committees, the elite has been able to secure a significantly larger share of the total funds available for loans; they have borrowed larger amounts and escaped with a poorer repayment record than have regular cooperative members. According to one study, overdue loans amounted to 1,354 takas for each managing committee member, while the overdue amount for each regular member was only 93 takas. (17) A generalized expectation for low cooperative-loan recoveries has spilled over into the Five-Year Plan; a 50% default rate is assumed during the first year. (18) The 15% rate of interest for these loans, now increased to 17½%, has proven too attractive to resist and the sanctions for non-repayment too easy to ignore. Regular cooperative members have higher loan repayment rates than those on the committee; they cannot afford to alienate the committeemen to whom they have traditional obligations. Moreover, they do not have alternative sources of attractive credit.

Early recognition of the elite's dominance has not been followed by a similar recognition that this dominance has led to the use of cooperative funds for non-crop activities, and to the "on-lending," or relending, of cooperative loans to cultivators. It has been found that cooperative members as a group use these loans to release mortgaged land, to buy added holdings, and even to lease additional land. (19) More recently, it has been reported that cooperative credit is complementing the supply of credit available to village traders and to wealthy farmers, who, in turn, lend these funds at normal market rates of interest to cultivators and other borrowers. We noted in Chapter 7 that similar conditions exist in the Thana Irrigation Program; TIP members "on-lend" their water to the actual cultivators. (20) For the same reason, the supply of subsidized fertilizers and pesticides by the Bangladesh Agricultural Development Corporation (BADC) serves the elite very well. These resource windfalls explain why TCCAs have fought successfully for the control of BADC's fertilizer distributorships within Integrated Rural Development Program thanas.

To finance crop production loans, and ultimately to ensure financial independence, Comilla cooperatives require members to make regular savings deposits. However, because of the low interest rates offered for savings and shares, an insignificant amount of money has been mobilized. The Five-Year Plan projects a savings and share contribution of 28 takas for each cooperative member, a level that represents a member contribution to the total loan target of only 6%. (21) In contrast, cooperative associations in Taiwan have been able to mobilize upwards of 80% of their own loan resources. (22)

Following Bangladesh's independence, agricultral credit became increasingly understood as a national development issue. The nation's financial institutions have been directed to extend agricultural credit, to expand their rural branches, and to experiment with alternative credit arrangements which could enable poor producers to obtain loans. Cooperative repayment records are improving, and the regulations governing conditions for loan forgiveness and roll-over are better defined. Village cooperatives are requiring each member to repay one loan before taking on another. The introduction of commercial banking controls and funds into the TCCAs will strengthen auditing procedures previously left to an internally appointed staff. The loan collateral requirement is slowly changing from land to crop hypothecation, and even to joint and group signatures. These collateral changes represent belated recognition that cooperative members with small farms have better repayment records than their managing committeemen. Despite these financial changes, the prime interest rate remains low; it has been increased from 5 to only 8% since independence. And Comilla's cooperatives still offer token savings and share rates to their members. The rural and, therefore, the national rate structure should be increased to 20 or 25% for savings and to 25 or 30% for loans if the cooperatives are to be financially self-sustaining. Their independence and the viability of other financial institutions generally require a wholesale restructuring of the cost of capital. It is noteworthy that this type of interest rate structure in South Korea caused a dramatic shift of financial resources from traditional into formal markets. (23)

The Cost of Agricultural Equipment

Of all rural programs, the gap between original purpose and actual experience is widest when it comes to agricultural machinery. As I have described in Chapters 6 and 8, virtually all agricultural equipment is subsidized in the name of ensuring its utilization by poor farmers. However, like cooperative credit, farm equipment is soon commandeered by the village elite.

Tractors, which were introduced early into Comilla cooperative thanas, are the most flagrantly misused of all costly imported equipment. (24) In the face of very small plots, complex growing patterns, and high social costs for operation and maintenance, the demand for tractors would have been extinguished in the mid-1960s if there had not been subsidies. The Academy would now have a wealth of experience on appropriate solutions to the problem of agricultural mechanization. The bullocks and traditional implements of rural Bangladesh are clearly in need of improvement, yet the Comilla Academy has not looked at this problem because of its preoccupation with tractors.

The accumulation of field experience is having an impact on resource prices. The government has reduced its subsidies on tractors, pumps, and other types of agricultural equipment, with the result that tractors are now being imported and pumps are increasingly available on the open market. Still, it will be many years before higher equipment prices cause rural institutions to discover more appropriate, labor-using processes. As Biggs has pointed out "cooperatives have been seen as an easy answer to making lumpy inputs (e.g., two-cusec low-lift pumps and tractors) available to small farmers when a great range of alternative techniques and institutions exist which may achieve higher outputs and distributive justice." (25) In time, as cooperatives and thana organizations pursue their training, informational, and participatory functions, they should see that higher capital costs are in their self-interest. Only with the rationing of scarce capital will rural organizations and techniques take cognizance of their labor-rich environment. (26)

The Price of Acceptance

With the defects of the cooperatives and other program shortcomings now evident, what justification was there for reliance upon subsidies? Because Comilla district's agricultural production did increase at a rate above 4% per year in the 1960s and early 1970s, there appears to be an _ex post facto_ justification for this investment. (27) Cooperative members obtained subsidized credit and services and, through the Agricultural Development Corporation, the simultaneous introduction of irrigation equipment, tractors, and fertilizer. If it had not been for these subsidies, some would claim, production would not have grown at this remarkable rate.

Only after Comilla's cooperatives had been set up did the new rice seed varieties become available. This has prompted one author to comment that the new seed helped to "bail out" the rural institutional programs of the 1960s. (28) By implication this suggests that the technological seed breakthrough, and not Comilla's institutions, caused the rapid increase in crop production. Other authors have noted that the cooperative program was successful because owners of medium and small farms accepted the new seed technology more rapidly than did the farmers with larger holdings. As mentioned in Chapter 7, this pattern may be explained by the degree of sharecropping and leasing practiced by owners of large farms. Research done at the Comilla Academy suggests a different thesis; although farms of less than two acres had absolutely higher yields early in the 1960s, their total yield increase between 1963-64 and 1969-70 was 78%, while the increase for farms with more than two acres was 125%. (29) With time, it appears that the owners of large farms caught up and surpassed those with smaller farms. This evidence, together with the cost of production data in Chapter 6, illustrates the profitability of the new seed and calls the use of subsidies for small farm oriented programs into question.

One clear casualty of subsidized agricultural inputs has been the growth of off-farm economic activity. Contrary to the intention of Comilla's leaders, cooperatives have been unable to expand their organizational scope to include food grain storage, marketing, and non-food enterprises. The ability to rely on low cost public resources has encouraged this result; credit and other inputs have continued to flow to cooperative members despite lack of performance and non-payment of loans. Managing committees have not become investment decision-making bodies.

Village markets are also less active than they might be and for a similar set of reasons. If Comilla's cooperatives and the Bangladesh Agricultural Development Corporation had not held a monopoly on subsidized agricultural inputs, the private sector would be maintaining agricultural equipment, distributing inputs, and could even be manufacturing pump units and engines. (30) The public-sector strategy to distribute the green revolution package precluded opportunities for private investment of several types. In Comilla district the case of the foot-powered pedal thresher for threshing rice is unique, and it is the exception that dramatizes what market towns can become. This thresher was introduced by the Japanese and by IRRI to the Comilla cooperative workshop in the late 1960s. By 1974, 12 private entrepreneurs, some of whom operated in bamboo shacks, were producing these pedal threshers at less cost. This was possible in part because at the outset the cooperative pedal thresher was sold without benefit of direct public subsidy. This one example dramatizes two possible courses for rural growth in the future: rural markets typified by vigorous entrepreneurial and commercial activity or "market towns" that are simply larger villages.

If rural institutions are to focus on the delivery of information and training as I prescribe, then consistency requires that the recipients of these services pay the full price for them. If agricultural inputs are profitable, then by extension should not model farmer-training be sold to cooperative members? In other words, are these services exempt from our earlier criticisms of subsidies?

The physical commodities required of the green revolution, such as new seed, fertilizer, pesticides, and irrigation equipment, are widely understood and accepted. Their profitability to the farm owner is easily demonstrated. (31) The new seed long preceded the knowledge revolution required for participatory rural development. Although they were production-oriented, Comilla's institutions were also designed to alter the rural decision-making process from one based on authority to one based on pluralization, from one of acquiescence to one of debate, and from one of exclusiveness to one of inclusiveness. Seen in this light, the success of the Comilla model has been limited. The supply of information and training from central ministries and the pluralization of thana government have yet to attract large numbers of people, and for good reason. Charging for these services now, when the knowledge revolution is still being defined, would stymie a fundamental prerequisite for participatory development. (32)

Rural institutional development in Bangladesh has been penalized for its reliance on subsidies. The social cost of this pricing philosophy within the institutional context of rural Bangladesh has outweighted its projected benefits because small farm owner programs have been so clearly subverted in favor of the rural elite. These owners never gained control of institutions designed in their behalf. Furthermore, these institutions have not been motivated to find processes appropriate for a population that will double in the near future.

CHECKS AND BALANCES

In our search for principles which will bring public resources to the rural population, an additional concept is required. Checks on public resource flows, the first provision of our third principle, are necessary to guide the allocation of public resources. Checks or controls on public resources are required because these flows should be conditioned upon cooperative performance, the effective utilization of resources and information, and the need for disaster or famine relief.

The pluralization of the thana decision-making process is the second provision of our third principle. The central administration of thana institutions must be balanced by village participation and, just as important, by the inclusion of local politicians. This further provision recognizes that rural programs should reflect village aspirations, and that rural political decisions are essentially about public resources. This third principle, like the first, is evident in the original concept of Comilla's programs.

Checks on Public Resource Flows

The Comilla model is rooted in the concept that institutions that work for villagers have to be founded on those villagers' own needs and capacities to plan and administer. In theory, the government is supportive of Comilla's programs but refrains from initiating and controlling them. In actual practice, this ideal was set aside in favor of Comilla's expansion. New village cooperatives had to be formed and new members recruited. Pressure to meet annual targets of program expansion in the late 1960s and early 1970s forced the open expression of cooperative needs to atrophy. The conflict between members' needs and Comilla's performance was resolved in favor of the Program.

There is evidence that cultivators' needs have been different from those anticipated by the new cooperatives and the BADC. Because agricultural inputs are administratively controlled, occasional low supplies and the consequent high black market prices have not elicited greater supplies from the government. Similarly, consistently low attendance rates at thana meetings have not brought about curriculum changes. Resources and services should not continue to flow through rural institutions in the face of signals that needs are not being met. Checks on performance should apply to recipients as well as to ministries. Only the repayment of agricultural credit, the maximization of irrigation command areas, and the maintenance of equipment should justify the flow of more resources and services.

The internal discipline of developmental programs has long been eroded by the relief tradition in Bangladesh. Newer credit programs cannot compete with relief, or _taccavi_, loans where repayment is not expected; the two forms of credit cannot coexist. The recent manifestation of this relief tradition occurred in 1974, when the annual floods proved to be excessive and severely affected the lives of millions of people. Gruel kitchens were opened nationwide without regard to early evidence that the targeting of relief food was required in only a few severely affected areas. In the same year, district officials organized rural works programs to employ the destitute; laborers were to be paid in food, and a local contribution was required of the projects' beneficiaries. A local contribution was not forthcoming from landowners who stood to gain flood protection for their crops, nor from the locally unemployed who were expected to work for low food wages. In short, the people who stood to benefit from the relief project knew that it would be financed without their contribution. As the political pressure to complete the project increased, so did the daily wage, which drew outside laborers into the area. The relief mentality on the part of both government and recipient prevailed. (33)

Complaints have long been raised about the debilitating effects that "easy" resources have upon disciplined programs. Akhter Hameed Khan noted this contradiction in the late 1960s. What few examples there are of renewed discipline in this post-independence period bear enumeration. The Integrated Rural Development Program has curtailed its cooperative expansion target until financial discipline can be established; new loans for some cooperatives are being withheld until past loans are repaid; and some tubewells have been shut down to force payment of maintenance costs.

The resource checks illustrated here, if applied across the board, will forge a closer alliance between the flow of public resources and an enlarged participation in productive processes. Such an alliance will signal to the poor that performance, demand, and need ensure access to public resources rather than influence.

The Balancing of Contending Interests

The allocation of resources on the basis of performance, demand, and need requires a greater degree of participation in the thana decision-making process. Cooperative members, other program participants, and local politicians need to be heard. Past processes indicate that future development programs will be implemented only when they reflect a balance of rural interests.

The TTDC concept and its affiliated Comilla institutions found their footings in the mid-1960s when the locally-elected members of the Muslim League, the Basic Democrats, were permitted to plan public resources in conjuction with their civil service compatriots. This merger has come to be known primarily for its shortcomings, yet a vast amount of rural infrastructure is now in place. Roads were built, miles of embankments were erected, and nearly 400 TTDC campuses and 150 Thana Health Centers were constructed. This occurred in part because the Muslim League forced the civil administration to perform. Eventually the Basic Democrats did prove to be politically destabilizing, and this ultimately led to the strengthening of the Awami League and to political independence. But the political events of this era, as important as they are in their own right, should not cloud a basic institutional point: the interaction of political and civil control built the rural institutional structures inherited by the Bangladesh Government. (34)

Following independence, the government attempted to restore the rural political system to its former role. The Awami League's popularity faded after Bangladesh attained independence, and the party lost its rural majority during the union elections in 1973. As a consequence of this defeat, thana elections were cancelled. With the change in government in 1975, union elections in 1977, and the scheduling of further elections, the country may reestablish its rural institutions as they were envisioned in the mid-1960s.

Comilla's institutions are also recognizing the need to allow greater political representation from within. Until recently, the TCCA cooperative structure was managed by civil servants. In part because of the commercial success of the Rangunia cooperatives in Chittagong district which elects its officials, Comilla's appointed officers are being replaced with elected ones. Line ministries, however, continue to "regard planning and supervision, sanctions and approvals, as their exclusive privilege." (35) It is understandable that villagers view governmental institutions as a one-way process open only to influence and pressure; what little involvement or expectation they enjoyed in the mid-1960s eroded when the country became independent. Villagers do not see the TTDC as an institution which welcomes their participation; most villagers have never even visited their TTDC campuses. (36)

THE CONTINUING CHALLENGE - JOBS FOR THE LANDLESS

In the eyes of Comilla's planners, the village landless were to find employment in expanding harvests and in the marketing and processing activities of village and thana cooperatives. As agricultural or non-agricultural laborers or as small merchants, the landless were to join the landed as viable cooperative members. This is not happening because the number of landless is far larger than originally envisioned, and rural laborers are the ones least able to compete for the few new job opportunities. The village cooperative has not become a cooperative enterprise that can expand nonfarm employment by taking on added functions. The subsidization of public resources without regard to cooperative performance arrested the development of cooperative disciplines and undercut the expansion of private investment opportunities. Even under the best of circumstances, the service and processing jobs created by the introduction of the new seed have generated far fewer jobs than had been originally envisioned. (37)

What is to become of the millions of landless laborers - that vast group of people who find only occasional work and must share others' income and toil much of the year?

There is little governmental awareness that the solution to the unemployment problem lies outside the realm of rural institutions. Although our three institutional principles include all rural people, these rural institutions, however modified, can do little by themselves to incorporate the millions of rural poor in productive processes. Rather, the productive capacity of the country is fundamentally determined by national policies. The major policy areas addressed in earlier chapters are seen as the economic preconditions of one development strategy. The increased flow of resources into agriculture, the use of labor-intensive techniques, and the establishment of progressive tenure relationships hold hope for employing some of these laborers. As prescribed by the model, rural earthworks and market towns must also be expanded to further the well-being of millions of people. It will be easier to reach the landless and the jobless through agriculture than it will be to meet the needs of a nation of destitute people.

WHITHER RURAL INSTITUTIONS?

The Comilla model has proven to be an enduring institutional innovation despite challenges to its integrity during the last few years. Program alternatives to Comilla have been short-lived, as I note in the appendix to this chapter. If it had not been for the Academy's vision, there would have been little institutional recognition of the distributive or participatory requirements of rural development. Comilla's three-tiered institutional formulation and its pluralization of developmental access are concepts necessary for development in nonrevolutionary Bangladesh. I do not foresee the addition of new institutions, or the wholesale alteration of existing programs. Modes of implementation, however, have allowed Comilla's objectives to be obscured in some programs and wholly lost in others. Civil service intervention at the village level should be gradually curtailed not only because it has been ineffective but because, with the broadening of economic opportunities prescribed here and in earlier chapters, the village as a whole should participate in productive processes. Relief programs should become less political and relief supplies should be delivered only to those in need. It is also recommended that Comilla's programs narrow their function to the provision of developmental information and training and to the encouragement of planning and participation.

Comilla's founders did not foresee the risks entailed in the public and cooperative administration of agricultural credit and other inputs. The penalty paid for this oversight has been severe: subsidies have diverted resources from intended beneficiaries; they have encouraged the erosion of cooperative discipline; and they have slowed private rural investment. Subsidies have created a "target group" of their own, and have killed the institutional search for appropriate forms of delivery systems and for appropriate mechanical technologies. Comilla's vision was not allowed to evolve according to the philosophical principles upon which it was founded. Subsidies should be reduced, if not removed, from all agricultural input, and the public sector, including cooperatives, should divest itself of the control and distribution of fertilizers, pesticides, and irrigation equipment.

Rural institutions must be alert to the demands of a massive population. What is conceptually relevant for the present may not remain so as this population contirues to grow. In Bangladesh, 80 million people face stagnant lives; an additional 80 million clearly cannot share in the institutions and resource policies currently in force. The Comilla Academy must once again anticipate and guide an ongoing experiment in survival.

NOTES

(1) I use the phrase "rural institutions" to refer to the new rural institutions and programs created in East Pakistan during the 1960s: the Comilla cooperatives, the Rural Works Program, and the Thana Irrigation Program, among others, originated from the pioneering work of Professor Akhter Hameed Khan at the Comilla Academy. I also include the rural programs of the Ministry of Agriculture, of which the Bangladesh Agricultural Development Corporation and the Extension Division are the most noteworthy, and the rural programs of the Relief, Health, and other Ministries. Even a simple uncritical description of these institutions, and their predecessors, would be lengthy. A summary has been attached as an appendix to this chapter for those who are unfamiliar with this experience. An early assessment of Comilla's small farm programs is provided by Arthur Raper (1970) and by Owens and Shaw (1972). A more recent view of this experience is provided by Myers (1974), Abdullah et al. (1973), and Blair (1974) and (1978).

(2) Princeton Lyman, p. 14.

(3) See Protocol by David R. Nalin, M.D., et al, entitled "Elimination for Need of Hospitalization for Cholera and Allied Diarrheas by Means of Early Therapy at the Village Level Using Available Personnel," Dacca: Cholera Research Laboratory/Johns Hopkins, 1976.

(4) Another example of this approach is the People's Health Center established by Dr. Zafrullah Chowdhury in Savar thana near Dacca. Cost-reducing modifications for the conventional thana health center in Companyganj thana have also been suggested by Dr. Colin McCord in "What's The Use of a Demonstration Project?" Dacca: The Ford Foundation, November 1976.

(5) When account is taken of the 40 to 50% of the rural population that is landless and of the Comilla cooperative's rule of thumb that farmers with less than three acres should not be encouraged to join, it can be said that Comilla's "small farmer" is indeed in the top quartile of the rural population.

(6) A bari is a cluster of family households. When grouped with adjacent households of relatives and neighbors, several baris are called a para. A village, or gram, generally contains several paras. A family that belongs to a para is a paribar. A respected paribar elder, a murabbi or matbor, heads the para. A group of murabbis and matbors, who form a common bond of social and religious authority, is a samaj. The samaj is, therefore, a grouping of leaders of contiguous paras and is far smaller than a village, as an outsider would know it. What has come to be known as a "village cooperative" is, in fact, a group of households that recognizes a common basis of traditional authority. Still, the samaj is not thought of as an economic decision making unit, nor are the fields of its members fully contiguous with their homes. Authority within the traditional village does flow from the ownership of land and from the ability to support one's family, an ability assured by the ownership of land. Though no single set of terms is recognized across Bangladesh to describe village relationships, the origins and uses of village

authority, as described in numerous reports, show little variation. These comments have been drawn from conversations with John Thorp, who studied a village in Pabna District in 1976. Also, Blair (1974); Abu Abdullah, Land Reform and Agrarian Change in Bangladesh, Dacca: Bangladesh Institute of Development Economics, November 1973; Peter J. Bertocci, "Social Organization and Agricultural Development in Bangladesh," pp. 157-184; and Robert D. Stevens, et al (editors), Rural Development in Bangladesh and Pakistan, Honolulu: University of Hawaii Press, 1976.

(7) Abu Abdullah, et al, 1974, p. 26.

(8) Articles by G. D. Wood in Exploitation and the Rural Poor, edited by M. Ameerul Huq, Comilla: BARD, 1976.

(9) Paper by Shapan Adnan and the Village Study Group, "Social Structure and Resource Allocation in a Chittagong Village," Dacca University/Bangladesh Institute of Development Studies (BIDS), November 1975, p. 19.

(10) See Akhter Hameed Khan's Tour of 20 Thanas, Comilla: PARD, 1971. As stressed in earlier chapters, particularly 5, 6 and 7, the veil of village order is becoming increasingly hard to maintain. Access to land and control of credit carry a greater premium now that the new seed is available. The word of village elders carries less authority; poor widows have to beg; the poor see the exploitation; and the elite see themselves in a struggle to maintain their position. The reduced flow of public resources, fewer outside opportunities and, particularly, population growth, are causing a compression of people in their villages that is noticeably changing their understanding of village life.

(11) Muhammad Yunus, in his "Planning in Bangladesh - Format, Technique, and Priority and other Essays," (Chittagong University, June 1976; p. 51) has summed up the dilemma very well: "Bureaucratic approach to rural economic change tacitly assumes that the rural people are passive, fatalistic, uninterested in initiating anything on their own, incapable of undertaking activities to change their lives, and therefore need constant prodding, supervision, and spoon-feeding. While this view does not do justice to the reality, the opposite view, which seems to claim that the rural people are fully capable and willing to change their lives if only the bureaucrats would leave them alone, is equally unreal. The second view refuses to see the class-structure of the rural society and the exploitative process within it."

(12) The weaknesses of the government's agricultural extension program in general, and of Comilla's model farmer program in particular, have been described by Melvin H. Goldman in his "Training and Extension: An Observer's View," Dacca: USAID, September 6, 1974, p. 40. The potential for rural radio is described by Benedict Tisa in his "Report on the Radio Survey Conducted for CARE in the Mirzapur Area, June 1975," Dacca: IVS, June 1975, p. 25.

(13) Akhter Hameed Khan, 1971, p. 7.

(14) These general conclusions are supported by reviews of the government's rural development programs, by the BIDS, and by Blair (1974), Thorpe (1976), and Abdullah, et al (1974).

(15) Akhter Hameed Khan, 1971, p. 6.

(16) Akhter Hameed Khan recognized that by 1971 20% of the village cooperatives in Comilla district had become "pocket" societies. (1971, p. 25) With the rapid expansion of the cooperative program to half of the country's thanas by 1974, it was inevitable that dilution of staff and resources would make it easy for the rural elite to dominate village societies. In a 1974 study by the Sonali Bank it was found that small farm owners have some representation in village cooperatives, but virtually none in the thana level TCCAs.

(17) Blair, 1974, p. 45.

(18) Five-Year Plan, p. 172.

(19) Anisur Rahman, p. 3.

(20) The practice of "on-lending" is noted in a USAID field trip report dated July 14, 1976, and in a newspaper account, "Cooperative Societies Instead of Repaying Outstanding Loans are doing Moneylending Business," August 25, 1976. Lipton notes this practice with respect to both credit and water (1977, pp. 301, 302).

(21) In discussions of Comilla's low savings rate, some authorities have cited the obligatory savings of village cooperatives as being high and reflective of members' savings capacity. Others have said these contributions are low, in part because of the general level of poverty. It is my view that neither argument holds, because crop production analyses (such as those in Chapter 6) indicate that short-term savings contributions, particularly after each harvest, can be considerably higher. I also note that all members appear to be the relatively better-off farmers. Therefore, these savings quantities represent, in my view, a minimal foot in the cooperative door on the part of the village elite in the event that additional resources are made available.

(22) Footnote in Owens and Shaw, 1972, p. 93. The large interest spread between the crop loan rate, and the rates for savings and shares, is absorbed by cooperative overheads. Only two percentage points of the 12 percentage point spread are allocated for relending. Any loan defaults, therefore, subtract directly from the cooperatives' ability to expand lending from their own resources. Because of high default rates, these reserves for both relending and overheads have been negative. In practice, TCCA overheads are paid directly by annual government grants. J.F. Stepanek, "Comilla Cooperative Production Loans - A Note on the Cost of Capital," in AIDF Spring Review of Small Farmer Credit, Vol. X. Washington, D.C.: USAID, February 1973.

(23) Gilbert T. Brown, Korean Pricing Policies and Economic Development in the 1960's. Baltimore: Johns Hopkins, 1973, Chapter 7, "Interest Rate Reform and Domestic Savings," pp. 179-211. Dale Adams has contributed greatly to our appreciation of the "high interest rate" argument, in Gordon Donald (ed.), Credit For Small Farmers in Developing Countries, Boulder: Westview, 1976.

(24) When it came to mechanical agricultural equipment, Akhter Hameed Khan saw the Massey Ferguson tractor as an answer. The experience has

been evaluated from an engineering point of view by L. Faidley and M. Esmay, "Cooperative Tractor Mechanization in Bangla Desh," East Lansing: Michigan State University (draft) 1972; by L. White, "Tractor and Machine Station Study," Dacca: CUSO, June 1973; and by Anwaruzzaman Khan, "Introduction of Tractors in a Subsistence Farm Economy," Comilla: PARD, 1962, p. 63.

(25) Stephen Biggs, "Appropriate Agricultural Technology in Bangladesh: Issues, Needs and Suggestions." p. 27, Bangladesh Government, Proceedings ... on Appropriate Agricultural Technology, 1975.

(26) The direct distributive impact of increasing the cost of credit and other resources may be described as follows: because the recipients of public resources, largely the elite, on-lend resources to cultivators, because agricultural wages and tenure terms are deteriorating, and because these rates vary with the cost of food, I hypothesize that resource cost increases brought about by the reduction of subsidies will not be passed on to poor people. That is, the rural elite, who are the cooperative members, will bear the increased cost of agricultural inputs. This is a mechanism for increasing domestic resource mobilization by the very group that has traditionally enjoyed the windfalls created by rural programs.

(27) Quazi M. A. Malek, "Rice Cultivation in Comilla Ktowali Thana," Dacca: BIDE, December 1973.

(28) Robert Evenson, "The 'Green Revolution' in Recent Development Experience," New York: Agricultural Development Council, 1974, p. 390.

(29) S. A. Rahim, "Rural Cooperatives and Economic Development of Subsistence Agriculture," Comilla: BARD, (draft) 1972, p. 36.

(30) East and West Pakistani market-town growth experiences are contrasted by John Thomas in Timmer, 1975, p. 48. The dynamic growth of diesel engine manufacturing in West Pakistan is analyzed by Edward H. Smith, Jr., with M. Tariq Durrani, in "The Diesel Engine Industry of Dasca, Sialkot District," Islamabad: USAID, April 1969, p. 12.

(31) See Chapters 6 and 7. Although the new seed technology is not widely utilized, cultivators throughout Bangladesh know it well. They decide whether to use the new seed on the basis of, inter alia, costs of credit and other inputs, tenure terms, taste, and expected harvest prices.

(32) Seen in this context, I do not quarrel with the cooperative practice of paying small per diems and travel allowances to model farmers, cooperative managers, and chairmen to encourage their participation at TCCA meetings.

(33) Zaidi Sattar, "Pandarkhal Shyamal Prakalpa; A Unique Experience in Organized Nation-Building," (draft) 1974.

(34) The rupee proceeds generated by the sale of largely U.S. financed food grain imports, and President Ayub Khan's desire to win rural allegiance combined conveniently and deliberately to channel resources through a civil service bureaucracy into the hands of a largely unpopular political party. Since independence, political emphasis has continued to be placed on the establishment of joint civil-political councils and on rural elections. There

has been no effort to shift the rural decision-making process entirely into either arena. This issue is discussed in USAID Mission Staff, 1974, p. 224.

(35) Anisur Rahman, p. 9.

(36) A rural survey by John Thorp (1976) in Pabna district suggests that 85% of the villagers had not visited the TTDC campus. With the possible exception of the thanas in Comilla district and those surrounding Rangunia thana, this finding is probably typical of all rural thanas.

(37) Akhter Hameed Khan did not foresee the numbers of landless laborers in rural Bangladesh, nor did he foresee that so few jobs would be created by agriculturally-related processes. For evidence on this point see Chapter 4, note 17.

APPENDIX

INSTITUTIONS ORGANIZING PEOPLE - AN HISTORICAL PERSPECTIVE

The Bangladesh government inherited more than 50 rural development programs that were instituted by East Pakistan during the 1950s and 1960s to effect the agricultural strategies popular at that time. These programs were overlaid on the remnants of the British Bengal administrative framework.

Our survey of these developmental programs starts in the 1950s, when the agricultural strategy of the period emphasized large-scale flood control and irrigation programs, tractor mechanization, and other Western models. In keeping with the view that cultivators made poor use of available resources, agricultural extension agents taught improved crop production methods. In time the lack of well-trained agents and the paucity of useful information which they had to convey - the new seed varieties were still 10 to 15 years away - forced the government to seek other approaches to agricultural modernization. Late in the 1950s a strategy known as "community development" came into international vogue. Under this approach, the Village Aid Program in Pakistan applied a mixture of sociology and psychology to practical village affairs through district-level "catalytic agents." In a few areas the approach made an impact, but it was neither sufficient nor comprehensive enough to prevent the stagnation of the agricultural sector in the 1950s and early 1960s. The bureaucracy censored the program, and the economic planners were disillusioned. The most vocal of the critics were the original agricultural extension advocates, who felt vindicated by the failure of the program and demanded a return to their production-focused role.

The advent of high-yielding rice varieties and small-scale irrigation techniques in the mid-1960s saw the abandonment of the Village Aid Program and the return to production-oriented strategies. When the new seed gave the extension program a technological breakthrough, the agricultural extension agents returned. With the Accelerated Rice Production Program (ARPP) and the Thana Irrigation Program (TIP), production objectives drew well ahead of the former community-development approach. Foodgrain self-sufficiency was to be achieved in five years. Attempts to reach the rural masses had come full circle, from production and extension to community development and back to production.

Since its inception in 1904 the cooperative movement in the region had been active, but aloof from governmental programs. This changed in the mid-1950s, when 4,107 union-level, multi-purpose cooperatives were organized by the government in a hierarchical position between the village and the thana to extend credit to farmers and other producers. This structure, like the Village Aid Program, once again proved to be too distant from the mainstream of village farming.

Although the extension approach and multi-purpose societies dominated the 1950s and early 1960s, in at least one district of East Pakistan a different approach was conceived and thrived; a decade of experimentation and revision was underway in Comilla. New approaches synthesized there in the 1960s are being replicated in the 1970s in the rural thanas of Bangladesh. The Comilla experimentation, begun in 1959, was a marked departure from previous approaches to rural development; it postulated that planning, credit, irrigation, and other developmental activities had to involve the villagers from the outset and that such activities could not be superimposed on villagers by centralized bureaucracies. The Bangladesh Academy for Rural Development (BARD), which was then the Pakistan Academy, concluded that anything done on behalf of villagers would succeed only if it arose directly from their felt needs and their own capacity to plan and administer; government should necessarily be limited to supporting services. The strategy was predicated upon the interaction between village people participating through their own organizations of elected local government institutions and cooperatives, and the government agencies which provided training, extension, and the supply of inputs. Village cooperatives could reach owners of small farms with credit and the new seed, and could ensure loan and savings disciplines at the same time. This model for rural institutional planning, tested on a pilot basis in Comilla Kotwali Thana during the early 1960s, became the foundation for much of rural institutional development in Bangladesh today. The Academy remains affiliated with the thana-based institutions it founded and continues to provide the basic training and guidance for their strengthening and expansion.

COMILLA'S THANA-LEVEL INSTITUTIONS

Following the collapse of the Village Aid Program in the early 1960s, the government concluded that its basic weakness had been the absence of effective administration at a level low enough to interact meaningfully with villagers. The district, from which the Village Aid Program had been run, was too remote from the villages; and, while the 4,055 rural unions would be ideal as points of village contact, it would be too costly for the government to reach all of them. Therefore, it was decided that the thana, shown to be viable by the Academy's experimentation, would become the locus of interaction; each of the 423 thanas in Bangladesh covers an area of between 100 and 150 square miles and has an average population of about 190,000. Based on this decision, the Ministries of Local Government, Rural Development, and Cooperatives built a thana-level development administration in the 1960s.

The Thana Training and Development Center

The system of Thana Training and Development Centers (TTDC) has become the principal public institution organizing and serving farmers. Here, physically apart from the offices of revenue and police, cooperatives and private citizens have access to development officers from 12 to 15 government ministries representing agriculture, rural development, health, family-planning, education, livestock, and several others. The thana Circle Officer-Development serves as chief executive of the TTDC. He coordinates the activities of all ministry officers posted at the TTDC and oversees their interaction with the officials elected to the union and thana councils. In addition, he serves as the principal implementing agent of the Thana Development Council (TDC), a group elected from the thana's unions for the purpose of formulating the development policy of each TTDC.

In addition to this thana administrative model, the Comilla Academy contributed four other development program concepts that are coordinated at the TTDC.

The Thana Central Cooperative Association

Of all the offices and programs represented at the TTDC, one stands out as the most important in extending the new seed technology to more small farm owners. The Thana Project Officer (TPO), a relatively recent addition to the TTDCs of Bangladesh, is charged with introducing and operating the two-tiered cooperative structure first developed in Comilla district in the early 1960s by Professor Akhter Hameed Khan of the Academy. The TPO forms the agricultural cooperative societies, Krishak Samabaya Samiti (KSSs), into a thana organization known as the Thana Central Cooperative Association (TCCA). The village KSS members meet once each week to formulate their crop production plans, make their savings deposits, and arrange their crop credit needs; annually, they elect an accountant, a manager, and a Model Farmer. The latter two go once a week to the TTDC for supplies and services, including credit and training. These leaders are change agents - extension agents from within - for their village cooperatives. It is this two-tiered, thana-village structure that is to bridge the rural institutional gap between the government and the agricultural producer. Together with the TCCAs, the nationalized commercial banks and the Bangladesh Agricultural Bank supply about 25% of the estimated credit required for the new seed. The remaining amount is obtained from traditional sources.

Model Farmer training is the extension component of the TCCA model that provides the education link between the TCCAs and their village cooperative members. The Model Farmer concept is an effective alternative to the traditional agricultural extension network of the Ministry of Agriculture. The ability of this program to reach all farm families with messages regarding nutrition, birth control, crop diversification, and marketing will be an important factor in improving rural welfare. In short, the Model Farmer Program may become the government's non-formal education system.

To the south of Comilla, in Chittagong district, is another cooperative experiment that parallels and yet is distinct from its northern neighbor. The Rangunia thana cooperatives were founded in late 1967 as a consequence of a severe flood. To Monatash Das and the thana's other leaders, recovery meant the rapid introduction of the new seed technology and not reliance upon relief supplies. Cooperatives were organized quickly and great importance was placed on the ready supply of agricultural inputs. From the outset, thana officials were elected from among the local elite and diverse types of high-value crops were marketed aggressively and were even exported. Rangunia's commercial orientation is often contrasted with the small-farm owner goals of Comilla's programs.

The Integrated Rural Development Program

The raison d'etre of Comilla's Integrated Rural Development Program (IRDP) is the creation of a sociopolitical structure at the TTDC that will make it possible for twice the present rural population to live and work productively, without regimentation, on the scarce land of Bangladesh. The TCCA concept is the production-oriented vehicle by which this goal is to be achieved. By June 1976, 162 of Bangladesh's 416 rural thanas were covered by the IRDP, with 18,888 affiliated village cooperatives and approximately 527,000 members. Because these cooperatives are given preferential treatment in the distribution of agricultural inputs such as fertilizer, the government expects membership to grow. By the end of the First Five-Year Plan in June 1978, IRDP coverage was to include 250 thanas, 39,000 KSSs, and 2,600,000 individual members.

The Rural Works Program

The Rural Works Program (RWP) is a well-known Comilla innovation. Established in part because of the failure of the major flood-control strategy to better the lives of villagers, the RWP provided minor roads and drainage canals and some flood protection at the village level. RWP project decisions were open to village discussion, schemes were planned in a thana plan book, and accounts were published. The Program's past success has led to its proposed expansion into other areas of labor-intensive construction in the 1970s.

The Thana Irrigation Program

The Thana Irrigation Program (TIP) is another Comilla Academy contribution to institutional development. The purpose of TIP is to organize farmers and their land around a technologically indivisible piece of irrigation equipment. A ten-thana pilot in 1966-67 grew to national coverage a few years later. TIP cooperative members prepare high-yielding variety production plans to utilize the irrigation command areas of a two-cusec, low-lift pump. In the mid-1970s, over 30,000 of these pumps were fielded each winter season by the Bangladesh Agricultural Development Corporation (BADC) to some 800,000 members in 20,000 TIP groups.

TEST RELIEF - FOOD FOR WORK

Test Relief, often mentioned in conjunction with the RWP is a much older rural relief program administered by the Relief Ministry. It is designed, according to its British origins, to "test" the need for below-market-rate wage work when crops are poor. According to Nyrop (p. 31) famine relief was made necessary by the zamandari system and the Indian Civil Service, which together had emasculated the villagers' sense of self-reliance.

Since independence, the Relief Ministry has been financing its rural projects with grants of imported food. Rural laborers are paid foodgrain to dig irrigation canals and drainage ditches and to construct embankments on a piece rate basis. The Relief Ministry is now responsible for completing many of the earthwork components of centrally planned flood-control projects.

THE BANGLADESH AGRICULTURAL DEVELOPMENT CORPORATION

The Bangladesh Agricultural Development Corporation (BADC) imports and supplies modern agricultural inputs for farmers. Founded in 1959, BADC has become responsible for the supply of chemical fertilizers, pesticides, and an array of tubewell and low-lift pump irrigation equipment. Because its resources are eagerly sought by villagers, BADC's influence far surpasses that of other rural development institutions. BADC is also responsible for the multiplication and distribution of new seed varieties produced by the country's seed research institutes. In 1959 the East Pakistan Government also founded the Water and Power Development Authority (EP-WAPDA) following disenchantment with community development and agricultural extension programs. The Water Board, since separated from the Power Board, is responsible for the development of flood control and major drainage projects. The Water Board and BADC together control the physical requirements of the new seed "package."

RURAL TRAINING AND RESEARCH

The country's crop production programs depend upon the new seed and an energized rural administrative service. Seed research is being conducted by the Bangladesh Rice Research Institute, the Agricultural Research Institute, and the Jute Research Institute. Each of these has sub-stations where adaptive work is undertaken and foundation seed is grown. Personnel training is provided by a network of institutions - seven Agricultural Extension Training Institutes, the Agricultural University at Mymensingh, the Cooperative College of Comilla, the Rural Development Training Institute at Sylhet, the Bangladesh Academy for Rural Development at Comilla, and various other institutions pressed into service on an *ad hoc* basis. In recognition of specific agricultural problems faced in northwest Bangladesh, the Comilla Academy opened a research academy in Bogra.

THE SHEIKH'S "SECOND REVOLUTION"

Independence offered the new government an opportunity to alter this rural institutional legacy. Changes were effected - some modest, a few radical. Comilla's institutions continued to be replicated, but with little official enthusiasm; BADC and the Water Board became relatively more powerful. However, the continuing emphasis upon crop production was interrupted, however momentarily, by two provocative programs that were to encompass vast numbers of rural people.

Prime Minister Sheikh Mujibur Rahman promulgated a "Second Revolution" two years after his "Socialistic Transformation," described in Chapter 2, to tie the rural poor into production processes. This second national kindling of the reform spirit the first having been the "Four Pillars of Mujibism," called for cooperative farming and was interpreted as a direct challenge to the landed elite. Although land titles were to be retained, the small bunds, or *ailes*, that physically demarcate the innumerable farm plots were to be leveled to facilitate cooperative farming. It was soon said that the Sheikh's party, BAKSAL, would be out of power before the *ailes* were leveled; and it was. The budget contained a token allocation for one communal cooperative in each district, but public support was weak from the beginning and vanished with the first coup in August 1975. However poorly supported and implemented, this attempt at radical reform reinforced fears in the minds of the landed elite.

THE SELF-RELIANT PROGRAM

Immediately after the coups in the fall of 1975, "self-reliance" was promulgated. Another rural development slogan, it represented an effort to institutionalize the grass-roots success of Chittagong district's Rangunia thana, where a natural disaster, timely leadership, and supplies of agricultural inputs led to rapid crop production increases in the early 1970s. A publicly administered "self-reliance" program, however, is inherently contradictory. It added almost nothing to existing priorities and seemed to consist of little more than repeated admonitions from government officials to fulfill existing programs. Many villagers saw only "self-reliant picnics;" civil servants toured the villages, ate lunches, and left.

This program should not be confused with the truly self-reliant efforts that followed the 1974 floods when local leaders obtained undisbursed funds from ministry accounts and organized work on irrigation canals and embankments to serve their villages. Despite their *ad hoc* character, these few successes are important for they were accomplished solely by local initiative.

THE INTEGRATION OF DEVELOPMENTAL AND POLITICAL STRUCTURES

The effectiveness of these development institutions at the thana level depends upon the cooperation of vast numbers of civil service employees and elected officials. The suspension of elections between 1974 and 1976 prevented these institutions from operating as they were originally envisaged. Even with energetic leadership from the central ministries, the thana's 250-odd civil servants representing 50 organizations present a formidable organizational challenge.

The suspension of elections meant that local members of developmental councils could not take part in thana decisions. This forced the formation of *ad hoc* governing bodies to fill in until the thana-elected representatives could sit with their civil service counterparts.

Even within the civil service the sorting out still goes on. The Circle Officer - Development, (the "C.O.,") acts as the thana coordinator for all developmental activity in the TTDCs. However, in the 162 thanas where the IRDP has been introduced, the relationship between IRDP's Thana Project Officer and the C.O. remains undefined. Not surprisingly, the activist IRDP Program is viewed by older thana officials, including the C.O., as an encroachment upon their authority. Developmental institutions do not easily displace administrative ones.

Historically, thana government has meant the police station and the revenue office and, before that, the land tax collection office, *zamindari kutchurry*. Village self-government existed before the East India Company arrived, but it suffered an erosion of responsibility and a lack of representation with successive administrative reform acts. Very recent public offices, the TTDCs, were constructed at the thana level to provide a new symbol of government, a point of developmental contact for thana citizens.

With independence and partition in 1947, President Ayub Khan renamed the union boards "Union Councils" and called upon all adult males and, for the first time, females to elect the Basic Democrats. Elected in 1959, 40,000 Basic Democrats formed the bottom tier of an electoral college system that served until the independence of Bangladesh; they elected chairmen of their Union Councils and, together with government officers, these chairmen formed the newly-renamed Thana Councils. The Basic Democrats also elected District Council members, drawn from the Thana Councils, and members of the Provincial and National Assemblies. It is said that Ayub Khan set up the Basic Democrats in the countryside to prevent the nationalistic Bengali Awami League from continuing to threaten his urban-based West Pakistani Muslim League.

With independence, the Basic Democrats were abolished and Union and Thana Relief Committees were formed as *ad hoc* governing bodies until the new government could conduct the long-promised Union and Thana Council elections. Many members of the Awami League were appointed Relief Committeemen because the civil service and the Muslim League were mistrusted. Elections to the Union Council, now called Union *Parishad*, were held in 1973 but proved to be sufficiently disruptive of Awami League aspirations that thana-level elections were suspended. As a consequence, the relationship between the thana civil service and the thana's politicians remained undefined. Developmental programs have suffered as a consequence of this political hiatus. Union and thana elections were held in 1977 and 1978 under martial law and show promise of inaugurating a new era in rural development. The institutional creativeness and vigor of the 1960s was not equalled or even exploited in the early 1970s. Elections in the late 1970s may revive Comilla's original concepts.

10 Assessment and Reflection

> Judged by the present scene, our case is hopeless. But such a judgment would not only ignore the possibility of change; more important, it would overlook the process of development which has led to the present situation. Ideas do not originate in vacuum. The abhorrence which intelligent people feel toward war in steadily increasing degree is more than a vague, emotional humanitarianism, and so is the abhorrence of poverty. Both express a deep and growing sense of travesty, a sense, still largely inarticulate but none the less genuine on that account, that poverty and war are not only shameful but quite unnecessary, that it is only our stupidity which permits poverty and war to flourish in the midst of plenty. We have not yet brought these ideas to full articulacy. As yet they seem to lack theoretical foundations such as the classical economists provided for the policy of laissez faire, and consequently the strategy of income redistribution as yet lacks the force of full conviction. But the facts of which such a theory of economic progress would be a formulation are there and are already dimly realized. Sooner or later we shall achieve a theoretical reformulation of the economic life process of which the strategy of income distribution will be the inexorable logical consequence and the prelude to a new age of economic progress.
> (Clarence Ayres, 1944, pp. 281-282)

The "inexorable logical consequence" of an analysis of Bangladesh is that a broadly participatory strategy of agricultural development is necessary. National survival - for this is the real issue - depends on it. (1) Although Bangladesh is fertile soil for the new seed revolution, its institutions are inappropriate, if not irrelevant, for "a new age of economic progress." Too many people are seeking to survive in an institutional milieu designed to serve the few.

Ayres' hopes for the future, have already been realized by poor people elsewhere. Equitable growth is taking place in several Asian countries where national plans have successfully united the developmental objectives of individual well-being and economic growth.

How will economic development be brought about in Bangladesh? A sense of "travesty" does not exist among her elite. There is no "abhorrence" of poverty in the sense conveyed by Ayres. Although the country's predicament is understood by a few leaders, elitist aspirations, ironically combined with the fatalistic insha Allah, are widely shared by rich and poor alike. This book has discussed the reasons for this enduring legacy. Sources of economic progress are less easily identified.

The growth model of Chapter 4 is a hopeful view of what is possible. Nevertheless, its throretical strengths are severely qualified in Chapters 5 through 9 because the model's underlying assumptions do not hold in Bangladesh - and yet no other strategy seems relevant. If my prescriptions could be implemented, broad participation in rural growth processes would not be the seemingly insurmountable task that it appears to be at the present time. Because this is such a large "if," the remaining sections of this final chapter are devoted to an assessment, in the light of earlier chapters' prescriptions, of what the government is doing to draw people into productive processes. Because the government's embrace of the status quo can be considered a strategy, the consequences of this course of action are also considered.

The institutional difficulties analyzed in the preceding chapters are not entirely, or even largely, the result of Bangladesh government policy. The country's economic legacies were so completely entrenched at the time independence was achieved that the new government could not possibly cast aside existing economic traditions. Aderence to the status quo was the only option - an adherence made inevitable, even desirable, in the face of massive foreign assistance. What role this assistance now plays in this book's prescriptions is an open question. Will this newest form of outside influence effect revolutionary changes in a very poor country? This important source of support, albeit an outside one, must also be evaluated.

Although governmental policy changes to date are, in my judgment, inadequate to the task, I believe that the opportunity exists for equitable growth. "There are enough things.... within the control of the decision makers of Bangladesh to convert present stagnation.... into forward motion." (2)

EQUITABLE GROWTH?

In the preceding chapters I have analyzed the consequences of the new seed's profitability and the consequences of other, much older economic institutions on a new seed-based, equitable-growth strategy. From this analysis, I have concluded that development will not occur until several fundamental changes are made in economic policy. What is the government doing to ensure equitable access to productive opportunities?

Unifying the Two Food Systems

The cultivators of Bangladesh plant rice to survive. Will they be motivated to plant for their country's development? Urban dwellers depend upon food imports for their comfort. Will they come to depend upon their own cultivators, and not foreign ones, for their well-being? The duality of the country's food system continues, with severe penalties for the poor and for development itself. Inadequate purchasing power veils the nutritional needs of a massive population, as well as the potential growth linkages of this agrarian economy. This stagnation is intolerable because there is an alternative; in the time it takes to launch a foreign food appeal and ship food to Bangladesh, the cultivators and the government working together could grow another, larger crop of grain.

To achieve the kinds of food policy objectives described in Chapter 5, the government has made some alterations in the food ration system. At the urging of the foreign donors, ration prices for grain are being increased toward prevailing market prices, and higher floor prices are being offered for rice and wheat at harvest time in the larger grain markets. However, modest changes in the right direction have to be weighed against those in the opposite direction. The fact remains that ration coverage has been extended to more cities and towns and to food-for-work. This expansion of food imports into an agrarian economy was not justified during 1976-78, and encourages still greater reliance upon foreign assistance.

What is the cost of this dependence on food aid? What is the motivation? These questions were addressed in Chapter 5 but their answers were incomplete. It is my judgment that the nutritional deterioration evidenced in Table 10.1 is one cost of this dependence; neither food aid nor agricultural development programs are contributing to the well-being of the poor. In fact, the case is made in these chapters that the so-called "development" programs are exascerbating their plight.

Table 10.1 Findings of National Nutrition Surveys in Bangladesh, 1962-64 and 1975-76

Food Intake (grams per day)	1962-63	1975-76	Percent Change
Cereals	537.0	523.0	-2.6
Tubers	55.5	52.3	-5.8
Pulses	28.0	23.8	-15.0
Fish/Meat	38.5	26.1	-32.2
Edible Oils	6.2	3.2	-48.4
Vegetables	135.0	126.0	-6.7

Source: Institute of Nutrition and Food Science, Dacca

With respect to motivation, the importance the government places on its ration system is reinforced by the willingness of countries with a food surplus to ship foodgrain in the name of humanitarian assistance. However these donors have evidenced a certain contradiction in their own purposes: food surplus disposal is not always compatible with the food and agricultural prescriptions they press upon Bangladesh. Only recently has Bangladesh and the food-surplus countries directed their often-conflicting food objectives towards a common goal.

If such a concept is to be accepted by the elite, the use of food for development must encompass the preservation of their privileged food supply, as I have suggested at the conclusion of Chapter 5. While urban food should become more costly, the risks of famine and very high food prices must be eliminated. Domestic food security, made possible by food-surplus nations, may be a way to implement those reforms that are a basic precondition for the country's development. This security will also allow the government to direct its energies to other development priorities.

Food development policies are important in a larger sense. Most of this book's other prescriptions depend on improved agricultural terms of trade and a host of production-oriented and rural development programs. The type of tenure and land reform recommended in Chapter 7, for example, can only be contemplated in a dynamic agricultural economy. Because the distribution of land and credit, as well as population growth, is seen to be the cause of poverty in Bangladesh, land reform should be attempted after agriculture receives the political and economic support its population demands.

The Relevance of the New Seed

It is readily apparent that higher food prices and expanded markets for agricultural products in urban Bangladesh will not benefit very many people. The rural elite can provide increased food supplies for the market, and will do so at a cost to the rural poor. To translate an agricultural strategy into rural well-being requires attention to the additional prescriptions described in Chapters 6 through 9. Yet each set of prescriptions is inevitably wrapped in its own qualifications. For example, the green revolution promised to bring increased crop production and farm employment to food-deficit countries, but Chapter 6 concludes that the new seed technology has not raised the income of the laboring population. The newer seed varieties are costly and provide high profits to the owners of land and credit, but little return to landless cultivators and laborers. The regressive tenure structure, made all the more unstable by a large and rapidly growing population, severely circumscribes the projected benefits of the new seed technology. With the institutional changes and population control prescribed in these chapters, the new seed technology would prove to be the force for equitable growth that it has been widely heralded to be.

The analysis in Chapter 6 might suggest to some that the green revolution is irrelevant to an equitable growth strategy in Bangladesh. However, because no other technical change holds promise of addressing both the country's production and distribution objectives, the new seed must be successfully introduced and spread across the country as rapidly as possible. Agricultural research is supplying a wide range of seed varieties for the complex agricultural zones of Bangladesh. This seed breeding record is impressive, as described in Chapter 6 and Appendix 4-A, but it is a slender reed upon which poor people cannot depend.

The slow acceptance of the new seed dramatizes the lack of other appropriate processes and products for a labor-rich, resource-poor economy. It is tragic that no comparable technical or organizational changes are taking place in the small industrial sector of Bangladesh. The experience of other countries in this regard serves as an important example. Several East Asian countries are aggressively manufacturing labor-intensive goods for their own markets and for export worldwide. It is possible that this appropriate industrial model may not be used to exploit the labor-rich potential of Bangladesh to serve her own internal market, or the international one as well. (3) The government's pricing and private sector policies are ample testimony to the continued reliance on the faltering public sector and the importation of basic consumer goods. Foreign assistance sustains this industrial structure and thereby slows the adjustment of domestic prices and the selection of production techniques to reflect the supply of domestic resources. As vital as the processes of induced technological change are for Bangladesh, I am not optimistic that price or policy-induced changes in the country's products or processes are occurring rapidly enough to contribute to an equitable growth strategy.

Harvests for the Cultivators?

For too long government officials have accepted legal definitions that portray Bangladesh as a country of owner-cultivators. It is now known that as much as 90% of the land is physically cultivated by laborers and tenants. This has detrimental consequences not only for individual well-being but for the employment and income linkages prescribed by the model. The age-old *zamindari* land tenure system has not been abolished; land alienation continues without effective contest from the government. Hints of reform will speed the day when the "owner-managing-his-serfs" model completely displaces sharecropping. If a ration system may be termed sacrosanct, why not present land ownership practices?

No land reform is possible in the face of population pressure and the present political realities. Even modest tenure reforms to associate effort with productivity cannot be implemented in this institutional milieu. Only in a dynamic economy, where nonfarm opportunities for income and asset growth are generously in evidence, is there scope for a land reform.

Even without central government support for prescriptions enumerated in these chapters, a restructuring may occur. The land elite knows that the terms of tenure are deteriorating and that resentment may burst into open opposition. In the face of mounting social pressure, tenure terms could shift in favor of the cultivators, with owners sharing equitably in the cost of agricultural inputs. A pious hope. There is no escaping the fact that "the nation's productivity is ultimately at the mercy of the social system." (4) A sense of futility for the land tenure situation is overcome only by my appreciation of the Bangladeshi capacity to endure.

Chasing Rainbows

The Bangladesh Water Development Board was created by foreign advice and financing and is now a willing hostage to this early investment. The penalty to Bangladesh, however, is severe. The long-promised benefits of Master Plan projects remain elusive; millions of man-years of on-farm work and millions of tons of foodgrain have yet to materialize.

The flood-control premise of the Master Plan retains its orthodoxy in the face of alternative land and water techniques created largely by the country's own cultivators. India's Farakka Barrage is also a constant reminder that past rainbows need replacing with present harvests. As India's irrigation coverage expands in response to its own food needs, what is now a political thorn to Bangladesh will turn into an economic reality.

Despite the evidence in support of less costly irrigation techniques and dry land crops and the abysmal failure of past strategies, government priorities and most donor financing continue to flow on behalf of major projects and deep tubewells. This financing has subsidized the exploitation of laborers and cultivators by the rural elite as well as the latter's purchase of land. For a few donors, these projects remain attractive because they are so expensive. Another decade may pass before the Bangladesh government acknowledges the evidence from its own fields and from its dwindling winter river flows.

Comilla for the 1980s

The Comilla Academy and its rural institutions were designed in the 1960s to ensure access to productive livelihoods for millions of poor farmers. In the face of the present worldwide concern for basic needs, it is interesting to note that in the days of East Pakistan many rural, farm-oriented concepts were tested. Whether on a pilot or even a provincial scale, programs for credit and the delivery of agricultural inputs, for health, education, and family planning, and for local planning and participation, were designed and replicated. It is this rich experience, a golden age of rural institutional experimentation and expansion, that has ground to a halt in the 1970s.

In practice, these rural institutions played directly into the hands of the very group they were designed to bypass. Reliance upon the civil service and upon a vast array of subsidies compromised Comilla's institutions at the outset. Comilla's scope proved to be inaccurately defined; the target group was far larger than was originally imagined, and Comilla's capacity to reach the poor, far smaller. As I have shown in my analysis of these institutions, subsidy policies and land and credit traditions govern access to the means of production, not programs for rural development alone.

Despite resource pricing and implementation difficulties, it is my judgment that Comilla's programs are conceptually sound and well-tested. The experience of the 1960s must not be set aside. Comilla's institutions should concentrate on a pluralization of participatory processes for planning, information, and training at the thana level. A reinstatement of Comilla's programs can encompass all rural people by being responsive to their economic needs and interests.

Although Comilla's institutions are not being altered along the lines suggested here, the rural processes that ensure Comilla's exclusiveness are now being identified. The credit cooperatives, the Thana Irrigation and Rural Works Programs, and the Thana Centers are being questioned for their effect on equity and rural accessibility.

Whether these thana programs will be reenergized depends upon political perceptions. The prescriptions of Chapter 9, like those of Chapter 7 on tenure, assume a dynamic agriculture, which, in turn, requires the market and administrative commitment to rural growth processes described in Chapters 4 and 5. If history is any guide, rural participation in any meaningful, political sense is seldom broadened voluntarily by the governing elite. Whether the elite will support policies to broaden participation depends upon their perceptions of rural political necessities. Comilla's institutions are not supported now because they are not seen as having the political relevance which they did in the 1960s. During the mid-1970s, rural allegiance is being purchased with expanded food for work programs, generous extensions of credit, more cooperative pilots, and village "self-reliance" sloganeering. The public provision of easy resources and gratuitous advice appears to be the formula for pacifying the countryside. Discipline and development must again command the center of the rural political process. (5)

Resource Subsidies

Although I have not intended to emphasize the issue, subsidies have been a recurring theme throughout these chapters. The government's doctrinaire adherence to cheap resources and to the public controls that this philosophy invites imposes severe penalties on the population. The supply of low-priced public resources appears to have sapped discipline, initiative, and productive opportunity throughout the economy. Whether it is the public food ration system, subsidized consumer goods, credit, or the supply of agricultural inputs, the beneficiaries are clear. The bureaucratic administration of goods and services, in the name of improved social welfare, has been a failure. Few people foresaw that the widespread use of subsidies in a poor economy would build powerful vested interests which, among other things, would divert resources from the intended beneficiaries. Furthermore, because of the prevalence of subsidies in the rural economy, villagers have come to rely on the government for resources; and the government, in turn, has come to depend upon outside assistance in order to maintain the subsidies. Once-strong village government has atrophied; foreign assistance has fostered a complex system of controls and patronage.

The reduction of subsidies and the decontrol of many public goods and services would allow the private sector to make investments and to search for less capital-intensive techniques of production. Whether it has been food, shoes, or farm implements, public involvement in the supply and pricing of these goods has made it unprofitable for private producers to compete.

It is a commentary on the inefficiencies of the public sector that the market must be relied upon to improve the distribution of resources. Increased market incentives would encourage private production to expand, which, in turn, would cause the scarcity premiums on public resources to fall. Movement in this direction is resisted because the public control of subsidized food commodities, other basic goods, and agricultural inputs yields large, secure rewards for a few. Vested interests do not have reason to seek less costly solutions to development problems. Private investments should be given greater scope for all the reasons cited in these chapters, and also because home remittances from other countries, growing larger each year, must be mobilized for development.

THE BASIC STRATEGY RECONSIDERED

Because my analysis raises as many difficulties as it appears to resolve, the model's underlying thesis bears re-examination. I posit in Chapter 4 that the well-being of the poor in Bangladesh depends on their productive employment. This employment is to be achieved by the expanded use of the new high-yielding seed varieties, by stressing rural works, and by the creation of secondary growth processes in market towns. It is apparent that this three-part strategy will not significantly increase employment and income and that malnutrition and underemployment will consequently increase. Two factors explain this: the enduring land and credit traditions, and the massive population. For these reasons, it is easy to conclude that the model presented in Chapter 4 is irrelevant.

In the face of this unhappy conclusion, one could recommend that the public sector distribute basic goods and services directly to the poor in order to provide them with an acceptable standard of living. In effect, this would de-emphasize a market-oriented equitable growth strategy. The link between the productivity of land and the rewards to cultivators would cease to be of central concern. Under this alternative strategy, the public sector would provide food and basic services; population control, education, and health programs would continue to be stressed, and hunger and malnutrition would be alleviated.

As attractive as such a strategy may be in humanitarian terms, it also has severe risks; an ever larger population would be further disassociated from the sources of individual productivity and the preconditions for economic growth would be eased. Unless this strategy envisions cash handouts the new "welfarism" would not generate additional demand for domestic food, a precondition of rural growth linkages. The provision of a humanitarian floor, in the face of a weak administrative structure and deteriorating wage and tenure patterns, would be very difficult to achieve. The resource burden for what would, in effect, become the world's largest camp for destitute people would be staggering.

The basic issue must be squarely faced: the present institutional structure must be altered if Bangladesh is to function as a nation.

LARGE PROMISES - SMOOTH EXCUSES?

The deeply-rooted institutions of Bengal have been shaped by foreigners over the centuries. Whether an independent Bangladesh continues on its present course or an altered one depends in part on the perceptions of today's aliens. My analysis would be inaccurate if I did not recognize the influence that foreign assistance has upon the country's economic decisions. This assistance sustains the economy on a collision course with disaster.

Each of the five institutional chapters could have included evaluations of development programs and projects financed by foreign aid. I have avoided this approach in order to focus on the origins and consequences of those domestic institutional processes that have been identified as being central to the model. Nevertheless, because of its scale and the manner in which it is provided, foreign assistance has a determining influence on the direction of the economy. Will this assistance serve only to maintain the appearances of the status quo, or will it become a force for aligning traditional institutions with domestic challenges?

The new international development rhetoric urges that attention be paid to the poor majority. This is a large promise. Improved well-being of the poor is the primary purpose of most foreign assistance. The implications of this goal for development priorities are slowly being recognized in Bangladesh. It is a major intervention on the part of the foreign aid community to promote what must ultimately be the wholesale restructuring of the present economy. Project lists are not the solution. The risk is that one list may replace another; lists of agricultural and rural development projects may be replaced by lists of publicly-supplied necessities and services. Neither approach will succeed in addressing basic issues of economic productivity and structure. Until policy and institutional changes occur, foreign resource transfers will fuel a further deterioration in the relative and even absolute well-being of the poor of Bangladesh.

The Bangladesh government receives generous levels of food aid and other commodities, as well as cash and project assistance. Because the level of non-project assistance is so high (see Table 2.2), the government pays inadequate attention to the difficult tasks of policy and program implementation. The absorptive capacity of project assistance remains abysmally low. We have reviewed some of the reasons for this in preceding chapters, but domestic difficulties provide only a partial answer. In the name of aiding one of the world's poorest countries, wealthy nations commit large amounts of assistance; the need is clear, yet the absorption of high levels of foreign aid necessarily means the expenditure of these funds for established systems in the economy and for those types of technological choices that are capital-intensive. It is because commodities and such things as tubewells are so expensive and can "soak up" aid that they retain their orthodoxy. The "resource" approach to development is self-reinforcing, and self-defeating.

Assisting poor people requires new policies and restructured institutions. New ways must be found to educate and motivate, to forge reward with productivity and security with labor. "People" projects, or "soft" projects, do not call for massive resource transfers, nor, necessarily, do the difficult policy changes. These changes do require energetic leaders and trained people, people who are being drained away in increasing numbers to foreign countries and multilateral institutions.

The competition among donors to "help" Bangladesh enables those donors with the lowest expectations to outmaneuver those who hold hope. Easy projects and easy money push out the hard projects and put off the hard decisions. Poorly-coordinated aid is one result. For another, pledges and promises are exchanged at donor meetings with infrequent glances at the preceding year's performance. It becomes apparent that the institutional difficulties of Bangladesh are compounded by the institutional necessities of the aid community. Smooth excuses may soon follow the large promises; the poor may prove to be more durable than the commitment to them.

It is not certain that the government will alter its economic and political priorities to encompass the population as a whole. What are the implications for the country of the present economic course?

For the government to adhere to traditional economic policies is to continue as circumstances were perceived before independence; the price of rice was stable, commerce prospered, and the countryside was quiet. To achieve the same stability again, with a larger population, will be a test of the world's generosity and the population's willingness to endure. The humanitarian crisis will continue to grow as the country's institutional logic works its inexorable inhumanity on man. These penalties of this "logic" may be ignored for now partly because the world chooses to feed its poor. Food for work may become the primary rural "development" program; food aid is easily justified when it goes to malnourished people. To ensure stability, international appeals for food and resources will have to be increasingly cloaked in humanitarian clothes, as will the responses to those appeals.

THOUGHTS ON A MASSIVE POPULATION

My prescriptions have not provided a clear path to national growth and individual well-being. The economy has not been "turned around" or "taken flight," nor has the employment gap illustrated in Table 4.1 been significantly narrowed. At best, I have identified processes that can associate effort and productivity with improvements in the quality of life. However, in the face of a burgeoning population these prescriptions may only buy time.

I have looked to the future of Bangladesh, and so portions of this analysis have been speculative. Nowhere am I more hesitant than in estimating a massive population's impact on the ability of society to function. Co-operation in any form may become very difficult under the extreme circumstances which a doubled population would present. Village tensions are increasing now. Traditional income-sharing mechanisms in agriculture are breaking down. The civil service may cease to function for the public welfare altogether. By the turn of the century, no social process may work well.

The extremely difficult period of 1974, which was described in Chapters 2 and 5, gives a glimpse of what can recur. During 1974 and on into 1975 death rates increased and fewer children were born. The rate of population growth fell from 3% per year to around 1% during these months. (6) Was this a gain for population control? No, this decline was a direct result of scarcities and inequities. Not until families can voluntarily reduce family size will per capita income grow and expenditure patterns diversify. Growth linkages emanate neither from Malthusian checks nor from the institutional rigidities described in these chapters.

This grim prospect should galvanize the government into action on several fronts. An aggressive population control program, for example, to parallel the government's development programs may encourage parents to have fewer children. The average number of children per family is now 6.7. Should the three-child family be achieved dramatically by 1985, the population of Bangladesh in the year 2000 will be 118 million people instead of the presently projected 178 million; and should the two-child family be achieved almost miraculously by the year 1985, the population of Bangladesh in the year 2000 will be only 101 million people. (See Fig. 10.1). These targets can be accomplished while still assuring an important decrease in infant and child mortality from the present death rate of 171 per thousand to 114 per thousand, the world's average, by the year 1985. A sharp reduction in family size must be accompanied by a similar sharp reduction in infant mortality in order for parents to be more confident of their children's survival. Both reductions will require vastly improved rural family planning and health services.

The implications of these alternative populations for the country's future need no elaboration. It remains to be seen whether family size will be reduced by Malthusian factors or by the processes of equitable growth. (7)

CONCLUSION

This book's prescriptions, taken as a whole, represent an act of faith. Good conscience forces me to admit as much. The recommendations are predicated on my perception of the facts and my judgment about who should benefit. Some may call these recommendations radical; others may call them naive and inadequate. I believe they are modest.

I conclude that Bangladesh does have one development option that serves the aspirations of individual well-being and economic growth; although its people are poor, the country is rich and green. I have focused on institutional processes to reconcile the two. In time we will know whether and in what way the Bangladeshi people will enjoy their full measure of prosperity.

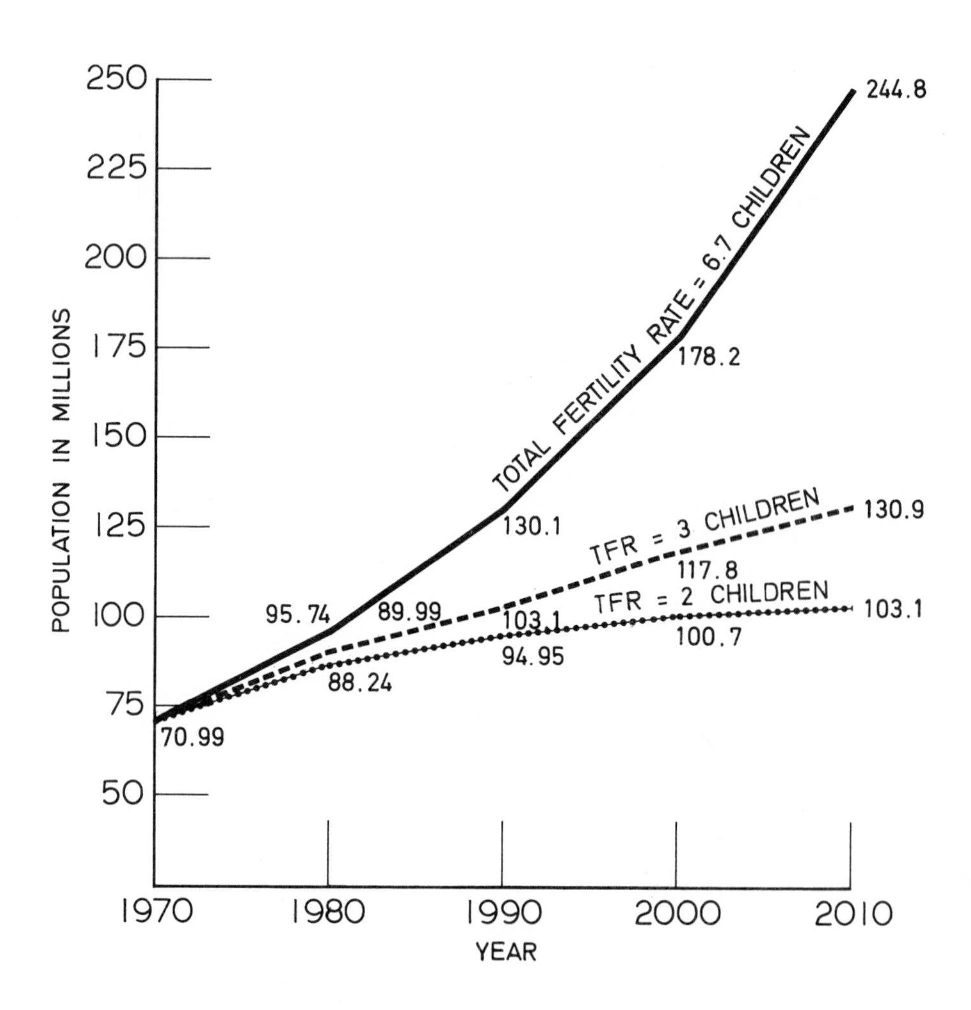

Fig. 10.1 Population of Bangladesh, 1970, and as Projected to 2010 Using Alternative Fertility Rates.

Source: Data drawn from Plato-Population Dynamics Program, University of Illinois (Washington office), December 1, 1976.

NOTES

(1) Drawn from USAID Staff, "Conversation with Professor Akhter Ahmeed Khan," Dacca: June 9, 1977.

(2) Gustav Ranis, p. 839.

(3) Even with further liberalizations in international trade, a late developing country is going to face difficulty in finding markets for its processed and manufactured goods.

(4) J. B. Stepanek, "A Comment on the Doctrines of the International Monetary Fund," (draft) p. 34.

(5) Comilla's programs in the 1960s were sufficiently large in financial terms and benefited enough laborers to cause real wages and the distribution of income to improve. Thereafter they deteriorated. See Chapter 2, note 16, and Table 6.2.

(6) Although this 1974 evidence is drawn from two thanas, other regions of the country suffered more severely during the 1974 famine. See studies by A. K. M. Aluddin Chowdhury, et al., and Colin McCord.

(7) Chen has suggested that an aggressive family planning program be administered in much the same way that the medical campaign eradicated the country of smallpox. Given the urgency of reducing the population growth rate, the important social, organizational, and technical differences that distinguish the two objectives can be overcome.

Selected Bibliography

Abdullah, Abu, Mosharraf Hossain, and Richard Nations, "SIDA/ILO Report on Integrated Rural Development Program, IRDP, Bangladesh - Issues in Agrarian Development and the IRDP." Appendix I. Dacca: June 1974.

Ahmed, Raisuddin, "Foodgrain Production in Bangladesh: An Analysis of Growth, Its Sources and Related Policies." Washington, D.C.: International Food Policy Research Institute, May 1976.

Ahmed, Raisuddin, "Foodgrain Distribution Policies in Bangladesh." Washington, D.C.: International Food Policy Research Institute, October 1976.

Akbar, Ali, 1974 Famine in Bangladesh. Rajshahi University, November 1975.

Alamgir, Mohiuddin, "Some Aspects of Bangladesh Agriculture: Review of Performance and Evaluation of Policies." The Bangladesh Development Studies, Vol. III, No. 3, July 1975, pp. 261-300.

Ayres, Clarence E., The Theory of Economic Progress. Chapel Hill: The University of North Carolina Press, 1944.

Bangladesh Government, Bangladesh Agricultural Research Council. Proceedings of the Workshop on Appropriate Agricultural Technology. Dacca: 1975.

Bangladesh Government, Bangladesh Rice Research Institute. Proceedings of the International Seminar on Deep-water Rice. Joydebpur: October 1975.

Bangladesh Government, Bureau of Statistics. Master Survey of Agriculture in Bangladesh 1967-68. 1970.

Bangladesh Government, Bureau of Statistics. Statistical Yearbook of Bangladesh 1975.

Bangladesh Government, Planning Commission. The First Five-Year Plan 1973-78. Dacca: November 1973.

Blair, Harry W., "Rural Development, Class Structure and Bureaucracy in Bangladesh." World Development. Vol. 6, No. 1, January 1978.

Blair, Harry W., "The Elusiveness of Equity: Institutional Approaches to Rural Development in Bangladesh." Ithaca, N.Y.: Cornell Center of International Studies, 1974.

Chowdhury, A. K. M. Alauddin, Douglas H. Huber, and George Curlin, "Fertility and Mortality - Recent Trends in Rural Bangladesh." Dacca: Cholera Research Laboratory, April, 1977.

Clay, Edward J., "Institutional Change and Agricultural Wages in Bangladesh." The Bangladesh Development Studies, Vol. IV, No. 4, October 1976.

Clay, Edward J. and Md. Selkandar Khan,"Agricultural Employment and Under-Employment in Bangladesh: The Next Decade." Dacca: Bangladesh Agricultural Research Council, October 1977.

Currey, Bruce, "Mapping of Areas Liable to Famine in Bangladesh." Dacca: Johns Hopkins, 1976.

Dumont, Rene, "A Self-Reliant Rural Development Policy for the Poor Peasantry of Sonar Bangladesh." Dacca: The Ford Foundation, May 1973.

Dumont, Rene, "Problems and Prospects for Rural Development in Bangladesh." Dacca: The Ford Foundation, November 1973.

Faaland, Just and J.R. Parkinson, Bangladesh - The Test Case for Development. Dacca: University Press Limited, 1976.

Farruk, Md. Osman, "Structure and Performance of the Rice Marketing System in East Pakistan." Ithaca, N.Y.: Cornell International Agricultural Development Bulletin No. 23, May 1972.

Huq, M. Ameerul, ed., Exploitation and the Rural Poor - A Working Paper on the Rural Power Structure in Bangladesh. Comilla: Bangladesh University for Rural Development, March 1976.

Jannuzi, F. Tomasson, "Preliminary Report Concerning the Need for Further Research on the Hierarchy of Interests in Land in Bangladesh." Dacca: USAID (draft), June 4, 1976.

Jannuzi, F. Tomasson and James T. Peach, "Report on the Hierarchy of Interests in Land in Bangladesh." Austin: University of Texas, September 1977.

Johan, Rounaq, Pakistan: Failure in National Integration. Bangladesh: Oxford University Press, 1973.

Johnston, Bruce F., "Agriculture and Economic Development: The Relevance of the Japanese Experience." Stanford: Food Research Institute Studies, 1966, pp. 251-312.

Kavalsky, Basil, and eleven member mission, Bangladesh - Development in a Rural Economy. Washington, D.C.: World Bank, 1973, in three volumes.

Khan, Akhter Hameed, Tour of Twenty Thanas - Impressions of Drainage-Roads, Irrigation and Co-operative Programmes. Comilla: PARD, February 1971.

Khan, A.Z. Obaidullah, "Rural Development in Bangladesh: Problems and Prospects." (draft) 1974.

Khan, Azizur Rahman, The Economics of Bangladesh. London: Macmillan, 1972.

Khan, Azizur Rahman, "Poverty and Inequality in Rural Bangladesh." pp. 137-160, in Poverty and Landlessness in Rural Asia. Geneva: ILO, 1977.

Lewis, John P., "Some Notes on Decentralized Development in a Poor Nonrevolutionary Socialistic Republic." Dacca: The Ford Foundation, October 1974.

Lipton, Michael, Why Poor People Stay Poor - Urban Bias in World Development. Cambridge: Harvard University Press, 1977.

Lyman, Princeton, "Issues in Rural Development in East Pakistan." Journal of Comparative Administration, Vol. III, No. 1, May 1971, pp. 25-59.

McCord, Colin, "What's the Use of a Demonstration Project?" Dacca: The Ford Foundation, November 1976.

Mellor, John W., The Economics of Agricultural Development. Ithaca, N.Y.: Cornell University Press, 1966.

Mellor, John W., The New Economics of Growth - A Strategy for India and the Developing World. Ithaca, N.Y.: Cornell University Press, 1976.

Mellor, John W. and Uma J. Lele, "Growth Linkages of the New Foodgrain Technologies." Cornell Agricultural Economics Occasional Paper No. 50, May 1972.

Myrdal, Gunnar, Asian Drama. New York: Pantheon, 1968.

Nyrop, Richard F., B.L. Benderly, C.C. Conn, W.W. Cover and D.R. Eglin, Area Handbook for Bangladesh. Washington, D.C.: U.S. Government Printing Office, 1975.

Owens, Edgar and Robert Shaw, Development Reconsidered - Bridging the Gap Between Government and People. New Delhi: Oxford and IBH Publishing Co., 1972.

Pakistan Government, Ministry of Agriculture. 1960 Pakistan Census of Agriculture: Vol. 1 - East Pakistan. March 1964.

Rahman, Anisur, "Aspects of Rural Development in Bangladesh." Dacca University, May 1974.

Ranis, Gustav, "Brief Reflections on the Central Issues of Policy in Bangladesh." The Bangladesh Development Studies, Vol. II, No. 4 October 1974, pp. 839-856.

Raper, Arthur F., Rural Development in Action: The Comprehensive Experiment at Comilla, East Pakistan. Ithaca, N.Y.: Cornell University Press, 1970.

Thomas, John W., "The Thana Irrigation Programme and Notes on Local Planning for Bangladesh." Dacca: Ford Foundation, April 1976.

Thorp, John P., "Power among the Farmers of Daripalla," Dacca: Caritas/Bangladesh, (draft) September 1, 1976.

Timmer, C. Peter, John W. Thomas, Louis T. Wells, and David Morawetzy, The Choice of Technology in Developing Countries - Some Cautionary Tales. Cambridge: Centre for International Affairs, 1975.

USAID Mission Staff, "Economic Growth in Bangladesh - The Case for Broad-Based Agricultural Development." Dacca: Development Assistance Program, December, 1974.

Name Index

Subject Index

About the Author

JOSEPH F. STEPANEK is presently with the Program and Policy Coordination Bureau of the Agency for International Development in Washington. His responsibilities include the development of policies and procedures to improve the developmental utilization of U.S. food assistance. During the fall of 1977, upon his return from a five-year tour with AID in Bangladesh, he was asked to join the staff of the White House Working Group on World Hunger.

Dr. Stepanek has a Ph.D. in economics from the University of Colorado.